Language, Structure, and Change

A NORTON PROFESSIONAL BOOK

Language, Structure, and Change

Frameworks of Meaning in Psychotherapy

Jay S. Efran
Michael D. Lukens
Robert J. Lukens

W. W. Norton & Company • New York • London

Printed in the United States of America

First Edition

Library of Congress Cataloging-in-Publication Data

Efran, Jay S.

Language, structure, and change : frameworks of meaning in psychotherapy / Jay S. Efran, Michael D. Lukens, and Robert J. Lukens.

p. cm.

Includes bibliographical references.

ISBN 978-0-393-33373-2

1. Psychotherapy. 2. Lukens, Michael D. 3. Lukens, Robert J. I. Title.

RC480.E345 1990 616.89'14—dc20 90-37807

W. W. Norton & Company, Inc., 500 Fifth Avenue, New York, N.Y. 10110
W. W. Norton & Company, Ltd., 37 Great Russell Street, London WC1B 3NU

1 2 3 4 5 6 7 8 9 0

This book is dedicated to the memory of Sidney and Sylvia Efran and Robert J. Lukens, Sr.

Contents

Acknowledgments

There is no way to thank all of the people who have contributed to this book. Our families, teachers, colleagues, students, clients, and friends from the past and the present have all inspired us, challenged us, complained to us, or agreed with us. However, a few people require special mention.

Michael P. Nichols and Richard Simon urged us to write this book, read early drafts, and told us what they thought our readers might want to know. Rich, as editor of *The Family Therapy Networker*, provided a number of opportunities for us to commit some of our notions about the psychotherapeutic enterprise to paper.

Two of the authors studied with Julian B. Rotter, a master teacher who is invariably able to cut through to the heart of basic issues. It is difficult for a student to have had contact with him without acquiring the habit of examining core suppositions and questioning the utility of traditional terms and concepts. One of the authors also had the good fortune to have studied with George A. Kelly, whose early contextualist formulation—personal construct theory—has strongly influenced the view of therapy to be found in these pages.

Over the years, insightful questions and comments from various groups of seminar students, colleagues, and clients have helped us hone what we now think we believe about psychotherapy. Particularly helpful were discussions late into the night with Etiony Aldarondo, Robert L. Chorney, Charles E. Gallagher, Christopher K. Germer, J. Herbert Hamsher, Jürgen Hargens, Kerry P. Heffner, Paul H. Himmelberg, Richard J. Leffel,

M. Penny Levin, Christopher J. Lukens, and Dennis H. Sandrock. William R. Knowlton, Alan J. Lipman, and Marc Zekowski all read parts of the manuscript and provided useful suggestions.

Assistance in locating reference citations was provided by Kimberly R. Hayden, Rodman E. Holland, Jr., William R. Martin, Robert H. Ouaou, and Paul L. Schneider. Elizabeth A. Muldawer-Gallagher transcribed early notes, and Jo Cobb provided notes of supervisory discussions.

Friends and family who provided us with encouragement, understanding, and take-out food while we labored over this manuscript (and often ignored them) included Heather Ascher, L. Michael Ascher, Mimi Bohbot, Rachelle A. Dorfman, Michael G. Efran, Eileen M. Lindinger, Anne N. Lukens, and Regina C. Palazzese. Daniel S. Efran initially convinced us that computers weren't all that bad (and that he needed his very own) and, as a member of the younger generation, prompted us to keep up with the newfangled world of fractals and metamagical themas.

A research and study leave from Temple University permitted the proposal for this book to be written, and Donald J. Parker and Richard A. Gisondi of the Atlantic Mental Health Center were remarkably flexible and understanding about the impossibility of two of the authors' being in two places at the same time.

Our editor at Norton, Susan E. Barrows, was patient with our changing deadlines and unflinching in her support of the project. Her kind words kept our motivation from flagging at critical junctures. Our live-in editor, Elsa R. Efran, insisted that each sentence be clear, each punctuation mark be appropriate, and each "which" be differentiated from each "that." She read every word and changed quite a few. She tactfully but persistently argued for the rights of the future reader, while at the same time massaging the bruised egos of the authors as they watched precious phrases bite the dust. She fended off phone calls and other interruptions and made sure that we were stocked with an adequate supply of food and coffee to soften the strain of long writing sessions. Moreover, she helped foster an atmosphere of calm and reasonableness at many moments of panic and crisis.

Preface

This book is about something that has proven virtually impossible to define—psychotherapy. Ever since the term was coined in 1889, many inventive, energetic, and committed practitioners have struggled to get this nebulous class of procedures to work at least reasonably well in everyday practice. In the process, they have suffered through more than their share of angst. It has dawned on some of these therapists—sometimes right in the middle of a session—that they had little idea what they were doing or why they were doing it. They may have understood that "just listening" helps. However, the question troubling them was: Did they, as professionals, have anything more specific to offer clients than general support, attention, and empathy?

Even experienced therapists—those who have taken many courses, read many books, seen many clients, and received extensive supervision—cannot necessarily give a succinct, coherent description of the nature of their craft. Some of these therapists have developed a pat reply for prospective clients who ask what psychotherapy is or how it works. However, despite having rehearsed a series of high-sounding vagaries and abstractions, many of them remain plagued by a certain insecurity about the exact nature of the services they render.

Deep skepticism about theory and method has arisen about every major school of psychotherapeutic thought. Moreover, no single position or combination of positions (of the 500 or so that have been proposed) has won the allegiance of the majority of today's clinicians. An alarming percentage subscribes to a fuzzy and confusing eclecticism (Garfield & Kurtz, 1974, 1976; Norcross & Prochaska, 1982a, 1982b; Prochaska & Norcross, 1983). They resort to using a potpourri of miscellaneous techniques, even though they cannot defend their choice of methods on the basis of any consistent set of theoretical premises (Omer & London, 1988).

Nevertheless, many clients do seem to improve, and they often attribute their improvement to the therapy they received. Clients believe that what they did with their therapists helped them even though they can't say precisely how or why. A former client of one of the authors, when asked to explain the value of his sessions, said simply, "It was just you being you."

Of course, there are also clients who do not seem to improve, no matter what you do with them, to them, or for them. Some of these therapeutic "failures" have been treated by more than one therapist and have sampled different therapeutic modalities. Despite having made valiant efforts to follow their therapists' directives or to get into the spirit of the enterprise, they remain essentially unchanged and dissatisfied after years, or even decades, of treatment.

Therapists are often at a loss to predict if or when significant progress will occur with a given client. Perhaps this lack of predictability accounts for the current increased popularity of the *borderline* diagnostic category—labeling a client *borderline* justifies, explains, and legitimizes a certain level of uncertainty. Any number of other diagnostic terms—narcissistic, paranoid, passive-aggressive—can also be pressed into service to rationalize setbacks and explain away weak outcomes.

In the absence of a theory that provides a firm basis for predictions, even positive outcomes may not be entirely satisfying to therapists. Since ours is a field in which success is not more easily understood than failure, favorable outcomes do not automatically serve as a grounding for the details of clinical practice. Therapists continue to crave—but for the most part have not been able to find—a solid footing in the amorphous theoretical and methodological landscape of the field.

Moreover, the field has historically been dominated by the misleading metaphors of medicine—for example, concepts like disease, patients, symptoms, treatments, cure, diagnosis, prognosis, and etiology. When applied to the "problems in living" (Szasz, 1973) that motivate many clients to enter therapy, these metaphors are stretched beyond all recognition. An impending divorce or fear of public speaking is not like an attack of the flu or acute appendicitis. In our opinion, it has been difficult to create productive psychotherapeutic role relationships fashioned in the image of traditional medical practice.

So, at a time when scientists and engineers are inventing replacement parts for many bodily tissues and organs and developing techniques to manufacture surgical instruments the size of a human cell, psychotherapists are still forced to debate the fundamentals of their field. Does therapy work? If it works, how? Why? What kind of training is needed to become good at it?

Psychotherapists naturally want to spend most of their time focusing directly on issues of human behavior, rather than on philosophical abstractions. However, a preoccupation with the immediate and the practical can be disadvantageous. Unless the foundational assumptions of our theories of psychopathology and psychotherapy are reexamined, our thinking about people will remain trapped within a limited range of conceptual possibilities. An examination of trends in mental health theory and technology over the last several decades reveals a certain shuffling of emphasis among the same several alternatives, none of which has proven entirely satisfactory. For instance, we have shifted around among biochemical, intrapsychic, and interpersonal foci. Emotions, behaviors, and cognitions have each been placed temporarily in the limelight. Also, we have alternately focused our attention on the individual, the family, and the sociology of the community. In our estimation, the murkiness that currently characterizes work in the field cannot be cleared up simply by inventing more techniques or by introducing additional theoretical refinements to existing models. To break out of the current conceptual morass will require a review of the core epistemological assumptions on which our thinking has been based.

A viable theory of psychotherapeutic assistance must be built upon a sound conception of how living systems operate. It is painfully obvious that the transfer of traditional theories from medicine and the social sciences has not yet provided adequate guidance to therapists in their attempts to deal with complex human behavior. Psychotherapeutic theories, from the Freudian to the behavioral, have been based on a Newtonian epistemology developed primarily in connection with the world of mechanics—theories about the movements of inanimate objects. This epistemology turns out to be inappropriate for understanding the operation of living systems in general, and human beings in particular.

In fact, it is now becoming apparent just how limited this mechanistic theorizing has been in accounting for even elementary details of the physical universe in which we live. When "chaos theory" (Gleick, 1987) came to the attention of scientists, it not only enabled them to take a new approach to the series of anomalies that had long been accumulating in physics, mechanics, and mathematics, but also revealed how limited our previous approaches had been. For instance, the quadratic equations we laboriously practiced solving in college and graduate courses turn out to apply to only highly limited, specialized problem categories—quite the exceptions rather than the rule. Once you begin looking through the appropriate lenses, so-called "chaotic" phenomena can be found everywhere, including in the swing of a pendulum, the undulation of a wave, and the fluctuations of the human heartbeat. Looking back, it is incredible that a class of phenomena so obvious and ubiquitous could have been so thoroughly "tabled" in science for so long. Yet that is the way it is. The explanatory schemes with which we grow up and become familiar lull us into overlooking or trivializing vast mysteries and glaring inconsistencies. For example, in psychology, there have always been documented cases of idiot savants—individuals who are mentally retarded but show unusual learning skills, such as being able to play an entire musical piece by ear after only one hearing, or being able to describe the weather for any date since they were young children (the film *Rain Man* portrays one such individual). Although these feats fly in the face of most traditional laws of learning, very few learning theorists have troubled themselves over the matter. They have simply continued to focus their attention elsewhere.

Understanding people requires a revised epistemology that takes into account not just the Newtonian world of forces, collisions, and impacts, but the self-created world of words, symbols, and meanings (Bateson, 1979). Fortunately, recent and converging developments in the fields of physics, biology, and cybernetics point the way toward a more consistent, integrated framework from which to discuss critical issues of living in human communities.

In this book, we propose a view of psychotherapy based on these new theoretical insights. In this approach, language is treated as an essential and core element in human events. A single coordinated set of principles is used to discuss and explain the total range of human behavior, from the cellular through the communal and the evolutionary (Maturana & Varela, 1987). Moreover, the creation of meaning in language is conceptualized in biological terms rather than being viewed as simply a collateral social or mental phenomenon.

This book is based on new epistemological and theoretical developments. It represents our attempt to ground the basics of psychotherapeutic practice in principles that seem more adequate and up-to-date than those derived from the older Newtonian, mechanistic models or extrapolated from the general field of medicine.

The epistemology to which we subscribe departs from the traditional "paradigm of objectivity." By contrast, the new view might be labeled the "paradigm of autonomy" (Durkin, 1981). The shift from objectivity to autonomy is radical—analogous, perhaps, to the shift from Newtonian to

Einsteinian physics. It implies a fundamental reorientation to ideas about the nature of human reality, the exchange of information, the wielding of social influence, and the process of change. Various concepts that derive from the older epistemologies, like *control*, *purpose*, and *cause*, will require reexamination in this new framework. In addition, therapy terminology from a variety of schools of thought—terms such as *transference*, *resistance*, *insight*, *active listening*, *reframing*, *assertiveness training*, and *counterconditioning*—will have to be either discarded or drastically redefined.

The new epistemology acknowledges that our lives take place mainly in a world of meanings—in "conversation." Problems, too, are packets of meaning. They arise in connection with certain kinds of social performances in a human language community. If psychological assistance is to be effective, it must take place in the very same space in which our living and our problems are enacted—in meaningful conversation. In other words, that which we have labeled "psychotherapy" must begin to be seen as a specialized form of dialogue—not as a medical treatment analogous to administering inoculations, performing surgery, or dressing wounds.

STRUCTURE OF THE BOOK

In this book, we will spell out the implications of the conversational metaphor for the practice of psychotherapy. We will indicate why some of our traditional thinking about working with clients has been off the mark. Instead of providing separate sections on theory and practice, we will weave issues of practice and theory together, since we view the distinction between them as more arbitrary than real; a theory mandates a practice, and a practice specifies a theory.

First we outline more fully the kind of trouble the field is in. We suggest that this state of affairs is inevitable given the historical and conceptual roots of the psychotherapeutic endeavor. Then we describe an integrated, biologically derived theory of living systems. That approach—structure determinism—takes into account the primacy of language in human interactions and provides a solid basis for developing better principles of psychotherapeutic practice. A succinct list of the essential principles is provided in Chapter 2, and the implications of these principles are fleshed out in the succeeding chapters.

We illustrate how people create meaningful lives for themselves by drawing distinctions and sharing narratives. Along the way we grapple with concepts that confuse people in their attempts to understand how they operate—ideas such as free will, purpose, choice, control, and change. We also redefine the term emotion, showing how older conceptions that divide a person's functioning into separate cognitive, behavioral, and affective components perpetuate misunderstandings about the nature of conflict. Finally, we bring the threads we have been developing together and describe therapy as an educational process—an inquiry into frameworks of meaning. Consistent with that conception, we outline the responsibilities of the therapist and the nature of his or her role.

AUTHORS' NOTE

This book has been a collaborative effort. As with all such efforts, there had to be some division of labor. In describing incidents there was some awkwardness surrounding the use of plural pronouns, such as "we," "us," and "our." To avoid unnecessary complication, we used those pronouns even if all three of us did not work together on a particular case or were not in the room together for a given session. Only when it seemed essential to distinguish among us did we use more cumbersome wordings, such as "The senior author did such and such," or "One of the authors noticed this or that."

We have described bits and pieces of cases throughout. Our intent in doing so has been to clarify points, illustrate principles, and convey the flavor of how we work. We have disguised our clients' identities. To accomplish this, identifying information has been substantially modified and, in some instances, separate identities and incidents were grafted together. In this process, we have striven to thoroughly protect identities and simultaneously to avoid misleading the reader about details of case management.

Language, Structure, and Change

CHAPTER 1

Professional Doubts

Although clients often report being helped by psychotherapy, neither therapists nor their clients seem entirely clear about what specifically has been offered or received. What's more, surveys indicate that no single set of premises about therapy is widely accepted by practitioners as an adequate grounding for what they do (Omer & London, 1988). At the moment, there is also little evidence to support the claim that high-level training in psychotherapy enables therapists to provide services that are either unique or uniquely effective (American Psychological Association, 1982; Berman & Norton, 1985).

In other words, it is hard to find proof that the specialties of the therapist are actually special. Paraprofessionals regularly seem to obtain results comparable to those of the more highly trained (Durlak, 1979; Hattie, Sharpley, & Rogers, 1984), and in some instances do even better than those with advanced degrees. In one well-known study, sympathetic college professors in other fields proved to be as effective as trained psychological counselors in ministering to students with problems (Strupp & Hadley, 1979). Likewise, a community psychology study found that bartenders, taxicab drivers, and hairdressers often served as effective "listeners," without benefit of advanced training in medicine or psychology (Cowen, 1982). The current state of affairs—in which psychotherapy cannot be shown to have specific properties and therapists cannot be shown to possess special expertise—is incompatible with the sustenance of a viable profession.

In this regard, it is revealing to sit back and observe professionals interacting at clinic case conferences. There is typically a disproportionate amount of time and energy devoted to describing the client—his or her foibles, history, complaints, and characteristics—as contrasted with the time and attention devoted to developing a specific treatment plan or evaluating the therapist's activities. The client's behavior is explored with great relish, but the therapist's behavior and the treatment plan are often disposed of in a few brief comments. Trainees and junior staff members are sometimes required to take "the hot seat" and permit their work to be scrutinized, but agency politics often allow senior staff members to avoid being placed in such potentially vulnerable positions. These staff members are generally more comfortable engaging in a kind of professional gossip about the client—or in questioning what underlings have done—than they are in saying specifically how *they* intend to approach a given therapeutic problem.

If one asks too many pointed questions about what the therapist will do or has done, one is apt to earn an unsavory reputation as a "spoiler." The convivial and collegial climate of such conferences can be fragile, and to be candid with colleagues about the breadth and depth of one's befuddlement about what to do next with a client may be regarded as a breach of professional etiquette. In some circles, even flat-out failures and instances of gross therapeutic negligence are expected to be glossed over. They can be readily masked by statements about a client's "readiness for treatment," his or her "degree of psychological mindedness," the existence of an "underlying borderline character structure," and so on. Professionals have grown accustomed to accepting such explanations from their colleagues. Family therapist Richard Rabkin, commenting on a certain lack of candor among psychoanalysts, once pointed out that when you question an analyst about what he or she does, you're not just talking theory—you're talking $200,000 a year!

THROUGH THE EYES OF NEOPHYTES

Students do not yet have years of investment in a particular approach. Therefore, they can more openly admit to being confused about who they are, what they do, and what they believe. They are still shopping for a point of view to fit their needs. At least among themselves, they tend to be more vocal about their disappointments and insecurities. We recall when we ourselves were students. We kept waiting to be admitted to that inner circle where the secrets of the profession would be laid bare. We floundered through sessions with clients, but we were certain that sooner or later we would learn important tricks of the trade that would decrease the frequency of such occurrences. It was hard to imagine that seasoned professionals could be experiencing as much uncertainty as we were.

Yet each course we took seemed to survey much but provide few operational details. We held onto whatever specifics we could get our hands on, becoming overly infatuated with approaches that seemed to offer concrete techniques. When we saw clients, we used a number of ploys to cover our lack of confidence in our role. For example, we frequently lapsed into a nondirective "reflective" mode, not because we were Rogerians, but because we were not sure what to say next to the client. "Reflecting" was an easy out. For similar reasons, we sometimes affected a posture of psychoanalytic silence, even though we had no particular affinity for analytic tenets. Most of all we asked questions. We relentlessly explored the history of the client's symptoms and the background of the problem: When did you first notice that? Is it the same when you are at work? And so on. Of course, such information can have legitimate treatment planning uses, but for us these question-and-answer series were mainly a stall. They successfully postponed that awful moment of truth when *actual treatment* would need to begin.

We found that clients were usually cooperative with these efforts, at least at first. They assumed that information-gathering was a necessary preliminary to the start of treatment and appreciated the sense of "being understood" that our attempts at reflection provided. They rarely realized at the outset that we had little idea what was coming next or where the therapy was headed. As novice therapists, we kept our "safe" procedures going as long as humanly possible.

When clients appeared to be demanding more immediate or concrete help than we had been offering, we tended to launch into lecturettes on the principles of good living. We doled out tidbits of practical advice on this subject or that. The advice we gave was usually invented on the spot, derived loosely from a combination of common sense and personal experience, having little relation to theoretical postulates, professional training, or scientifically validated information. We were plagued by the nagging concern that "real therapists" don't do this. Indeed, we had been warned by supervisors to scrupulously avoid lecturing or advising. We were also vaguely aware that the advice we gave was not necessarily different from what the client had already heard a million times before from friends and relatives. Nevertheless, the desperation to offer *something* substantive induced us to traffic in cheap homilies and to invent instant prescriptions for problem-solving. Again, the clients were pretty good sports about all this. They generally listened appreciatively to what we had to offer, nodding in agreement from time to time and even promising to try out our suggestions. Naturally, they didn't always do what they had promised.

Psychotherapists—the experienced as well as the inexperienced—seem deeply ambivalent about the giving of advice. Most formal theories recommend against it, but common sense and impulse continually push us toward it. When we are in trouble in our personal lives, we too may experience a need for advice. Clients often crave advice, and when therapists steadfastly refuse to provide it, they often seek it out elsewhere—from friends, relatives, teachers, religious advisors, and so on. We will have more to say about the value of advice-giving later.

In later years, we discovered to our surprise that students were not the only ones experiencing distress about playing the role of therapist. Even seasoned therapists report finding themselves in an agonizingly ambiguous role, feeling somehow obliged to offer solutions they do not think they possess. We have noted that in these circumstances such professionals tend to use exactly the same time-filling and structuring devices that we thought we had invented as students, but with a degree of polish and panache we would have envied.

Evidently, history repeats itself. Today's students report the same role confusions we endured, and they continue to grasp at straws. Trainees we have spoken to confess that, despite extensive classroom training, they still feel at a loss when confronted with a live client. Moreover, practicum and internship supervisors often fail to provide them with the basic "how-to" information they feel they need. Supervisors often act as if these *basics* are simply too obvious to discuss. However, the central tenets of practice are never obvious to trainees, and their befuddlement about how they are supposed to "cure" anyone by just talking to them may last for years. They, too, feel as if there is a conspiracy of silence about the fundamental underpinnings of psychotherapeutic practice. They will quickly learn to speak the language of professionals—substituting therapy jargon for commonsense constructs—but they may still feel like outsiders. The struggle to fill in the missing pieces of the puzzle continues.

Faculty members of training programs are often chagrined to learn that their own students have rejected the utility and validity of the models they are attempting to teach them. This is particularly true in academic programs where faculty have lost contact with the exigencies of everyday practice or never had such contact in the first place. As Kovacs (1987) writes, "Even today in most APA-approved programs, students will still tell you that professionally oriented courses are taught by professors who denigrate their contents and who themselves are not engaged in the activities about which they are teaching" (p. 14).

In these programs, where what is taught cannot be practiced and what can be practiced is not taught, students may secretly seek exposure to alternative models "on the side," through reading, attendance at workshops or training institutes, and participation in late-night bull sessions with other students.

If their programs do not encourage open discussion of doubts and misgivings, they may keep their own counsel, biding their time and fulfilling their degree obligations until they have obtained the credentials they consider necessary to advance their careers. After they get their diplomas, they pursue those models and practices that made the most sense to them, or they go looking for additional inspiration elsewhere.

PSYCHOANALYSIS AS A COVER

When Freudian theories were more universally in vogue, it was easier for practitioners to hide their insecurity about psychotherapeutic practice behind arcane and esoteric concepts (e.g., superego lacunae, penis envy) bandied about without any real understanding of drive theory or the essence of psychic conflict. At that time, therapy was *supposed* to take a long time, so it was easy to rationalize a certain apparent sameness in a client's situation from week to week and month to month. However, the advent of the behavioral approaches and the increasingly sophisticated use of medications have changed all that. They ushered in an era in which increased therapist activity and directness not only have been encouraged but are expected to result in fairly immediate, measurable client change. Therapists have been urged to describe problems and procedures in more operational terms, to establish specific therapeutic goals, and to provide clients, insurers, and government agencies with estimates of treatment duration.

It is no longer considered acceptable for therapy to ramble along for years without clear goals and without concrete indications of progress. Insight without observable behavior change has begun to be viewed with suspicion, especially because clients (or third parties) are being asked to invest large sums of money and resources in an open-ended process that (a) might be based on mistaken premises and (b) could conceivably end without any discernible benefits having been attained. It could be said that whatever else behavior therapy and drug therapies have accomplished, they have forced psychotherapists to face the issue of accountability more squarely than before. Reiss (1987) goes further than that. He points out that it was the advent of behavior therapy that "made clinical psychology a science" (p. 865).

THE BEHAVIORAL LEGACY

Prior to 1950, it was virtually impossible to find a single controlled outcome study. "Mental health research consisted mostly of psychodynamic interviews and speculation about unconscious processes" (Reiss, 1987, p. 865). The experimentation with briefer, more direct behavioral interventions called into question both the necessity and the desirability of therapists' meeting with clients for long periods of time, discussing with them the obscure dynamics of the mind, symbolic equivalencies, or details of childhood.

Meanwhile, although behavior therapists had succeeded in unsettling the complacent practices of some psychodynamic therapists, they found themselves confronting a thorny array of theoretical and practical problems in their own backyard (Breger & McGaugh, 1965, 1966; Costello, 1963; Efran & Marcia, 1972; Kazdin, 1979; Lazarus, 1971a; London, 1986). It became increasingly clear, for instance, that the claim that behavior therapy techniques were founded on well-validated, laboratory-derived conditioning principles was not justified. Perhaps therapy was not a science after all.

Behavior therapy represented, for many, a glittering promise that ambiguities of practice might be vanquished, once and for all. Specific therapies would be devised for specific problems and, over time, scientific studies would provide clear evidence of the superiority of one method over another. Techniques could be taught, and outcomes could be measured. Obviously, this dream of finding a concrete technology for complex human problems had a great deal of appeal for those who had been wallowing in uncertainty. Moreover, it initially seemed plausible to base a theory of change on a popular, scientific-sounding, and distinctly American psychological invention—learning theory. If habits of behaving could be learned, why couldn't we devise and test practical strategies for replacing them with better habits? If only life were that simple.

To an outsider, the world of learning theory may have looked neat, tidy, and scientific, but researchers in the field of learning knew full well how little agreement there was about even the most basic postulates. In addition to the fact that the learning principles themselves were still matters of debate, the connections between learning-laboratory findings and the phenomena facing psychotherapists in the real world were very tenuous—based more on wish than reality. Many who looked into the matter closely questioned the validity of the analogy drawn between the performances of elementary organisms that were operating in simplistic laboratory environments and the symptoms of suffering individuals who were arriving voluntarily at the doorsteps of psychotherapists (Breger & McGaugh, 1965; Efran & Marcia, 1972).

For example, Levis (1988), a behaviorally oriented therapist with many years of treatment experience, clearly acknowledges the gap between learning laboratory and clinic: "I have become increasingly aware of how conceptually shallow, oversimplistic, and unrelated to clinical experience are the vast majority of behavior techniques. Not only do these techniques appear to be developed in an academic vacuum but their incorporation of learning principles and theory are all too often naive, simplistic, and lacking integration, let alone creative thoughts" (p. 95).

Even studies using human subjects can yield misleading results, since the subjects–often college students–have complaints and motives different from those found in clinical practice. To complicate matters further, careful observers of well-known behavior therapists at work (e.g., Klein, Dittman, Parloff, & Gill, 1969; Metzner, 1963) reported that they didn't necessarily practice what they preached. Although they described and explained their results strictly in learning theory terms, their actual sessions with clients contained potentially crucial elements that had little to do with theories of learning or with any laboratory-based procedures. In the course of administering treatment, the therapists also gave advice, provided social support, instilled hope, encouraged alternative viewpoints, intervened with family members, explored images and memories, and so on. It became difficult to determine which elements might have contributed to any change produced.

In any event, behavioral methods have not proved to be the panacea originally hoped for. Significant weaknesses and inconsistencies remain at both the theoretical and practical levels. For example, many people who receive a round of assertiveness training–even those who successfully send an overdone steak or two back to the restaurant kitchen–report that they continue to feel painfully shy inside. Ironically, their motivation for sending the steak back may indicate a continuation of, rather than the amelioration of, their lack of assertiveness. Such individuals may be attempting to win their therapists' approval by complying with the behavioral assignment–they are still being "good." Although they may be behaving differently, their pattern of being overly concerned with what others think persists unabated.

The current generation of behavior therapists has become more vocal about the many failures and disappointments connected with the use of behavioral methods (Franks, 1987). For example, there has been an increase in frank discussion about clients who drop out of treatment or who seem unable or unwilling to carry out the necessary behavioral homework assignments. There is more discussion about the difficulty of getting results to generalize to significant life arenas and of maintaining changes in behavior over the long haul (e.g., Foa & Emmelkamp, 1983). Behavior therapists have also been frustrated when faced with those vaguer "existential" complaints that clients often present. Many clients first offer some circumscribed complaint, such as a phobic fear of flying, but soon get around to more global concerns about personal identity and the meaninglessness of their lives. What good is it to an acrophobic to learn to go to the tenth floor of a building if he or she still experiences life as dreary and pointless?

Surveys have repeatedly shown that a rather large proportion of behavioral therapists—about 50 percent—have sought personal therapy from nonbehaviorists (Franks, 1987; Gochman, Allgood, & Greer, 1982; Lazarus, 1971b; Norcross & Prochaska, 1982a, 1982b, 1984; Norcross & Wogan, 1983; Prochaska & Norcross, 1983). Although these statistics can be interpreted in a variety of ways, they fit our observation that a significant number of behavior therapists distrust the techniques they practice when it comes to dealing with their own personal issues. For the most part, they do not want to be desensitized or reconditioned. In private they acknowledge what they might prefer to deny in public—that their own problems seem too complex and "existential" to be solved by simple conditioning procedures.

As behavioral practitioners discovered limitations in the techniques proposed by pioneers such as Wolpe and Stampfl, they made up *additional* techniques on an ad hoc basis (see, e.g., Lazarus, 1971a). Some of these ad hoc methods have only a tenuous connection with the principles of behaviorism. Despite the presumed commitments of behaviorists to validating their techniques scientifically, these methods were pressed into service with virtually no theoretical or evidentiary backing. In commenting on trends in the field, Franks writes, "The gap between theory and research, on the one hand, and clinical innovation, on the other, is . . . widening. In the early days, the major thrust was toward the clinical application of principles established in the laboratory. . . . The first volume of *Behavior Therapy*, the official journal of the AABT, included numerous references to experimental psychology. Today, some two decades later, the situation is different, and references to basic research have practically disappeared from *Behavior Therapy*'s pages" (1987, p. 38).

Employing techniques with no established validity is generally defended as a necessary and temporary expedient. One hears the argument that practitioners cannot always sit around waiting for the outcomes of controlled laboratory investigations or clinical trials. However, many behavior therapists have, with respect to this issue, attempted to have their cake and eat it, too. They have rather freely modified existing techniques or invented brand-new ones, yet they still wish to be known as the branch of psychotherapy that bases practice on scientifically established procedures. Even though behaviorally oriented practitioners often take a somewhat holier-than-thou stance about "science," few of them conduct research or bother to assess case outcomes in an acceptably thorough, systematic, or objective manner.

In fact, leaders of the behavioral movement have repeatedly chastised members of their organizations for neglecting the principle that clinical techniques be validated via objective evidence of effectiveness (Kazdin, 1979; Marks, 1982). Reiss (1987), for example, bemoans the fact that today's practitioners are neither reading nor heeding the research literature. He notes that only a handful of practitioners have a continuing interest in contemporary learning theory developments. The well-known experimental psychologist Robert Rescorla (1988) goes further—he claims that the academics who *teach* these clinicians are not really up-to-date with regard to recent learning theory developments either. Therefore, they are proffering to clinicians outdated and inaccurate versions of the basic learning theory paradigms.

COGNITIVE-BEHAVIORISM COMES OF AGE

In the midst of such sobering reappraisals of behavior therapy, and in connection with a renewed interest in the operations of the mind, the so-called cognitive-behavioral movement has gained popularity. Understandably, some of the pioneers of the behavioral view have regarded the ascendancy of this hyphenated amalgam with great trepidation (Ledwidge, 1978, 1979a, 1979b; Lieberman, 1979; Locke, 1979; Mahoney & Kazdin, 1979; Meichenbaum, 1979; Wolpe, 1978). They have considered it a potential throwback to the days of introspectivism and armchair psychology. After all, many of them had spent the majority of their careers arguing the dangers of mentalistic explanations and had lectured against relying too heavily on introspective methods and self-report data. They therefore felt betrayed by the emergence of a movement that appeared to represent a return to the earlier focus on cognition, conversation, and common everyday parlance. They saw it as a resurgence of the unhealthy fascination with postulated internal events that could not be directly observed and measured.

On the other hand, proponents of cognitive-behavioral methods argued that behavior therapy had never successfully avoided mentalism and inferential processes in the first place because (a) images and imaginal processes were central to such behavioral procedures as systematic desensitization and implosion therapy and (b) therapeutic sessions always involved much verbal interaction, self-report, and direct instruction. In their view, it was high time to give more explicit recognition to the role that cognitions, expectations, and beliefs play both in everyday life and in the treatment process (e.g., Kendall & Bacon, 1988).

Cognitive-behaviorists conceptualized depression, panic, anxiety, and many other symptoms as caused by faulty conclusions clients drew based on flawed reasoning processes. Therefore, it followed that the job of the therapist was to help clients learn to think more logically—that is, to retest the validity of their habitual interpretations. Instead of blaming clients' troubles directly on the *events* or circumstances of their lives, cognitive-behaviorists blamed the subjective *beliefs* that the clients had formed in connection with those events.

Our objections to the cognitive-behavioral model are along slightly different lines. We believe this currently "hot" approach is actually a theoretical cul-de-sac. It promotes techniques that tend to be superficial, bearing an uncomfortably strong resemblance to the commonsense solutions one's grandmother might have proposed. Cognitive-behavioral theorists have great difficulty stating the exact relationships between events, cognitions, and behaviors (not to mention the role played by emotions, intuitions, and preferences). Yet the potential value of such an approach hinges entirely on the precision with which such relations can be specified. As Eysenck (1988) puts it, "There is no 'cognitive theory' to set against 'learning theory'. . . . So-called cognitive theory . . . is simply a ragbag of promissory notes on a nonexistent bank account; an appeal to processes that are seldom described and defined in a unique manner, obeying laws that are never specified and mediating behavior in ways that remain ever more mysterious" (pp. 52–53).

Moreover, research evidence calls into question the central assumption of cognitive-behavioral thinking—that emotional disorders, such as depression, are *caused* by faulty thinking patterns (see, e.g., Barnett & Gotlib, 1988; Coyne, 1989; Dohr, Rush, & Bernstein, 1989; Lewinsohn, Zeiss, & Duncan, 1989). Although the thinking of a depressed person may be "faulty" according to some standards, this may be a *symptom* of the depression rather than the *cause* of it. When the episode of depression clears up, so does the faulty thinking. Wiener (1989) makes a similar point, noting that in the cognitive-behavioral literature it is unclear "whether learned helplessness and cognitive distortion are considered signs, antecedents, correlates, consequents, or causes of depression" (pp. 303–304).

THE FAMILY SYSTEMS APPROACH TO THE RESCUE

While the behavioral and cognitive-behavioral therapists have been fighting among themselves, another group—the family and strategic therapists—have argued against focusing on the individual as the site of problems and have been developing methods based on larger diagnostic and intervention units. They hold that problems do not reside in individuals but must be understood instead as byproducts of how a family system operates as a whole. Social systems create and maintain the predicaments of individuals rather than vice versa.

Family systems workers were once regarded as the new kids on the block, and they took pains to emphasize their separateness from other schools of thought. Although there were striking theoretical and practical differences among family systems theorists even from the outset, they all agreed that the traditional focus on the individual was limiting and misguided. However, over time, even this basic point of agreement has been called into question, threatening to blur the very distinctions that originally gave family therapists their rallying cry. That some family theorists and practitioners are now "rediscovering" the importance of the individual is suggested by a recent book on family therapy titled *The Self in the System* (Nichols, 1987). The "Self in the System" was also the theme of the 12th Annual Family Therapy Network Symposium, which was subtitled, perhaps prophetically: "Is It Time to Rediscover the Individual?"

These developments indicate how approaches that are at first quite distinctive grow to resemble one another over time. The behavioral revolt against inner mechanisms developed into cognitive-behaviorism, which now embraces a concern with thinking and consciousness. Human emotion, which had been relegated to a subsidiary role by most cognitive-behaviorists, is now making a comeback. A recent publishing brochure heralds the coming "affective revolution" (Lawrence Erlbaum, 1989). Family therapists who once eschewed psychodynamic approaches are now unabashedly incorporating object relations thinking into their systemic formulations (Scharff & Scharff, 1987). All of this might be taken to lend support to the aims of the integrationists, who advocate combining principles common to various schools of thought (e.g., Goldfried, 1980; Messer & Winokur, 1980; Wachtel & Wachtel, 1986; Wachtel, 1977), and to eclectic therapists, who, as we describe below, borrow techniques somewhat shamelessly from wherever they can.

THE DRIFT TOWARD ECLECTICISM

In the face of the skepticism and confusion that has erupted in each of the major therapy models, many practitioners have drifted toward either a loose eclecticism or a permissive pluralism (Omer & Alon, 1989; Omer & London, 1988; Patterson, 1989). Therapists who began their careers as practitioners of a single point of view are now practicing a hodgepodge of techniques often chosen on the basis of personal preference and spur-of-the-moment decisions. Moreover, the technique they use with a client on Monday may have little or nothing in common with one they plan to use on Tuesday. The same client may be invited to do a gestalt therapy "empty chair exercise" one day and to negotiate a behavioral contract with a spouse the day after. Techniques used in successive sessions not only are apt to be unrelated to one another but may derive from theories that propose incompatible images of humanity or incommensurate philosophies of science.

The eclectic therapist generally does not feel an obligation to justify his or her choice of methods on other than purely pragmatic grounds, and even *that* claim is open to serious question. The truth of the matter is that most therapists, including eclectics, do not necessarily do what "works best." They choose their techniques from only a limited subset of the available methods, and—except in a few special instances, such as exposure methods for obsessive-compulsive disorders or paradoxical intention for some cases of sleep-onset insomnia—cannot offer any empirical justification for their choices (Dance & Neufeld, 1988). Although articles in professional journals extoll the virtues of systematically matching clients and problems to therapists and methods, in actual clinical work this is rarely feasible and almost never practiced. Research in the field has simply not progressed to the point at which clear guidelines have been established for determining which approach to use with whom. The logistics of doing so—even if our knowledge base were more secure—would indeed be formidable. Also, one would have to make the dubious assumption that clinicians could use techniques interchangeably, regardless of whether they liked them or felt they were compatible with their personal style. In any event, the techniques that have shown sufficient superiority to be considered "treatments of choice" in given situations are few and far between.

In the large majority of circumstances facing the average clinician, the selection of therapeutic strategies is still a seat-of-the-pants operation, guided more by personal predilections, intuitions, and financial considerations than by hard facts. Note, for example, the resistance and controversy stirred by the American Psychiatric Association's recent attempt to publish a handbook of acceptable, standardized procedures (American Psychiatric Association, 1989; Goleman, 1986; "Treatment book," 1989). The project was vociferously criticized from the outset by many who doubted that a meaningful set of guidelines could be produced and who worried that the existence of such a compendium would create a falsely optimistic impression concerning what was known about mental health approaches.

FROM SPECIFICS TO NONSPECIFICS

Another result of the current state of theoretical disarray is the increased acceptability of explanations of therapy effects in terms of so-called "nonspecific" factors. Meta-analytic reviews of psychotherapy outcomes (Luborsky & Singer, 1975; Miller & Berman, 1983; Shapiro & Shapiro, 1982; Smith, 1982; Smith & Glass, 1977) reveal that placebo-control treatments—designed to be facsimiles of treatment, but without the presumably critical components—work, for the most part, about as well as the therapies with which they are being compared. In addition, psychotherapy dropouts (including individuals who came only for a single intake session) have been shown to do as well as patients who completed treatment or who stayed with their therapist for a prolonged period of time (Fiester & Rudestan, 1975; Pekarik, 1983).

Short-term therapy seems to be about as effective as long-term approaches, with the maximum benefits of each coming in the early stages (Dell, 1982a; Green & Herget, 1989; Howard, Kopta, Krause, & Orlinsky, 1986; Smith, Glass, & Miller, 1980). Statistics from a study of many years' duration, conducted at the prestigious Menninger Clinic (Parloff, 1987; Wallerstein, 1986, 1989), revealed that clients who received supportive treatment profited as much as those who were exposed to more esoteric and intensive psychodynamic methods—the approaches that professionals had for years considered their "heavy artillery." Furthermore, all the treatments studied, including those that were supposed to be more purely psychoanalytic, contained a large proportion of general commonsensical and supportive elements.

All these findings point to an inability to distinguish clear differences *between* therapeutic approaches. Research has consistently reached the so-called Dodo bird's verdict: "All major forms of therapy seem to be effective, but approximately equally so" (Omer & Alon, 1989, p. 282).[1]

Therefore, some researchers are now maintaining that virtually all positive effects are attributable to those general relationship and expectancy factors common to all therapeutic approaches (Horvath, 1988; Prioleau, Murdock, & Brody, 1983). According to this argument, the "nonspecifics" of therapy are more important than the specifics.

The growing acceptance of this point of view is, of course, a mixed blessing. On the one hand, it is reassuring to know that most therapies are associated with positive results. On the other hand, it is embarrassing to discover that our vaunted interpretations and techniques may have no discernible *discriminative* effect on outcome—that therapy may be mostly a matter of rekindling "hope" and providing clients with a supportive, wholesome, and empathic relationship (Frank, 1973, 1987; Schofield, 1964; Truax & Carkhuff, 1967; Zilbergeld, 1983).

---

[1]As you may recall, at the end of the caucus-race in Lewis Carroll's *Alice in Wonderland*, the Dodo bird announces, "*Everybody* has won and *all* must have prizes."

One clinical theorist (Fish, 1973) suggests that therapists admit that they are, in effect, the modern equivalent of the shamans of older cultures (Torrey, 1972). Fish advocates accepting that role graciously; he believes that therapists should manipulate client beliefs as skillfully as possible, employing whatever devices (bogus or otherwise) are needed to get the job done.

From our point of view, this way of thinking moves the definition of therapist uncomfortably close to the definitions of the medicine man, fortune teller, and the con artist—job titles most of us would understandably be reluctant to embrace. Why would anyone bother being trained in complex theories and techniques if psychotherapy was assumed to be nothing more than an elaborate (albeit well-intentioned) hoax (Masson, 1988)? And, as word spread that therapists were just modern-day charlatans, what would keep clients coming back?

If therapists want to be considered more than benevolent hucksters, then they have to establish that there are indeed "specific" elements in psychotherapy and that well-trained practitioners can produce better effects than soothsayers and gypsies. To be taken seriously as a professional, a therapist needs to do more than demonstrate that people enjoyed their sessions or derived some benefit by ventilating their troubles to a sympathetic listener.

Furthermore, if the term "psychotherapy" is to mean something useful, it must designate services that are sufficiently unique and reliable to be recognized as such. A stroll in the woods with a friend might be "therapeutic" for a troubled individual, but—clearly—it is *not* psychotherapy. Similarly, taking a vacation, reading an inspiring book, attending church services, changing jobs, or volunteering one's services at a local Red Cross chapter might all provide a needed lift for people in the midst of various life crises. Again, however, a term like psychotherapy needs to be reserved for something more distinct than the multitude of activities that individuals in a culture like ours find of use in ameliorating distress. If there is to be a "profession" of psychotherapy, some distinct form of training or preparation must be a prerequisite for properly rendering such services.

MYTHOLOGY IN THE MAKING

There is a distressingly wide gap between what therapists write and what they do. For example, many students of behavioral and cognitive-behavioral methods are unable to get the methods they have read about to work well for them in actual practice. This discrepancy between theory and practice is not entirely a function of inexperience in using the method or subtle misunderstandings about its implementation. As described in the literature, the techniques can seem straightforward and virtually foolproof. However, attempting to produce the same dramatic, consistent, and positive outcomes with real people in one's own practice can be a very different matter. Although the "how to" texts make it sound as if cures are regularly and easily produced, the "accumulated evidence of the effectiveness of therapy suggests that gains are made, but that cures remain elusive" (Kendall, 1989, p. 363).

The unending supply of smoothly run cases with simple diagnoses and happy outcomes that is apparently available to writers and workshop presenters seems to be denied to most of the rest of us. Even those clients who (according to the published studies) ought to be ideal candidates for the techniques in question refuse, in real life, to play by the rules. Evidently, they didn't bone up on the material in the standard manuals before arriving at the therapist's office.

Many writers and workshop presenters understandably put their best feet forward when describing what they do, giving in to the all-too-human tendency to exaggerate outcomes and gloss over complications, failures, and dropouts. Obviously, some do more than simply exaggerate and "language up" their procedures—they fabricate whole scenarios, sometimes justifying these practices to themselves and others as necessary "teaching devices" or harmless hyperbole. Unfortunately, readers and workshop attendees can end up disillusioned and blame themselves for failing to recreate the successes that those presenters reported.

Even under the best of circumstances, one needs to be wary of the validity of case-history material. It usually consists of the selective account of a clinician, told from a necessarily biased perspective and designed to make a particular point. Rarely is there an opportunity for clients to rebut the interpretations the therapist presents to the profession or to explain their point of view about what transpired or about which aspects of the process were meaningful (Efran, Lukens, & Lukens, 1989; Spence, 1987). Corroborative data, if there are any at all, are rarely obtained independently and are usually selectively filtered through the clinician's biases.

Moreover, there is hardly ever an adequate "control" against which either client or therapist can sort out and assess with precision the effects of therapy. Undoubtedly, there are instances of both over- and underestimation. Sometimes clients initially enthusiastic about therapy outcomes will become more jaded about them later, and vice versa. Recently, a client left a session ecstatic about the new insights produced. By the following week she was complaining that the session had done her more harm than good. She had to admit that what had been said during the session was true enough, but thinking about it mainly caused her to fret all week long.

A field like ours rapidly develops mythologies about treatment procedures. New, apparently miraculous therapies tend to lose some of their allure when they have been around long enough to be tested in the crucible of everyday practice. Systematic desensitization, for example, was initially said to be effective after a very few sessions, and with a large majority of nonpsychotic clients. Its operation was initially portrayed as practically automatic. However, over time, the percentage of reported successes decreased, while the estimated number of sessions needed to produce salubrious effects increased. At the same time, researchers and theoreticians challenged the validity of the conditioning mechanisms on which the method was initially thought to rest (e.g., Berk & Efran, 1983), and demonstrated that some of the results produced were not dependent on presumably crucial elements in the procedure. Over time, the value of systematic desensitization's "stock" has declined in the eyes of many therapists, including many who were initially enthusiastic about its potential.

The same sort of history—initial enthusiasm followed by a more realistic appraisal, increasing skepticism, and at least partial disillusionment—has characterized virtually all techniques and approaches in our field. Traditional psychoanalytic practice, transactional analysis, neurolinguistic programming, gestalt therapy, and systemic family therapy have all gone through such growing pains, and one could fill a catalog with once-promising approaches that are now rarely mentioned.

The creation and sustenance of mythologies in the field are aided and abetted by the fact that some authors write as experts about techniques with which they have had little firsthand experience. One overview after another simply reiterates what was previously written, whether or not anyone has recently verified that the procedures described work "as advertised" in day-to-day clinical operation. Techniques thus gain an undeserved reputation simply through their having been cited prominently and frequently in the literature.

For instance, during "Grand Rounds" in a psychiatric department some years ago, the issue of symptom substitution (a cherished article of faith in clinical lore) was raised by someone in the room. This occurred at a time when most workers still assumed that the premature elimination of a symptom without full resolution of the underlying problem would lead to the almost automatic creation of another—and perhaps more pernicious—symptom. At this point in the discussion, one of the older psychiatrists had the temerity to ask: "Has anyone actually *seen* a case of symptom substitution?" No one had. In a room crowded with experienced mental health professionals, not a single case of symptom substitution could be recalled. Yet everyone had been convinced that it was a prevalent danger in working with clients. It was prominently featured in almost every reputable textbook, and its existence as a hazard of practice had been emphasized in everyone's training.

One of the authors recalls teaching confidently for years about the operation of symptom substitution without having had any direct experience in the matter, and with little awareness that the facts of its existence might be open to question. Lectures in undergraduate and graduate psychopathology courses are undoubtedly filled with information about syndromes that instructors have simply read about and have never seen in the flesh. They are passing on what they themselves have read—but not experienced—to yet another generation of students and professionals. Unfortunately, the very texts on which these instructors rely are themselves written by authors who may not have had much hands-on experience with the phenomena they are describing. One even suspects that many syndromes that are carried forward from one revision of the Diagnostic and Statistical Manual to the next (but seem rarely to be diagnosed in actual practice) are retained largely through force of habit—they may be figments of our collective imagination.

Another firmly held but dubious belief among practitioners is that sociopaths are extraordinarily adroit at pulling the wool over people's eyes. However, we remember a staff conference at a Veterans Administration Hospital during which this fabled ability of the sociopath was being questioned: Those present soon recognized that this bit of clinical gospel had to be an exaggeration, since everyone in the room appeared to know exactly who the sociopaths at the hospital were and had been able to discern for themselves the nature of their machinations.

It is, of course, useful for mental health professionals to believe that sociopaths are fiendishly clever, that clients with character disorders are inevitably poor treatment risks, and that borderlines can be expected to become irrationally angry with authority figures. Obviously, these views all have a self-serving component.

We consider it essential that mental health workers remain alert to the status of the profession's knowledge claims. Otherwise, it is too easy to participate unwittingly in disseminating and reifying false, misleading, and outdated information. A professional community often seems to operate more like a giant rumor mill than a repository of carefully sifted information. In this field, it seems as if conceptions are more likely to be self-fulfilling than self-correcting.

MEDICALIZATION

It is no secret that psychiatry is currently becoming re-medicalized—that is, it is returning to more strict adherence to the tenets of the disease model, relying more on biochemical interventions and less on "talking cures" (Goleman, 1989; Wright & Spielberger, 1989). A number of recent professional and popular books dealing with mental health problems (e.g., Gold, 1989; Levinson & Carter, 1986) have propounded the message that much of what you thought was "in your head" is really a matter of physiology and biochemistry. For example, changes in mood and mental functioning are being attributed to thyroid disorders, premenstrual syndrome, hypoglycemia, and so on. Psychiatrists are increasingly using drugs to treat panic attacks, obsessive-compulsive disorders, and other conditions once considered to be exclusively psychological in nature. Many psychiatric residents have lost interest in the practice of psychotherapy, even though there are still human predicaments in which biochemical remedies are obviously of secondary importance and to which the medical model is singularly inappropriate. Factors accounting for this trend include the recent explosion of knowledge about nervous system physiology and the increased sophistication of the medicinal arsenal. Nevertheless, psychiatric residents frequently seem quite ready to forsake the vagaries of psychotherapeutic practice for almost anything that appears to give them something concrete to offer—another sign that the field is in trouble.

SO WHAT?

The field of psychotherapy seems to have lost its bearings. Theoretical breakthroughs are announced at regular intervals and each new technique is auditioned for a place in the hearts of therapists. Some of these approaches fail even their initial tryouts. Others generate enthusiasm at first but then begin to lose luster as clinicians experiment with them in everyday practice. Approaches that at first seem attractively simple and straightforward become increasingly esoteric and complex as practitioners attempt to get them to work. For example, proponents of transactional analysis gradually "discovered" more and more "games people play," as well as sub-characterizations for the initial three ego states—child, parent, and adult. Techniques pulled from gestalt therapy and elsewhere were then grafted onto the basic therapy modes described by Eric Berne to give the approach more oomph (e.g., Goulding & Goulding, 1979).

All of this makes us pessimistic in assessing the current state of the field. Despite the proliferation of approaches since 1889, when the term "psychotherapy" was first coined, nothing remotely resembling a consensus has been achieved, and the thoughtful therapist can hardly be faulted for experiencing self-image problems. Consequently, professional burnout seems to be on the rise and is getting increased attention at mental health conferences and at staff in-service workshops (e.g., Ackerly, Burnell, Holder, & Kurdek, 1988). Some workers have drifted toward careers in allied fields, such as behavioral medicine and health psychology. Some have left altogether. One talented former student, after having given up on health psychology as well as more traditional forms of psychological intervention, quit clinical psychology and became a chef in a gourmet restaurant. As he put it, "When you prepare a meal for others, at least you know immediately whether or not it was a hit."

A NEW BEGINNING

This may therefore be an opportune moment in which to undertake a wholesale reevaluation of fundamentals. Not only is there widespread disappointment with all of the preexisting models, but, at the same time, a new option has been emerging out of recent developments in the biological sciences and the field of cybernetics. These developments, to which we now turn our attention, allow a more sophisticated description of how living systems operate and potentially provide some of the leverage necessary for creating better understandings of how human problems might be resolved.

CHAPTER 2

A Better Alternative: "Structure Determinism"

At the same time that many clinicians have begun to question the hows and whys of their profession, some theorists have seen the need for unhitching psychotherapy from the medical-model bandwagon (Kovacs, 1987). Although the medical model has validity when one is dealing with broken bones and raging viruses, it has proven less useful as a tool for understanding interpersonal and social relations—domains in which language plays a paramount role. This departure from a familiar model has left therapists even further in the dark, wondering if there are any governing principles whatsoever that underlie what they do. As the King of Siam sings in ***The King and I***, "It's a puzzlement."

We believe that answers to the dilemmas of theorists and clinicians alike have recently been emerging from a rather unexpected source—one that is outside the mental health profession entirely. Over the past two decades, a shift in philosophy has been occurring in the biological and physical sciences; this new emphasis is providing answers to previously thorny questions of epistemology and ontology—what we know and what we are. These answers have been making sense to investigators in *all* branches of science—psychology included.

This recent emphasis in the sciences turns away from the philosophical stance advocated by John Locke, the founder of British empiricism, toward the viewpoint espoused by Immanuel Kant, the 18th-century philosopher. The Lockeans assume that the outside world essentially etches a direct copy of itself onto our initially blank, "tabula rasa" minds (Rychlak, 1981). The

Kantians, on the other hand, assume that the human mind is never blank, even at birth. Therefore, knowledge must always be considered dependent on the characteristics of the knower and on how he or she interacts with the environment.

This shift in epistemology is in keeping with the progression from Newton's description of a static universe, in which the bias of the observer could be minimized or eliminated, to the relativistic descriptions of Einstein and quantum physicists, in which the position of the observer must necessarily be taken into account. The emerging acceptance of the continuity between observer and observed gives increased urgency to the study of how human functioning shapes knowledge and, in particular, how language affects what we think and do.

The insights of Chilean biologists Humberto Maturana and Francisco Varela (Maturana & Varela, 1987) speak directly to this issue. As Karl Tomm (1989) puts it, "As clinicians . . . we have observed again and again how mental phenomena are generated, maintained, and modified through social interaction, but we cannot explain it. Maturana can and that is the reason we are attracted to him" (p. 8). Tomm also adds that "understanding human conversation appears to be at the core of these processes" (p. 9). What we are coming to appreciate is that words and symbols are as basic to humans as claws and teeth are to animals of the jungle. They are as thoroughly consequential and just as "biological."

The approach we propose preserves some aspects of the action-oriented and behavioral psychotherapies—the emphasis on problem-solving and accountability—but it does not treat human problems simply as conditioned responses, skill deficits, or illnesses of the mind. Previously, therapists felt forced to choose between therapy as either an art *or* a science—and to construe themselves as idealistic humanists *or* hard-nosed realists. However, the new epistemology makes it possible to synthesize useful elements from each of these positions and to better appreciate the connections between them. Moreover, in this framework, terms that were often viewed as polar opposites, such as thinking and acting, are seen as different sides of the same coin. Language, for example, is not separate from action—it is a particular *form* of action.

Maturana (1970, 1984) describes human functioning, including language operations, from a biological perspective. His approach has two additional advantages. First, his theory of knowledge recognizes the inseparability of the observer and the observed, and is thus in tune with recent developments in epistemology, biology, and the philosophy of science (see, e.g., Overton, 1984; Thompson, 1987). Second, his theory is made up of well-defined and precisely integrated terms. It therefore provides an antidote to the sort of muddle-headed conceptual mess Gregory Bateson and others have accused social scientists of having gotten themselves into. Bateson (1972), for example, argues that most previous mental health and social science constructs—notions such as ego, instinct, and self—are "so loosely derived and so mutually irrelevant that they mix together to make a sort of conceptual fog which does much to delay the progress of science" (p. xviii).

Not all of what Maturana has to say about human functioning is new. His theory echoes elements of constructivist philosophy, Piagetian developmental theory, Darwinism, systems thinking, contextualism, and even radical behaviorism. However, his theorizing knits insights from these diverse sources together into one coherent fabric.

Since Maturana is not himself a psychologist or psychotherapist, his approach to living systems must be further interpreted and augmented if it is to bear directly on issues of concern to therapists (e.g., Dell, 1982b, 1985; Efran & Lukens, 1985; Hargens, 1989; Hoffman, 1988a; Mendez, Coddou, & Maturana, 1988; Tomm, 1989; Varela, 1989). Very little of this interpretative work has been done until now. One of our goals in this book is to point out the practical, clinical implications of Maturana's postulates.

A SHORT COURSE IN STRUCTURE DETERMINISM

Maturana's theory of science, epistemology, and living systems is known as ***structure determinism***. It developed out of his research with organisms other than human beings. However, as we have noted, the principles of his approach can be extrapolated to the domain of human interaction. In this domain, they provide a sound basis for understanding people—and, as a result, can lead to more effective ways of doing psychotherapy.

Structure determinism is not an easy theory to grasp. Its concepts are tightly interrelated—even circular—and very abstract. Most who have tried have found it difficult to imagine how such a theory can be directly applied to psychotherapy. In a way, of course, it can't—structure determinism is not a pat formula that can dictate what is to be done when in a clinical setting. What structure determinism can do, however, is give therapists a new way of thinking about the world and how it operates. Because it frees us from a number of misconceptions that have undergirded the ways therapy has been practiced up until now, this view can be immensely liberating—for therapist and client alike.

The basic principles of structure determinism, which we will discuss in some detail as we go along, can be stated here succinctly:

(a) Living systems are self-creating entities—what Maturana calls "autopoietic."
(b) Science can only study structure-determined entities.
(c) Living systems are informationally closed.
(d) Keeping "objectivity" in quotation marks reminds us that we manufacture that which we think we know.
(e) Fundamentally, life is a purposeless drift.
(f) Survival requires maintaining an adequate structural coupling with the medium.
(g) All our ostensibly rational systems are based on arational starting premises.
(h) Language, biologically speaking, is a specialized form of communal action—it results in the creation of domains of distinction.

At this point, these terms and ideas may seem esoteric. Nevertheless, in the interest of laying our conceptual cards on the table, we state them here. They will become the leitmotifs of everything we have to say later about clinical practice. As we define and explain these principles, we can begin to show how they can be useful in thinking about clients and their problems. Although language appears last in the list, we intend to say something about it first, because of its unique status: It is both a major component of human functioning and, simultaneously, the tool with which we attempt to explain that functioning. This dual status leads to a series of logical paradoxes, of which the master paradox is that language generates the very conundrums it is supposed to help resolve. Let's begin by describing the paradox-ridden, self-referential world in which people—using language—find themselves.

LIFE IN A SELF-REFERENTIAL WORLD

A man who has been smoking for 25 years comes to the therapist's office for help in "making himself" quit. He is attempting to do something to himself that he simultaneously wants to avoid or postpone doing. He is both the person who wants to keep smoking and the person who is trying to outwit that "smoker within." Therefore, as in the theater, the conversation between smoker and therapist is apt to contain "stage whispers" and asides, as if the therapist and client could conspiratorially say, "Come over here where that smoker can't hear us." The client periodically steps outside of himself in order to plot against himself, and then steps back inside to see if the plot he hatched is working. "Nope—that didn't do it—I'm still smoking. We'd better try something else."

This scenario is not unusual. Something similar pops up whenever we talk to ourselves about ourselves—which is most of the time. The struggle to understand ourselves and to modify ourselves is ubiquitous. So are the "splits" produced as self-as-subject and self-as-object converse. Clearly, at no time is the individual actually split—he or she remains whole and complete. So how are we to explain the undeniable experience of different personae within the individual?

In the past, psychotherapy theorists have accounted for these splits in a variety of ways, beginning with Freud's well-known division of the mind into the superego, ego, and id. Eric Berne gave us a more interpersonally focused version, labeling transactions in terms of parent, adult, and child ego states. Carl Jung liked to work with polarities such as the anima and the animus, the rational and irrational functions, the persona and the shadow. Fritz Perls encouraged the person's "top-dog" to have a talk with his "under-dog"; he worked to help the person reunite presumably split-off and under-represented aspects of himself or herself into a coherent gestalt. Harry Stack Sullivan's version included the "good me," "bad me," and "not me," as well as various other personifications. More recently, family therapist Richard Schwartz (1987, 1988) has described people as collections of "multiple selves" derived from family influences. Similarly, contemporary object relations theorists fill the person with introjects, part objects, and imagos of self and influential others.

In our view, all of these conceptualizations attempt to grapple with the same basic phenomenon—self-reference—but none gets it quite right. Each approach brings with it an unfortunate side effect—the tendency to create a series of conceptual homunculi—little inner persons that bicker, fight, and transfer control back and forth to one another. Although the theorists themselves generally recognize that these terms do not literally refer to actual internal agents, there is a strong tendency for clients to forget that fact and to reify "strict superegos," "nurturing parents," and "bad me's" into warring mind entities and mini-personalities that vie for control (Akillas & Efran, 1989; Rotter, 1954). Such reifications ultimately complicate rather than clarify. A person operates as a unity—not as a loose federation of agencies.

There is, however, a central grain of truth in all these conceptualizations: Because of our capacity for language, we are self-aware and lead self-referential lives. Self-awareness is a mixed blessing, being both a powerful conceptual tool and also the key that opens a Pandora's box of self-referential paradox.

The paradoxes of self-reference are parodied in Gilbert and Sullivan's *Mikado* when Ko-Ko, a criminal under sentence of death, is suddenly elevated to the post of Lord High Executioner. His first official act as executioner is to cut off his own head—a feat that he protests as being awkward in the extreme. Nevertheless, some of his fellow citizens suggest that, although he might not succeed completely in the task, he should at least be a good sport and make the attempt.

The self-referential paradoxes we routinely run into in life—and in therapy—are only slightly less awkward to manage than Ko-Ko's plight. For example, a married couple fights about whether or not they should continue fighting. A man and a woman have a soul-searching discussion about why they're *always* embroiled in soul-searching discussions. Parents work harder and harder to get their children to be *spontaneously* interested in school work. A person decides the only way to affirm an important life stance is by committing suicide. Self-referential paradoxes are not—as it was once believed—rare events, esoteric theoretical issues, or novelties of logic. For systems that use language, they are endemic to life itself.

In the Newtonian, objectivist paradigm, such paradoxes were treated as linguistic errors or logical anomalies to be eliminated. Various prescriptions for avoiding them were developed, including the well-known theory of logical types put forth by philosophers Bertrand Russell and Alfred North Whitehead. However, with hindsight, it is now apparent that all such attempts to fully separate subject and object were destined for failure (Brown, 1972; Hofstadter, 1979). In fact, within the usual system of logic, when one paradox was eliminated, another—at a higher level—was generated. Such paradoxes cannot be resolved by being banned or outlawed. The "message" contained in paradox is that our ordinary system of logic is insufficient to handle life as it is experienced in language. This requires an expanded epistemology within which self-referential paradoxes can reside harmoniously—an epistemology that acknowledges the basic indivisibility of subject and object, knower and known. Maturana's theory of structure determinism does exactly that. Its use therefore decreases the probability that the Ko-Kos of the world—people who live in language—will make a general mess of things.

SELF-REFERENCE AND THERAPY

From Freud's day on, psychotherapy has been construed as a process of self-examination. It thus behooves therapists to become experts in matters of self-reference and self-referential paradox. Inspect practically any randomly chosen segment of a therapy transcript and you will come across instances in which both therapist and client speak about and analyze the very processes in which they are involved—often at the very moment they are involved in them. Their conversations reference their own conversations. Problems that come to the attention of a therapist do not consist simply of sets of unpleasant circumstances—such as being poor, receiving a failing grade, living far away from one's family, weighing too much, or having a drug-addicted spouse. Moreover, they do not necessarily represent deficits in a client's repertoire of behavioral or cognitive skills. Psychotherapeutic problems are fundamentally issues of self-reference. That is why some forms of treatment that have been labeled "paradoxical" can be surprisingly effective, even though practitioners of those methods are not always sure why their techniques work.

It is not much of an exaggeration to say that when a paradox is clarified a conceptual problem disappears. Take people who complain about "test anxiety." They usually envision themselves as having been attacked by mysterious, alien "symptoms" over which they have no control (Lukens, 1989). They want to be calm, but are nervous instead. However, once a person's nervousness is seen to be a direct consequence of how he or she approaches school, courses, and examinations, the underlying paradoxes are resolved. What had initially seemed to be a peculiar ***external*** factor is now understood as a natural and expected facet of the educational strategy being adopted.

For example, a person with no real interest in studying or learning mathematics is faced with having to take a math exam. The person is hoping to finesse the requirement without actually coming to grips with the subject matter. Such individuals know that their math is weak, but all they want to do at the moment is get past the exam. The math requirement seems to them imposed from the outside, and obtaining a firm grasp of mathematics is way down on their list of priorities. These conditions make such individuals ideal candidates for "test anxiety." For them, an examination is not an educational tool but instead a dangerous and annoying roadblock. With regard to mathematics, these students are essentially educational frauds, hoping to avoid detection. Therefore, it makes perfect sense that test-taking would constitute a hazardous and frightening experience for them. Test anxiety is not a strange symptom—it is a reasonable system response to the danger of being revealed as an imposter. Additionally, once test anxiety has been created, it becomes a convenient explanation to help the individual rationalize poor performance (Efran, Germer, & Lukens, 1986; Lukens, 1989).

PARTIAL VIEWS

We are always juggling partial views of ourselves and of our world. We attempt to see ourselves as others might see us—a view from the outside—and then we rush back inside to compare those "outside" perceptions with what we think we know about ourselves from the inside. The two views never jibe completely; in fact, they are often diametrically opposed. Furthermore, no single view or combination of views is fully accurate. The outside view is not really drawn from the outside, nor is the inside view truly independent of what is happening in our surroundings. Bateson describes the peculiar fix we find ourselves in when we try to understand who we are in our world: "[A person's] beliefs about what sort of world it is will determine how he sees it and acts within it, and his ways of perceiving and acting will determine his beliefs about its nature. The living man is thus bound within a net of epistemological and ontological premises which—regardless of ultimate truth or falsity—become partially self-validating for him" (1972, p. 314).

In other words, the opinions any of us—clients included—have about ourselves is circularly determined. Likewise, a client's conception of psychotherapy partly determines what his or her psychotherapy will become. Furthermore, opinions about oneself or about therapy can be rendered obsolete the moment they are thought or spoken. The very act of thinking or verbalizing opinions can change the context of operation that gave rise to them. So, a client who says "I don't trust you" to his or her therapist has taken a potentially important step toward generating a level of honesty and trust that didn't exist the moment before.

We recall a case in which little progress was being made. Halfway through the third session the client announced that he was quitting. Going to therapy had been his girlfriend's idea, not his. He had no affection for psychology or psychologists, nor did he believe that therapy helped people. However, the act of taking that oppositional stand turned out to have a strong liberating effect on him. Several months later, to everyone's surprise, he recontacted the therapist and announced that he wanted to return to therapy. He was, at that point, eager to get down to work. What had initially been someone else's idea was now his own. Paradoxically, by clearly demonstrating his right to object to therapy he had paved the way to fuller participation. After all, saying "yes" doesn't mean much until or unless you are sure you can say "no." Upon his return, he proved to be a remarkably rewarding client with whom to work, and rapid progress was made.

As we have indicated, the self-referential "loops" of life and therapy cannot be adequately described within the lineal straitjacket of Newtonian, objectivist formulations. Life is not a series of causes that lead, in straight-line fashion, to a series of effects. In fact, because living is a continuous fabric of connections, dividing it into separate events is an arbitrary act of observation and classification by an observer operating within a particular (and limited) observational tradition. In the larger sense, everything is connected to—and "causes"—everything else. Or, alternately stated, no particular "thing" really causes any other.

Contemporary physicists understand this. They recognize the observer-dependent, fluid, and recursive nature of the world as we know it. They understand that the behavior of the observer affects that which he or she observes (Capra, 1976; Overbye, 1981; Zukav, 1979). Ironically, it is workers in the social sciences who have fallen behind in efforts to take self-reference into account. In a curious way, our envy of the presumed objectivity of the hard sciences has put psychology and psychiatry out of step with current developments in the very fields we have tried to emulate. While the hard sciences have been rapidly overcoming—or at least recognizing—the constraints of the Newtonian model, many social scientists have, in their own plodding way, clung to this limited and limiting objectivist conception. In attempting to practice science ***the way it used to be practiced***, mental health workers are still trying to locate the observer outside the observation.

This is an impossible stance, and it is especially troublesome in the realm of psychotherapy, where self-reference is the name of the game. It is perilous for therapists to think they are diagnosing and repairing objectively determined defects that remain unaffected by the diagnostic context they create. It is equally disadvantageous for them to believe they are objective commentators on the actions of their clients, as if they were watching a play that would have unfolded similarly with or without their participation. Even actors and actresses know that the audience is part of the show. They cannot create exactly the same effect for a Wednesday matinee audience that they can for a Saturday night crowd. As actress Shirley Booth put it, "The audience is 50 percent of the performance." The audio-animatronic robots of Disney World can perform their roles largely immune from audience influence. However, in human affairs, the notion of a passive audience—one that watches but does not influence—is an illusion. In the field of psychotherapy, Harry Stack Sullivan (1962) had it right when he insisted on describing the therapist as a "participant-observer."

The location of the observer is important even when a scientist studies something inanimate, such as a rock or an elementary particle. However, in understanding living systems—particularly human beings—the position of the person as observer is absolutely critical. Human beings don't just sit around inertly waiting for events to happen around them. They go looking for trouble.

An anxious client called her therapist between sessions. Although he took the call, she began to worry afterward that he was angry that she had called and bothered him. These thoughts made her all the more anxious, and she began to regret having called. She was half-tempted to call back and apologize. As her ruminations continued, she decided to stay home from work, since she "couldn't take" any more rejection. When she returned to work the following day, she found herself discomforted trying to explain why she had been absent. She couldn't wait to get home. She felt that her co-workers were prying into her private affairs and basically disapproved of her. By the time of her next session, she had seriously contemplated quitting her job. A series of small incidents had become welded into a crisis of major proportions, with each element providing substantiation for all the other elements in the picture. In such scenarios it eventually becomes impossible to say exactly what caused what, just as in protracted arguments it becomes difficult to establish who started them. Recursively, everything feeds into everything else.

This is why people's movements and reactions, unlike those of rocks or billiard balls, cannot be satisfactorily predicted or explained simply by combining the presumed effects of various pushes, pulls, vectors, forces, and impacts (Bateson, 1979). People—using words and symbols—invent meanings, generate goals, contemplate trajectories, and appraise outcomes. If thrown out of windows, people fall in accordance with the usual laws of gravity, aerodynamics, and the like. However, unlike rocks, they also ask themselves, "Why me?" and do some pretty noisy complaining on the way down. The social sciences—which have basically tried to make do with simple billiard-ball causality—have not done justice to the autonomous and self-referential processes that characterize the functioning of either a person who falls out a window or one who confides that he or she is considering taking the plunge. Neither the concept of reinforcement (from learning theory) nor that of cathexis (from psychodynamic theory) is up to the task.

LANGUAGE AND PARADOX

Most living organisms don't speak. Obviously, therefore, life itself does not hinge on language operations. However, most of that which we consider essential to our humanity does. Heidegger wrote "Language is the house of being. Man dwells in this house" (Steiner, 1978, p. 127). It is through language that we become conscious of ourselves as beings and can contemplate and evaluate our destinies. Self-reference and language are, of course, intertwined.

Biologically, languaging includes the use of both words and symbols and cuts across some of the traditional distinctions between verbal and nonverbal behavior. It is rooted in our propensity to live in close proximity with one another for sustained periods of time, and therefore to develop intricate patterns of coordinated action. In fact, languaging is defined by Maturana as the *consensual coordination of consensually coordinated actions*. Notice that in this definition cognitive processes are considered neither separate from nor preliminary to behavioral processes. Biologically, cognizing *is* behaving.

Despite the fact that *individuals* speak and gesture, we must break away from the time-honored practice of explaining cognition primarily as something that individuals do in their heads. Instead, our attention must shift to the communal organization in which symbolic functions arise and without which language could not, and would not, have come into being. Languaging requires the possession of a highly developed nervous system—there is no doubt about that—but it also requires the intimate communal contact that permits complex patterns of living to evolve and to be passed on from generation to generation. That is why Maturana argues that language, as a biological phenomenon, does not take place primarily in the head, but rather in the community. Rather than just examining the cortex of individuals in our attempts to understand human cognition, we must look elsewhere—on the battlefield and the playing field, in the boardroom and the classroom, at the dinner table and the TV nook—the arenas in which life's games are pursued. Cognition occurs in the space of interaction between people. Cognitive patterns are, as Wittgenstein (1922/1971) hints, the games people play.

Thinking, planning, imagining, wishing, analyzing, evaluating, and so on—all the symbolic functions—coordinate social performances and serve to greatly extend the range of human possibilities. Moreover, once a person begins to operate with language, words and symbols become such ubiquitous and integral parts of a person's experience that it becomes virtually impossible for him or her to determine how the world would look without the glasses that those functions provide. However, as useful as our language lenses are, they also blind us—more or less permanently—to some basic truths. It becomes hard to tell which aspects of perception are due to characteristics of the lenses rather than the shape of reality itself. For example, we find it difficult to keep in mind that "time" is *not* a directly perceived aspect of physical reality. It is an organizing scheme—a language formula for observing (Fraser, 1987; Ossorio, 1978). Different formulas yield different realities. Members of other cultures, using their own distinct concepts of time, develop perceptions of the universe that diverge significantly from our own (Rabkin, 1970). Within our own culture, there have been changes in "formula" from time to time, such as when physicists recently adopted the notion of the "space-time continuum."

In other words, once we have started using semantic tools as perceptual aids, it becomes impossible to ever again observe naively—to separate the influence of our perceptual equipment from that which is seen.

SEMANTIC SPACE

Because our semantic space and our perceptual space are so intricately related, some version or another of psychotherapy—the "talking cure"—will retain importance, despite the invention of psychotropic medications and other forms of physical treatment. The existence of psychotherapy is a recognition that a client's problems are at least partly semantic. Not all people who lose money gambling become "compulsive gamblers," and not all individuals who are deeply affected by a marital separation have "adjustment disorders." Although we may attempt to standardize the meanings of such terms in our diagnostic manuals, they do not—in the final analysis—point to objective, identifiable disease processes. They represent social conventions and communal action possibilities. They say something about how we live together and what we can expect from each other. People have smarted over misfortunes in love since time immemorial. Only lately have some of them become "adjustment disordered," requiring the attention of a mental health professional.

Even outside of therapy, the common descriptors that we use to evaluate ourselves and each other on a daily basis—terms such as happy or unhappy, rigid or flexible, shy or assertive, successful or unsuccessful—are wedded to language operations and are not simply statements of objective fact. For example, some individuals who consider themselves "all washed up" in terms of their careers are corporate executives making more money in a year or two than most of us will see in a lifetime. Moreover, many highly "successful" individuals continue to feel alone, unloved, and unwanted. Eartha Kitt, for example, confessed in a recent interview on *60 Minutes* that she still considered herself an abandoned waif despite her lengthy string of artistic, interpersonal, and financial triumphs. She may have acquired the "objective" trappings of fame and fortune, but not the languaging to render them "real" for her.

Language designations such as "up and coming," "over the hill," "fortunate," or "cursed" are anything but trivial—they can make the difference between a person's wanting to celebrate or deciding to commit suicide. However, since such designations are symbolizations rather than concrete actualities, they do not necessarily map neatly onto empirical criteria. That is why so many standard questionnaire and behavioral test instruments fail to live up to their promise.

For better or worse, we live in a world of language—not just in collections of facts and observations. It is in languaging that meanings are created. Without language, life would have to be lived moment-by-moment, minus narrative, evaluation, comparison, or contemplation. We would not know who we are, where we are going, or whether or not we have gotten there—the very issues clients bring to their therapists' doorsteps.

Although we can never truly stand outside ourselves in order to see who we are, language enables us to act as if such a thing were indeed possible—it creates an "observer." Furthermore, we come to believe deeply in the validity of our individual and collective acts of self-observation.

We can never apprehend the world as a simultaneous, unified whole. To "see" it, we first use language to divide it into a series of separate, definable objects and events. Unfortunately, we become so accustomed to the parts we have created that we act as if these divisions were intrinsic aspects of nature and that they predated our arrival on the scene. We reify our basic distinctions and become so attached to them that we can hardly imagine other ways of doing it. Yet new alternatives—new categories of perception—will continue to evolve, and these also will come to seem obvious and natural.

The objectivist believes that our conceptual distinctions yield increasingly accurate and sophisticated understandings of the outside world as it actually exists. Maturana reminds us that this isn't true. Even our most elegant "maps" of the universe are constrained by our biology. They tell us only how our own nervous systems happen to be operating in connection with the surrounding medium. We see the world only in terms of ourselves. That is why he urges that we put terms like "reality" and "objectivity" in quotations marks.[1] This is to remind ourselves that what we think we know about the world is always determined by the exigencies of our own situation. Truly objective knowledge is, and always has been, chimerical. Neither science nor any of our other human pursuits yields privileged access to the pure sort of information of which a diehard realist dreams. Science, for example, is not a way of knowing an objective world independent of us. It is simply the development of specialized languages—particular ways of living together that tend to work for us.

Although, in the abstract, we are aware that people are always coming from their own idiosyncratic perspective, we are sometimes startled when clashes of perspective affect us directly. For example, many therapists are

---

[1] Maturana actually calls this "objectivity in parentheses," but we think that the meaning in English is closer to "in quotation marks," when quotation marks indicate that a word is not being used in its usual sense.

puzzled that their clients see them only as the potential source of magical relief—not as individuals with lives and needs of their own. Clients can, of course, be sublimely oblivious to their therapists' personal values, shortcomings, desires, and frustrations. However, this is not necessarily because they are pathologically immature or lack consideration for others. In matters that count, most of us—including those who would never dream of seeking psychotherapeutic assistance—operate from a very personalized perspective. Any of us, when we are hungry enough, are only able to "see" food. Or, as the old expression goes, when a pickpocket meets a saint, all he sees are his pockets. Again, our "objectivity" never leaves quotation marks.

Language makes possible the most mundane human arrangements, such as meeting a friend on a street corner, as well as our loftiest achievements, such as designing and building the cathedral at Chartres. It is both a blessing and a curse. The same faculty that makes it possible to arrange a date makes it hard not to imagine various upsetting scenarios if the other person is late. A bear can get its paw caught in a trap, but—not having the "gift" of language—it doesn't wonder why it bothered to get up that morning. Animals experience immediate pain and discomfort, but only humans, through the use of words and symbols, worry about how long their suffering will last, and whether the punishment fits the crime. Language leaves people open to more pervasive forms of suffering and despair than those that beset members of other species.

It should be clear that we use the term *language* broadly. It includes all the forms of symbolization of which people are capable. This use is defensible, once you see cognition as communal action—not merely as vocalization. In our use of the term, language expressions are not abstractions—they are consequential acts. As Maturana points out, language hurts: Hitting people over the head with a bit of language can be as potent as hitting them over the head with a two-by-four. Furthermore, the strictures imposed by particular "languaging" modes can be as formidable as walls of steel. Words, just as surely as bullets fired from guns, change the structure of people and their lives. However, words would not have such power if they were not woven so completely into the fabric of our existence.

SUMMARY

The Biblical fall from grace was indeed a fall *into* language (Jaynes, 1976). Language changes everything. Nothing has more importance for us than how events are languaged. Without language, there is only "now"—life unfolding moment by moment without self-consciousness or meaning. With the advent of language, an observing "self" is created and experience is evaluated. Those evaluations continuously and recursively modify what is being experienced, leading to the self-referential quagmire that generates business for psychotherapists. Because Maturana's theory of living systems addresses these self-referential, language-based processes head-on, structure determinism offers clinicians a more useful guide to psychotherapeutic practice than the more traditional, objectivist formulations.

In this chapter we described the view of language embodied in Maturana's theory. In the next chapter we move on to describing the most fundamental operation of a living system – the drawing of distinctions. Acts of distinction are the building blocks that give rise to language and all other human phenomena.

CHAPTER 3

Making Distinctions

At the root of living is distinction-making. The drawing of boundaries is our most primitive and fundamental operation (Brown, 1972). It is the operation that creates a world of "things"–including the "thing" we call ourselves.[1]

The book of Genesis similarly portrays creation as a series of divisions or separations (with accompanying labelings). The folk stories of many other cultures contain equivalent descriptions. For example, members of Australia's aborigine tribes tell how their ancestors "sang" things into existence by calling their names. They maintain–as do we–that "nothing is nothing" until it has first been distinguished and then given some sort of name or symbol (Wallach, 1989, p. 60).

The words and symbols attached to distinctions enable people to take "action at a distance": An object right in front of us can just be picked up. However, if it is farther away in space or time, perhaps in the next room, in the trunk of a car, or in a plan for the future, it helps if it has been given a name.

Each set of distinctions creates new action possibilities. For example, in education, the invention of such notions as adult education, community college, work study, cooperative education, and correspondence courses all

[1]By making distinctions, we bring things into existence. The word *exist* derives from the Latin *existere*, meaning "to stand out from." Therefore, saying that something exists simply means that it has been discriminated from a background. A "this" has been separated from a "that." Things exist for human beings when they have been given definite, defining boundaries.

generated options that were not previously available. At one time psychotherapy was considered strictly an individual affair—clients were seen in private, one at a time. Concepts such as "family systems," "network therapy," "encounter groups," and "psychodrama" made other arrangements possible. Divisions that seem obvious today are those that are in widespread use in the culture. However, as history repeatedly demonstrates, many of today's unusual—even frivolous—divisions are apt to become essential to tomorrow's citizens. New ways of dividing a terrain are always being invented.

It is tempting to believe that there are some divisions so fundamental that they will be of long-time significance, yielding permanent objective truths. However, periodic surprises in "knowing" are the rule rather than the exception. As Bateson put it, "The division of the perceived universe into parts and wholes is convenient and may be necessary, but no necessity determines how it shall be done" (1979, p. 38).

As long as life continues, divisions will continue to be generated. Even in heavily explored domains of human activity, only a very few alternatives have yet been put to use. In that sense, one can never cover a subject completely—after all has been said and done, there is still much more to say and do. Of course, this applies to the domains of client problems as well: Every client situation can be phrased and solved in multiple ways. Most of these possibilities will, at any given point in time, escape notice. Perhaps it is this realization about the practically endless number of options that prompted Adlerian therapist Harold Mosak to remark (at a conference) that *something* can always be done for a client, even though it isn't always clear what that something is. George Kelly (1969) operated with a similar credo: that no event was so fixed in nature that alternative constructions of it were not apt to come along and open new doors.

Although it is important to emphasize the multitude of ways in which distinctions hypothetically might be drawn, it is also imperative to recognize that for a given person, at a given time, there are limits to what can be distinguished. Those limits are set by the person's structure, in interaction with the medium. The proof positive that something *can be* construed a particular way is that it *has been* construed that way. What is, is. A system takes a certain path and can take no other. Paradoxically, the discussion of hypothetical alternatives creates those alternatives, at least as something to discuss.

Consider patients on a ward. In how many ways can they be subdivided and classified? Hundreds? Thousands? Millions? There are the obvious possibilities, such as grouping them by family of origin, appearance, sex, intelligence, years of education, musical ability, place of birth, blood type, financial status, and the multiple descriptors contained in the latest Diagnostic and Statistical Manual. They could also be grouped on the basis of their preference for (a) watching Bill Cosby rather than Sherman Helmsley, (b) eating red meat or being vegetarian, (c) voting liberal or conservative, (d) reading *Time* or *Newsweek*, and (e) being pro-life or pro-choice. We could pick out all those whose occupations begin with an early letter of the alphabet, who have traveled outside the country, or who have seen a particular motion picture. Those whose small intestines contain a given strain of bacteria or whose cholesterol level has reached a particular point could be separated from the rest. Then there are those who acted in school plays versus those who were too shy to do so, those who have tried cocaine versus those who have not, those voted most likely to succeed by their classmates versus those ignored by their peers, and those willing to pay a premium price for Ben & Jerry's ice cream versus those content to stick with Breyers. In other words, there is an infinity of ways of distinguishing. Each split is legitimate in its own right, each has potential usefulness for human endeavors, and each represents only one of an inexhaustible supply of possibilities.

LEGITIMACY OF DISTINCTIONS

The realities available to us are those established by our collective acts of distinction-making. The distinctions made by *any* person's nervous system are legitimate—even when unique—and they have enormous potential significance for his or her life pattern. That some distinctions disturb social harmony is a separate matter. Systems do not make illegitimate distinctions. Distinctions widely shared in a culture will, of course, be seen as more "real." In other words, reality is always a matter of consensus. The consensus must derive from one of two sources. The person compares two realms of experience, having decided which one of them should be given precedence: "If I can touch it, it's really out there." Or, the person compares his or her experience with someone else's: "Did you hear that also?" People getting ill ask, "Is it a fever or do you feel warm, too?" or they take their temperature—which is just a handy way of taking a survey (Gergen, 1982). A person going to a therapist wants to know, "Am I crazy, or do others have similar perceptions?" As in television's *Family Feud*, we always want to know what the survey says.

Many disagreements between people are, at root, quarrels about the rules of precedence to be followed when data from disparate domains of experience conflict. For example, a child wants to stay home from school, but mother's thermometer registers precisely 98.6° Fahrenheit. A "delusional" individual refuses reassurance from family members that no bombs have been planted on the premises. A husband maintains that psychotherapy was worth the price, but his wife can't see any change in his behavior. A therapist's "gut feelings" suggest that a confrontation is needed, although his or her supervisor advises a more conservative approach. A hospitalized patient concludes, against medical advice, that the power of prayer is preferable to the power of Thorazine.

In each of these instances, two sets of distinctions fail to coincide. From our point of view, when distinctions conflict, disagreements about which are to be sustained and which are to be discounted are inevitably political debates. However, they are often languaged as something else—maladaptive thinking, lapses of objectivity, symptoms of psychopathology, the work of the devil, and so on. Such characterizations imply a world view in which somebody or some group of people has privileged access to the way things actually are—an objective standard against which the validity of all other distinctions must be measured. However, reality is always established by conferring with others (who are more or less in the same circumstances). In other words, everything said to establish a reality is said from within a particular, fallible tradition (Maturana, 1988a, 1988b; Varela, 1979).

THE POWER OF CONSENSUS

The powerful illusion of the realist that absolute knowledge can be produced is fostered by the fact that we consult with one another. We both look through the same microscope or telescope. We apply the same theories to what we see there. Since we have similar nervous systems, we often see roughly the same thing. Where there is consensus, we tend to assume objectivity. However, the consensus is never static, and it is apt to shift when voting rights are extended to additional groups of people.

A mental hospital staff meets regularly to discuss diagnoses. Staff members congratulate themselves on achieving a high degree of agreement. However, there is nothing surprising about this, since they were trained to agree. They were groomed to play a role in sustaining certain traditions. They were selected for similarity in interests and professional affiliation. They went to the same schools—sometimes the exact same school—studied the same authorities, and read the same textbooks. Some institutions are specifically identified as being "psychoanalytic," "cognitive-behavioral," or "family systems" oriented. Within these broad groupings, staff members may make further distinctions, paying attention only to the opinions of a subset of colleagues whom they "respect" or who share their affinity for a particular theorist or viewpoint. Thus, consensus is not coincidental—it has been prearranged. Hospital staff members are not assessing raw reality—

they are celebrating commonality within a club with restrictive membership rules. In these contexts, which pull for consensus, it is the disputes that are interesting—not the agreements.

Recently, the director of a large mental health agency experimented with allowing representatives from patients' rights groups to participate in staff conferences. This produced an immediate and cataclysmic reaction. Staff morale dropped precipitously and there were wholesale threats of resignation. Suddenly, every diagnosis, treatment plan, and patient disposition became a source of controversy. The director was soon forced to abandon the practice of allowing participation by "outsiders," causing an even bigger political commotion than the one he had hoped to avoid.

Similarly, the National Alliance for the Mentally Ill has managed to puncture the self-congratulatory balloons of many professionals—particularly family therapists (Bales, 1988; Johnson, 1988a, 1988b). Members of the alliance have taken umbrage at principles and practices that these therapists have long taken for granted. Such bitter controversies between mental health professionals and members of the groups they presumably serve are not new. Self-help groups like Alcoholics Anonymous have a long history of strained relations with the medical community. Recently, at a national conference, a psychologist who is also a recovering schizophrenic had an opportunity to admonish his colleagues concerning the cavalier, imperial, and insensitive manner with which they often approach the mentally ill and members of their families (Buie, 1989). Such interchanges between professionals and those they serve are potentially useful. They remind us that what one group considers self-evident and scientifically validated facts are, to another group, just a collection of narrow-minded, parochial, and self-serving opinions.

Sometimes when clients show up at the psychotherapist's door, all they really want is an ally in their fight to maintain consensus. They want the therapist to help substantiate that they have indeed "tried everything" to get along with a particular relative; that their addiction—not a lack of talent—prevents them from being promoted; that their history of childhood abuse explains (and excuses) their romantic failures; that having a manic-depressive son cannot be said to be their fault; and so on. For many, psychotherapy is mainly a social negotiation in which attributions and statuses can be established or revised. "According to my doctor, your having been arrested is definitely not my fault." "You can't throw me out now, just when I'm finally getting back on my feet and making progress in therapy." "At least I have recognized my problem and I'm trying to do something about it."

We recall a spat between two lovers—each of whom was seeing a different therapist. In the middle of the argument, the first announced,

"My therapist thinks it's self-destructive for me to stay in this relationship." "Oh, yeah?" said the second, "Well, *my* therapist said breaking up now would be the worst thing I could do. It would just be a repetition of my cycle of rejection." A mutual friend of the couple suggested that they might save time and energy by having their therapists fight it out directly.

MYTH-MAKING

In the realm of human activity, we must accept that all our so-called "discoveries" about the world are only tentative, tradition-bound human inventions. Other inventions will be along soon. In fact, in the mental health field, most of our favorite beliefs have not had a good track record. They have been revealed as mythologies after relatively short periods of time. Not long ago, professionals were convinced that masturbation was highly detrimental to mental and physical health. Early in his career, Freud wrote of the mental health dangers of premature ejaculation and coitus interruptus. Male homosexuality was long thought to be caused by weak fathering, while lesbianism was considered an outcome of penis envy and masculine striving. Schizophrenia and autism were attributed to "icebox" mothering. (The fact that many of these same mothers had other—perfectly normal—offspring didn't seem to make a dent in people's opinions about this.) Infant crib deaths in institutions were regularly considered a fatal form of depression resulting from the lack of a distinct mother figure (Ribble, 1943; Spitz, 1950, 1965). Public-speaking fears were interpreted as manifestations of castration anxiety. Manic-depression was presumed to be associated with excessive achievement strivings.

Today's myths-in-the-making are not apt to fare much better than those of the previous several decades. In fact, the persistence of mental health beliefs—and the earnestness with which they are held in some circles—is truly remarkable. Some beliefs persist in the face of readily available contradictory data. The everyday experiences of therapists as parents, children, workers, and citizens ought to be enough to cause some of these beliefs to be immediately abandoned or at least viewed with skepticism.

A vivid example of this is the curious case of a psychological investigator named Garcia. About 30 years ago he produced good evidence concerning conditioned food aversions (Barker, Best, & Domjan, 1977). Most of us can recall times when we developed a rapid and long-standing aversion to a food simply because we got sick soon after having eaten it, even though we knew the food had nothing to do with the illness. This is exactly the phenomenon Garcia was documenting. At the time, however, no editors would publish his work, because they could not make sense of his findings within the framework of the learning-theory tenets of the time. Had these editors examined their own experience, even briefly, they would have recognized that Garcia was on the right track and was exploring a widespread and important phenomenon of learning. The editors were unable to "see" the obvious.

There are many other examples of how, as "professionals" trying to be "objective," we tend to lose sight of the insights gained through everyday experience. For instance, when we ourselves are depressed, we know that our thinking becomes sweepingly negativistic—nothing seems right with the world and small problems loom large. When our mood shifts, these gloomy thoughts dissipate and problems seem easily manageable once again. Given that we have all had this kind of experience, how could we so readily have concurred with theorists who were arguing that depression is caused by maladaptive thinking patterns of long duration? Clearly (as the research we cited in Chapter 1 seems to show), shifts in thinking are secondary to depression—not the cause of it. This obvious conclusion is further reinforced by the fact that drug therapies for depressed individuals work about as well as therapies that attempt to retrain thinking patterns.

Minuchin (1974) points out that family therapists—who ought to know better—continue to operate with an idealized image of family life derived more from novels and Hollywood fantasies than from real life or research investigations.

> Somehow, the prevailing idealized view of the normal family is that it is nonstressful. In spite of sociological and anthropological studies of the family, the myth of placid normality endures, supported by hours of two-dimensional television characters. This picture of people living in harmony, coping with social inputs without getting ruffled, and always cooperating with each other, crumbles whenever one looks at any family with its ordinary problems. It is therefore alarming that this standard is sometimes maintained unchallenged by therapists, who measure the functioning of client families against the idealized image. (pp. 50–51)

Some of these workers appear to implicitly promise their clients that their family life will soon resemble the scenarios of *Father Knows Best*, *The Brady Bunch*, *Leave It to Beaver*, and *The Cosby Show* all rolled up into one. Their own family lives are not this way, nor do these glossy expectations fit the lives of families they have witnessed firsthand. Yet these unrealistic expectations persist.

Most of us are familiar with people who have grown up to be delightful, well-adjusted, and successful despite having had childhoods characterized by parental neglect, trauma, and abuse. On the other hand, we know people who have done relatively poorly despite having had pleasant parents and ordinary upbringings. Our brothers and sisters may have turned out very differently from us, despite having been brought up by the same parents and having been exposed to similar backgrounds. Such life experiences ought to have created skepticism about the postulated relationships between adult psychopathology and childhood upbringing. Again, however, we tend to compartmentalize our knowledge, using different "rules" for clients than for each other.

When pressed, we explain away differences in siblings by arguing that birth-order makes a difference or that traumatic occurrences—seen and unseen—may have played a role. However, the research evidence on birth-order effects has not been compellingly positive (e.g., Tierney, 1983). Moreover, recent studies of identical twins reared apart should dissuade us from placing much faith in that line of reasoning. They show, for example, that identical twins may develop the same phobias even when they have been raised by different parents in different countries and under different circumstances (Tellegen, et al., 1988; Watson, 1981).[2]

Yet, despite formal and informal evidence to the contrary, many therapists persist in believing in simplistic formulations concerning the relationship between childhood experience, adult personality characteristics, and mental health status. Most of the time, they overemphasize the influence of parents on children and underemphasize the influence of children on parents. One probable reason for this bias is that adult clients want their therapists to show them how the past is connected to the present, and they want the story told from their point of view. On the other hand, few children arrive at a therapist's doorstep demanding explanations of how it is that they are driving their parents to distraction.

We might be less susceptible to professional myths if we took Maturana's advice and kept "objectivity" in quotation marks. Otherwise, we become carried away with each new pronouncement by the authorities, from the latest dental association recommendation about which way to brush to the newest formulation concerning the etiology of agoraphobia. We think that people should stay informed about what the experts are saying; however, at the same time, they should recognize that expert opinions are still just sets of distinctions and are subject to change without notice.

---

[2]These twins seem *more similar* than those raised together, presumably because they did not live with someone from whom they felt a need to differentiate.

DOMAINS

Distinctions generate domains of activity. Domains may have points of intersection. For example, the domains of chess and checkers include similar playing boards. However, by definition, each domain is separate and distinct; it is closed. Chess permits only chess ploys; religion permits only religious ploys; psychiatry permits only psychiatric ploys. Strictly speaking, the moves of chess never transport one outside that game, and religious practices lead only to more religion. Although bishops exist in both chess and religion, they serve separate functions and are not interchangeable.

Sometimes it may seem as if a person can get "out" of one domain using "equipment" that belongs to another. Certain religions, for example, encourage psychotic individuals to pray for relief from their symptoms, and football players—who invariably seem convinced that God is on their side—pray for victory over the opposing team. However, football teams win by scoring points and, thus far, psychotic symptoms seem to respond best to a decrease in stress or an increase in medication. If prayer decreases stress, leading to less hallucinating or better scoring, then the analysis becomes more complex, although the principle that domains are closed and self-contained remains the same.

People do, of course, operate in many diverse domains in close temporal proximity, and they can switch rapidly between domains. A famous basketball player, who was having trouble scoring from the foul line, tried to improve his game by making the sign of the cross before each shot. When that didn't work, he consulted a well-known hypnotherapist. This player employed, in rapid succession, operations from several different domains—religion, basketball, and hypnosis. The *domains* do not intersect, but the player can travel rapidly between them. Unfortunately, in this instance, neither God nor the hypnotist delivered the goods, and the player's team lost the championship.

Many clients are consternated by their failure to understand the separateness of domains. They try to get satisfaction in one domain while operating in a totally different one. For example, a person keeps hoping that the next job promotion will lead to happiness. But job promotions generally lead to more job promotions, not happiness. People fail to appreciate that the "solution" being sought is unavailable in the domain being searched. In other words, they keep looking in the wrong place. Similarly, therapists become so wedded to certain models that they are unable to spot alternatives for providing assistance that would otherwise be obvious. For example, not everything a therapist does needs to be a "treatment" or a deep psychological analysis. A few of our jobless clients appreciated being directed toward a good book on preparing resumes instead of being subjected to lengthy discussions of their self-defeating tendencies.

Not all domains of distinction are language domains. After all, frogs and paramecia make distinctions although they cannot speak, and so do infants. However, many of the most interesting distinctions—particularly from the point of view of psychotherapists—are those that are embodied in language acts. Even domains of experience that appear to be relatively language-free usually incorporate linguistic components. Pain, for example, is not simply an accumulation of raw sensation. It is sensation filtered through a set of language percepts. A number of years ago, we did some research on the cold pressor task, in which subjects are asked to leave their hands in circulating ice water (Efran, Chorney, Ascher, & Lukens, 1989). The degree of difficulty the subjects had with the task and the sensations they reported were dependent on how they construed the task. Some were frightened even before they tried it and approached it with trepidation. Others thought of it as an exciting challenge—an opportunity to prove something to themselves or to best someone else's record. Similarly, the discomfort of a phobic dental patient is largely conceptual; it begins long before a drill comes in contact with his or her tooth. Dental anxiety is 5 percent sensation and 95 percent conversation.

Once it is recognized how much of an experience is a conversation about an event—not just the event itself—then a number of mysteries associated with psychotherapeutic practice clear up. For example, it has long been recognized that some of therapy's benefits are linked to the generation of hope (e.g., Frank, 1973, 1987). Most traditional theories have not been able to provide a satisfactory explanation of this or other so-called "nonspecific" factors. When we realize, however, that therapy is an alteration of conversation, there is no surprise in finding that different conversational pathways modify how events are perceived and experienced. This would be true wherever the conversations in question happened to take place.

When you distinguish something differently, its identity shifts. However, this does not mean that you have the power to change anything at will just by giving it a new name. You cannot, for example, turn a chair into a table just by saying so. If you attempt to do this, the chair will remain a chair, but people will consider you deranged. Language distinctions represent community practices, and you cannot remain a community member in good standing if you engage in capricious word magic. Even individuals in profound psychotic states generally know better than to call a chair a table. A paranoid individual may believe that the chair has been electrically rigged by a hostile foreign government or that the table transmits thought waves.

Nevertheless, he or she is usually clear about which one to sit on and which one to put a meal tray on.

Acts of distinction carry profound implications. Human beings live their distinctions. As was demonstrated when Salman Rushdie's book, ***The Satanic Verses***, was published, a verbal turn can instigate widespread rioting and bloodshed. Similarly, the recent Supreme Court decision allowing flag-burning deeply disturbed many citizens. On the one hand, the American flag is just a piece of cloth. At the same time, it is a symbolic distinction. The furor over how it is to be treated underscores the fact that our distinctions are us.

SUMMARY

Living consists of making distinctions. Every distinction brings something into existence. Domains of distinctions are the sandboxes in which we play life's games. These domains are self-contained—they have their own boundaries, vocabularies, and grammars of interaction. In each "box," you have to play by a particular set of rules. If you want to play a different sort of game, you have to move from one box to another.

New sets of distinctions are constantly being invented, and old ones fall into disuse. Even those paradigms we regard as most stable—those that seem to mirror reality itself—are subject to change. However, consensus does not confer objectivity. By keeping "objectivity" in quotation marks, as Maturana recommends, we remind ourselves that our distinctions are human contrivances—not ultimate truths. All distinctions, including unpopular ones, are legitimate. Mental health percepts, like any other sets of distinctions, must be judged on the basis of their workability in enabling us to live well together.

Distinctions are the fundamental building blocks of life. In the next chapter we look at a larger picture—the kinds of meanings that people generate by linking distinctions together. As we shall see, life is a meaningless drift, to which we add our own meanings as we go along.

CHAPTER 4

The Drift of Living

People like to believe that the human race is the pinnacle of nature's achievements. Distinguished paleontologist Stephen Jay Gould likes to remind us that such a notion is merely a human conceit (Gould, 1989; Mehren, 1989). In evolutionary terms, humans are an accident of nature—a lucky afterthought. We are the tiniest of twigs on a very large tree. It wouldn't have taken much for the branch we are on to have broken off somewhere along the way, leaving us out of the picture altogether.

People also like to think of their individual lives as being part of some grand scheme and serving some specific purpose. Here again, the long view suggests that such beliefs are egocentric and misguided. Biologically speaking, both the general pathway of evolution and the unfolding of an individual life are about as random as you can get. An average existence consists of a series of accidental happenings and twists of fate—relationships that crisscross and intertwine, break off, and take unexpected turns. In other words, life is a *purposeless drift*.

An individual is like a passenger on the ship of life—along for the cruise but not the captain of the voyage. When things are going smoothly, each passenger likes to think of himself or herself as being at the helm. Yet, when the seas are rough, few are eager to shoulder full responsibility for the direction the journey seems to be taking. When clients come to us for therapy, they perceive that the ship has veered badly off course and might be about to sink. Sometimes they want to know how it got that way. More often, they would be content if someone—anyone—would just set the rudder straight.

THE LIVING SYSTEM—AUTOPOIESIS

Maturana defines living systems as *autopoietic*—a word he invented.[1] Autopoietic entities, because of the way they are structurally organized, are engaged in the process of producing more of themselves. This process is manifest at every level of organization, from the cell to the colony. Cells grow and split, forming additional like-structured cells. Parents have offspring, perpetuating the family line. Missionaries go around the world replicating aspects of their community of origin. Living, from the ingestion of food to the excretion of waste, consists of cycles of self-production. For a living system there is a unity between product and process: In other words, the major line of work for a living system is creating more of itself.

Autopoiesis is neither a promise nor a purpose—it is an organizational characteristic. This means that life lasts only as long as it lasts. It doesn't come with guarantees. In contrast to what we are tempted to believe, people do not stay alive because of their strong survival instincts or because they have important jobs to complete. They stay alive because their autopoietic organization happens to permit it. When the essentials of that organization are lost, a person's career comes to an end—he or she disintegrates.

Any organism survives by maintaining successful couplings to the surrounding medium. In other words, it retains its basic organizational features despite bombardments from the outside. Even though many structural changes are taking place inside and outside, the organism's shape remains sufficiently stable to be recognized by an "observer." The career of a living system is nothing more than an organizational constancy measured against a backdrop of internal and external perturbations.

NATURAL DRIFT

Life, as a purposeless drift, is a series of accommodations an organism makes as it moves through a medium. By definition, every accommodation is successful except the last. As the person falling off a forty-story building

---

[1] Although biologists routinely study living creatures, they had not previously developed a satisfactory, all-encompassing definition of what being alive means. It is not unusual for a field to avoid coming to grips with its basic definitions. The assumptions that shape the nature of an endeavor are often so thoroughly taken for granted that they remain in the background, eluding direct examination. (As the old saying goes, when you want to know something about water, don't ask a fish!)

said as he passed the second-story window: "So far, so good." He could make that statement because he was still an instant away from the one final destructive interaction to which we are all—like it or not—entitled.

In the structural drift of life, there are no goals, no set directions, no promises. Imagine a boat afloat in the ocean without benefit of motor, rudder, or sails. The directions in which the boat floats are entirely a function of its shape and how it interacts with the randomly changing patterns of wind and waves. The boat continues as an entity until it either sinks from view or breaks apart, losing its identity. The boat isn't going anywhere in particular.

However, an observer watching the boat probably will *infer* purposes and motives. The boat will appear to know what it is doing and where it is heading. It may seem to have a mission to fulfill and the "guts" to remain afloat until that mission has been completed. Likewise, people readily attribute intentions to their houseplants, their pets, and even their household appliances. Many people, for example, are convinced that their plants develop root-rot or other dread diseases just for spite. One of the authors is sure that some of his appliances (particularly the dishwasher and the refrigerator) break down only on weekends—especially weekends when the house is full of company. A car skidding on an icy roadway seems to have a knack for heading directly into a roadside tree, even if it is the only obstacle for miles around.

If we are inclined to attribute intention to the inanimate, we are even more compelled to interpret our own lives and the lives of others in terms of purpose and intent. Living—to the person doing it—seems anything but random. Religious and cultural teachings reinforce the belief in a "just world" (Lerner & Simmons, 1966) in which there are definite goals and in which hard work and good deeds are rewarded while evil practices are eventually exposed and punished. Good works not adequately compensated in this life may be rewarded in an afterlife.

People are also encouraged to invent and believe in a series of fictitious devices to account for moments when they don't feel in control: They were in the throes of emotional turmoil. The devil made them do it. They lacked sufficient willpower or courage to stay on track. They were swayed by their addictions to various substances (e.g., cocaine, alcohol, tobacco) or activities (e.g., gambling, sex, eating). They were at the mercy of powerful unconscious motives.

Of course, since we participate in communities organized by such ideas, even entirely fictitious explanations can have powerful effects on our lives. In the days when witchcraft was a popular organizing principle, people were tortured or burned at the stake because someone had decided that they were possessed. These days, the dividing line between acceptable scientific-sounding explanations and those based entirely on verbal fictions is more subtle: People lose jobs because they "lack drive"; children are criticized for being "lazy" or "unmotivated"; therapists steer away from clients who "lack ego strength." Such concepts, when recognized as rough-and-ready summaries of behavioral patterns, can be useful to members of the community. However, when people think of these explanations as being valid descriptions of inner mechanisms, they confuse semantics and operations.

It behooves professionals to keep their conceptual houses in order. Psychotherapists are the experts designated to help people understand and improve themselves. When they themselves use and endorse hazy concepts, their interventions have the opposite effect—they contribute to the inarticulateness that keeps people stuck.

A client who is trying to "increase her self-control" is on a fool's errand. Self-control is a verbal fiction—it cannot be willfully increased or decreased. There are no system operations to which it directly corresponds. Recently, at her first session, a client reported that she had slept with a casual acquaintance because she lacked "self-discipline." She wanted therapy to make her more disciplined, so that she could avoid such guilt-provoking, unproductive, and risky entanglements in the future. Of course, therapy cannot do that. In therapy, clients are invited to clarify their options and desires, evaluate the costs of actions, distinguish between the actual and the hypothetical, and speak plainly and responsibly about who they are. As they accomplish those tasks, their need to use ambiguous and misleading concepts, such as "self-control," diminishes.

SEMANTIC VENTRILOQUISM

The brother of one of the authors once had a dog named Woody. He would impress guests with how obedient and well disciplined Woody was by instructing the dog to do whatever he was already doing. When the timing was right, it looked to the visitor as if Woody was following orders: "Okay, Woody, walk over this way. Now pause a while. Good dog. Now keep right on barking. That's right. Okay, that was enough barking."

Hypnotists do something similar. They amplify subjects' receptivity by shadowing their actions and reactions: "You are beginning to be aware of your left hand." "Something interesting is happening in that hand." After a while, subjects aren't sure who is leading whom, and they don't have much time to puzzle it out. The hypnotist's suggestions gently meld with their own thought patterns.

Likewise, in life, our typical language patterns foster the confusion of prediction with control—people "hypnotize" themselves into believing that their description of what is about to happen is actually what makes it happen. They say "I have decided to go and get some lunch" instead of "In the past, when I felt these sensations, I found myself getting something to eat." Running commentary gets mistaken for control.

CONTROL AND CHOICE

In some theories of therapy, it is assumed that we are normally in control of ourselves except under special circumstances, such as when defense mechanisms cloud perception or unconscious drives interfere. We take a different position. We assert that behaviors—including thoughts and feelings—are not controlled by an ego or a particular set of motives—conscious or unconscious—but by our composite structures, which are continuously in the process of adapting to internal and external perturbations. Terms like "control," "self-control," and "choice" are language ***metaphors*** applied after the fact. They are not operational realities. Having a chat with ourselves about increasing self-control does not impel action—such pep talks are *part* of the very changes they presumably instigate.

A well-known cybernetic principle states that a part of a system cannot control the system of which it is a part (Dell, 1982a; McCulloch, 1965; von Foerster, 1981; Wiener, 1961). Being part of your self, you are unable to control yourself. The nervous system you seek to master is you. That much is simple cybernetics. Yet, as humans, we use language to break ourselves up into portions—ego, self, impulses, drive states, defense mechanisms—that can presumably control the whole. Some such assumption is a central component of almost every theory of psychotherapy: Cognitions are said to control emotions; emotions are said to control cognitions; behavior is said to control both; behavior is said to be controlled *by* both; the adult is said to control the child; the need for self-actualization is said to control achievement striving; and so on. However, a system operates as a unity—component parts are not hierarchically arranged. The governor of an engine does not—despite its name—govern anything. It is just an integral component of a machine that, as a whole, manifests the property of regulated speed. Moreover, with regard to changes in speed, the governor is as much the slave as the master. It has no more "choice" about the speed of the engine than any other component has.

Concepts such as self-control, free will, and self-determination cannot be taken literally. The implication that people can motivate themselves—literally picking themselves up by their bootstraps—is misleading. Operationally speaking, whatever you find yourself doing is "it." At that point, there are no alternatives. All those "ifs, ands, and buts" are just discussion—additional language actions that add to and enrich the picture but are not "in charge" of it.

Neurons fire or they don't. They don't take "votes." We don't choose when they should fire. Also, we have no choice over our birth date, our parents, or our country of origin. We don't select whether to grow up male or female, short or tall, musical or artistic, athletic or poorly coordinated, rich or poor, even-tempered or emotionally labile, nurtured or abused. We don't decide on our food likes and dislikes—or on when we will find the courage to modify them. Falling asleep is automatic—and sometimes we toss and turn, upset that it hasn't happened yet. We do not determine what we will think or feel next, when we will decide we have had enough, or when the urge to "reform" will hit us. In fact, we don't really decide anything. The structure of our language gives the appearance of choice where none exists. Paradoxically, being told "It's your choice" may change a situation. It can put us on the spot and "force" us to respond in ways we hadn't predicted and cannot control.

We choose neither our motives nor their intensity. To the extent that we know something about what drives us, it is because, as language observers, we have had the opportunity to watch ourselves operate time after time. By recalling what we have previously done, we attempt to predict what we will do next, staying a bit ahead of the game wherever possible. In other words, knowing from experience that we are approaching the time when we will probably want something to eat, we begin preparing some food.

Despite frequent errors in self-prediction, our faith in our ability to run the show generally remains unshaken. In speaking to ourselves and others, we paper over the surprises that pop up in our own behavior. For example, when a friend reminds us that we are not studying, although we had announced earlier that we would be, we can provide a ready explanation: "Oh, I changed my mind at the last minute." Or, "Yes, and I was just getting down to work."

The friend's comment has an impact on what we do next, even though he or she may not be able to predict the direction of the impact. The question may hasten our getting down to work or prompt yet another "change of mind." Every query, from the outside or the inside, becomes incorporated into the ongoing flow of system adjustments. After a while it is impossible to fully discriminate one source of influence from another. However, in talking about what happened, the friend's role in the evolving drift is apt to be overlooked or underacknowledged. We prefer to think that we decided—on our own—whether to study or not.

Our accepted rhetoric, particularly in the American can-do culture, is that of the self-made man or woman who—by dint of hard work, good planning, and determination—makes crucial decisions, carefully controlling the essentials of his or her destiny. The image is wrong on many counts. First, most major decisions—changing jobs, getting married, deciding on a career—are made intuitively rather than rationally. Although we make lists of pros and cons and assign "weights" to all the factors, in the final analysis a decision just feels like the right thing to do. When it doesn't, we postpone deciding, make new lists, consult additional advisors, add information, and so on. Sometimes we decide "finally" and "logically" several times over.

Second, the American image of the individualist ignores the fact that our lives are lived within a community. We think in the language the community provides and judge our successes or failures by reference to communal standards. We don't typically grow our own flour, bake our own bread, raise our own sheep, or sew our own clothes. We ride in cars and elevators others have invented and built, read books others have written, listen to music others have recorded, and watch TV programs others have produced. Very little about our lives is genuinely separate or individual. We may defiantly say "Who cares?" concerning someone else's evaluations, but ultimately our identities are the sum of such reactions and our counterreactions. From our possessions to our obsessions, we are embedded in—and embodiments of—the communities in which we develop.

Third, as we have been explaining, we have little actual control over either ourselves or our destinies. We drift—interacting, changing, and commenting, but not controlling. The nervous system is a "conversation." With regard to that conversation, we are eavesdroppers—not dictators. We hear thoughts that bubble to the surface, and as observers we become aware of some of our action patterns. Much of what we do remains in the background—unnoticed—not because it is hidden or unconscious or because we have powerful defenses, but because only highly abstracted and selected aspects of our total system operations are ever symbolized in language. The rest does not enter directly into our conversations with self. Moreover, we do not get to make the selections. When we speak aloud, we hear our sentences at about the same time other listeners do. We aren't privy to the process by which particular words are chosen and strung together into sentences and paragraphs.

If, while listening to ourselves speak, we were to suddenly discover that we were not making sense—an experience common in certain neurological disorders and when mind-altering drugs are ingested—we would probably find ourselves helpless to straighten matters out. People suffering from certain aphasias and apraxias, for example, may "know" they want a pencil or a piece of paper, but are totally unable to find or utter the right words.

Another person may begin brushing his or her teeth, only to have the sequence inexplicably break off midstream. The person is left in perplexity, holding the toothbrush, understanding that something is amiss, perhaps even knowing what that something is, but being incapable of fixing it. As often as the person starts over, he or she cannot bring the sequence to a satisfactory conclusion.

MELDING VERSUS PUSHING

Many readers will no doubt have trouble with the image of humankind we are presenting. The notion of life as a drift is more in tune with Eastern mysticism and European existentialism than American pragmatism. Stereotypically, the Easterner is more willing to meld with his or her surroundings, but the Westerner insists on dominating and controlling self and environment. (Of course, neither contemplative Easterners nor pragmatic Westerners *choose* their preferred adaptive style.)

In America, in particular, we resist acknowledging the haphazard, chancy, or fateful nature of existence. Thus, perhaps more than people in any other culture, Americans can be devastated by a crippling injury, a serious illness, a sudden change of mood, or a failure at love. Such events thwart our craving for mastery and independence. They come as unwelcome reminders of our vulnerability, and of the potential capriciousness of life (Yalom, 1989).

Although the picture of life we are presenting—a meaningless drift to which we ourselves add meaning—may startle those who have grown accustomed to something else, the portrayal is not intended to be gloomy or pessimistic. In fact, the notion of life as a meaningless drift can be liberating and uplifting. When individuals grasp that meanings are not carved in stone, they are freed to investigate, experiment with, and invent meanings of their own—meanings that may be more compatible with their pattern of interests and needs than those with which they started. They find themselves cultivating affiliations that afford them wider latitude of self-expression and reducing their participation in groups where the ideological "fit" is strained—groups to which they previously experienced a stronger obligation to belong.

THE ASTUTE DEPRESSIVE

Depressed individuals, for example, tend to cling tenaciously to roles and expectations that they are unable to fulfill. They are trying to be the good mother, the diligent worker, the model citizen. However, a gap develops between what they have promised themselves and others and what they are able to deliver. Their evaluation of their performance is not necessarily off base. In fact, research shows that depressed people make more veridical judgments than nondepressed people do (e.g., Alloy & Abramson, 1979). Therefore, the "breakdown" the depressed person suffers is not a breakdown of perceptual or cognitive skill, but a rupture in the link between his or her image of life and the way life happens to be unfolding. He or she may visit a therapist hoping that the linkage can be repaired.

Our method of working with such individuals, when contrasted with the approaches of other therapists, is similar in some important respects but different in others. Like most therapists, we avoid direct attempts to cheer up a depressed individual. However, unlike other therapists—particularly cognitive-behaviorists—we make no attempt to strengthen or spruce up their cognitive or perceptual skills. In fact, we do our best to further erode what some consider an already weakened grasp of reality. Beck, Ellis, and other cognitive-behaviorists (Rorer, 1989a, 1989b) have all expressed concerns about the depressed person's all-or-none thinking patterns and his or her tendency to overgeneralize—for example, treating minor, temporary misfortunes as major, permanent calamities. We, on the other hand, urge the depressed person to make still more sweeping generalizations. This is in keeping with our hunch that the depressed person has glimpsed a bit of the truth about life but resisted taking his or her line of reasoning to its logical conclusion. By stopping midway, the depressed individual becomes stuck between two world views, neither willing to plunge ahead nor able to retreat comfortably back to his or her earlier conception. We want the person to take the forward leap.

To put it starkly, the depressed person comes in thinking that there must be a right path that he or she either hasn't found or hasn't been able to adhere to. From our point of view the path the person is trying so hard to locate doesn't exist—it is, and always has been, a mirage.

One such client complained that his career was "meaningless." We argued that this made perfect sense to us, since *all* careers are meaningless. Even the loftiest of careers is ultimately a waste of time, going nowhere. After some heated but interesting discussion around this point, he began to see that he might be among the lucky, rather than the unlucky. He was having *his* mid-life crisis early—avoiding the general rush. Others would later come to question whether the goals that they had worked most of their lives to achieve were worth the sacrifices they had made along the way. Did even the applause really mean anything substantial? When they finally got around to asking the big questions—such as "What was it all for?"—they might find themselves locked into pathways that were then too costly to abandon. Because our client was asking himself the existential questions now—at the outset—before he had acquired a large mortgage, he would still have time to take remedial action, should it be required.

People like this, in the throes of disappointment and disillusionment, are very susceptible to the "grass is greener" phenomenon. Such individuals are tempted to trade careers, locations, mates, or life-styles, hoping to find a better set of circumstances than the one they are used to. Most of the time, such changes simply postpone the inevitable—that day of reckoning when they discover that the differences between good and bad circumstances aren't as consequential as had been believed, and that circumstances, per se, aren't really to blame for their discontent. In fact, most people can—and do—create the very same kinds of dissatisfaction whatever their circumstances. They change jobs or partners, but after a short while they develop similar complaints. As someone once said about why vacations so often turn out to be disappointments, "Unfortunately, we always take ourselves along."

In any event, this client resisted the temptation to switch careers. He stayed at his job but maximized those aspects of the work that he found personally satisfying, instead of spending his time worrying about "getting somewhere." He realized there was no place to get to and that he could find fulfillment right where he was.

Another client, also experiencing career conflicts, turned the corner when he finally gave himself permission to take an extended vacation that he had been putting off for years. He, too, had been living life as a waiting game—banking on the *next* promotion, or certainly the one after that, to fill the void. He exemplified the sort of men described by Margaret Fuller, 19th-century literary critic, who "for the sake of getting a living forget to live." He knew something was wrong, but he couldn't put his finger on what it was. In therapy, he realized that no matter how many promotions he received, they would never be enough. Each accolade that came his way would be only a momentary "fix" and would soon be sullied by the fruit bats of self-doubt and self-criticism (Jackins, 1965). No matter how much he achieved, real or imagined competition from others would continue to plague him and associates would continue to ask, as they always had, "Yes, but what have you done for us lately?"

This client's waiting strategy would have made sense if he had been able to identify something really worth waiting for. He couldn't. Finally, appreciating that life is lived *now* and not later, he took off on his long-delayed vacation. An enormous burden seemed to have been lifted from his shoulders.

IS CHANGE CONTROLLABLE?

It is sheer hubris to think that as therapists we control other people's lives when we cannot even control our own. Even jailers and dictators do not control the lives of their subjects, much as they might like to. They can sometimes extract high prices for public acts of noncompliance. Nevertheless, some political prisoners—like Valentin in the film *Kiss of the Spider Woman*—may, even under extreme torture, resist believing the thoughts or having the feelings that the dictator demands. They might avoid even giving an *appearance* of compliance—to them the torture is worth it.

People are basically unable to predict in advance how they will react when faced with a given stressor. One of the authors was held up at gunpoint several years ago. Much to his surprise, he fought back, risking death and injury, for no particularly good reason. He wasn't carrying much cash, and he knew what the police advise—comply, comply, comply. However, as the event unfolded, compliance was the farthest thing from his mind. A variety of unanticipated reactions were evoked. For example, unbelievably, he found himself knocking the gun out of one attacker's hand and then chasing the two assailants down a nearby embankment. Fortunately, they ran faster, since it is anybody's guess what might have transpired had he caught up with them.

Our unpredictability extends to matters both small and large—from job choices to menu choices. For instance, a person looks forward to ordering a particular dish at his favorite restaurant. He tells everyone exactly what he will be having. However, when the waiter arrives, he orders something completely different. The person is as astonished at this "change of mind" as anyone else. It just "seemed right" at the time. Such choices can always be rationalized later, but they cannot be predicted or controlled. This isn't a matter of psychopathology, and it isn't mysterious—once you appreciate that humans are autopoietic entities involved in a natural drift.

In a world of flux, everything is always changing. Change is the one thing that can be counted on. Move around and you change. Sit still and you change. Go to a therapist and you change. Quit treatment and you change. Refuse to change and you change. However, what we *call* change is another matter entirely and itself keeps changing. As Einstein suggested, the subset of changes we focus on are only meaningful in relation to a background of changes that, for whatever reasons, are less interesting to us. In other words, there are differences and then there are differences that *make a difference* (Bateson, 1979). An observer singles out and punctuates certain shifts as the noteworthy ones. Therefore, when clients (or therapists) declare that after months of treatment "still nothing has changed," they mean only that the changes that have been occurring are not the ones in which they were interested. They were looking for and expecting something else.

Psychotherapists cannot change people any more than they can control them. As most of us know, a judge may insist that a client be "seen" by a therapist, but the court cannot mandate that their sessions together prove therapeutic. Parents can send their children to bed without dinner but cannot thereby ensure that the kids will learn to respect their elders. They can bribe a teenager to clean his or her room, but this will not necessarily instill an intrinsic appreciation for neatness. For that matter, most of us are at a loss to explain how or why *we* suddenly changed into neatniks after a childhood of unrestrained messiness, and we would be hard-pressed to know how to produce the same effect in others.

Client and therapist can interact, and that's about all—yet that can be sufficient. Change is the automatic and inevitable byproduct of interaction. People cannot wish themselves into making a particular change. It either happens or it doesn't happen. Statements such as "I want to change"—even when uttered in full sincerity and with the best of intentions—do not guarantee that a particular change is around the bend.

For example, individuals frequently proclaim that they are definitely going on a diet. They mean it—but they don't do it. They didn't know they weren't going to follow through on their resolution until they found it wasn't happening. On the other hand, radical shifts in pattern—when they do occur—sometimes arrive unannounced and when people least expect them. People wake up one morning and really do begin keeping track of calories or make a beeline for the nearest Weight Watchers group. Now, what previously seemed like an enormous or complicated undertaking happens practically automatically and with little sense of struggle.

Although people know that something is different, they cannot always give a plausible account of the genesis of the change that has taken place. It is interesting to watch them try. Better still, watch yourself try to explain why your exercise program "took" this time, why you snapped out of your depression, or why a complete plan for a project you are working on popped into your head—full-blown—while you were showering. People's explanations of differences between successful and unsuccessful instances are hardly compelling. For example, whether or not a diet worked, dieters offer the same reasons for having started it: Their clothes weren't fitting, friends had made pointed comments, and so on. Usually, the person has no good idea why the "magic button" got pushed this time. As research tends to indicate, dieters may ultimately be successful using the same methods with which they had previously failed.

The truth of the matter is that because every "input" strikes a different—changed—organism, there is no telling when a different response will be evoked. The drift is continuous, and we are never the same way twice. Only a single straw is needed to break the camel's back, but no one—not even the camel—knows, until after the fact, which one it will be. There is always the possibility that a scientist's experiment was abandoned one trial too soon—the next trial might have produced an exciting discovery. Clients and therapists, too, have often given up on a strategy which, if pursued just a little longer, would have paid off.

People can only tell afterward what they "meant." As Bette Midler acknowledges, "I never know how much of what I say is true." The only proof that people are "ready" to change is that they do so. Moreover, all the statements a person makes *about* changing interact with, and are part of, the process of change itself. Therefore, they cannot be taken at face value as having direct causal significance.

WHEN IS SOMEONE READY TO CHANGE?

Some therapists evaluate potential clients in terms of "treatment readiness." But treatment readiness is a very slippery concept. Over the years, we have lost confidence in our ability to discriminate between easy and tough cases. Sometimes miracles are accomplished with resistant, unmotivated individuals, including those who have been abandoned by other therapists as hopeless. On the other hand, we have run into unexpected difficulties with individuals who ought to have been ideal therapy candidates—bright, earnest, hardworking, psychologically minded, and adventuresome. Of course, we still make continual predictions about how therapy will go. However, we view all such prognostications with a healthy skepticism. An investigatory process has to be allowed to take unexpected turns. Furthermore, as investigators, we confess to deriving a certain perverse pleasure in discovering just how wrong some of our initial, sensible-sounding hypotheses turned out to be.

As a youth, one of the authors remembers being taken on family automobile outings. One of the special delights of these excursions was getting lost on back country roads and thereby making new discoveries. These accidental wanderings were often more exciting than the planned destinations—the enjoyment was heightened by that slight edge of mystery associated with the unknown and the unfamiliar. Therapy, as a voyage of discovery, can make good use of those same attributes. Instead of waiting for people to be "ready" or picking and choosing "YAVIS" clients (Schofield, 1964),[2] we are willing to dance with practically anybody who comes through the door.

In many self-help groups there is a needless reliance on concepts such as

---

[2]Young, attractive, verbal, intelligent, and successful.

readiness and commitment. The statement "We can't help you because you're not really *ready* to stop drinking" is a double-bind—and not necessarily a therapeutic one. Faced with that sort of pronouncement, a drinker might be well within his or her rights to reply: "When I'm *that* ready, I doubt if I'll need your help."

In a less flippant mood, however, the person might inquire earnestly about the next step: "Okay, but where can I go for help in getting ready?" That question is far from trivial. In fact, it symbolizes the underlying dilemma confronting anyone who wants to be different but doesn't seem to be moving in the desired direction. Mental health professionals and representatives of self-help organizations rarely provide an adequate answer.

Behaviorists, for example, have discovered that hand-washing compulsives can benefit from "exposure" treatments in which the person intentionally resists performing his or her rituals. However, many clients are unable or unwilling to comply with this anxiety-provoking procedure. Investigators have labeled their noncompliance "lack of treatment commitment" (Foa, Steketee, Grayson, & Doppelt, 1983). But this description doesn't really explain anything—it is being used tautologically. Other, deeper tautologies lurk in the logic of exposure treatments: An exposure treatment consists basically of taking actions opposite to those that constitute the problem. In other words, a person who complains of an irresistible urge is asked to resist the urge anyway. Therefore, by definition, those who can comply with the treatment are better off, at least temporarily, than those who—for whatever reasons—cannot (Efran & Caputo, 1984).

Similarly, in cases of alcohol abuse and other addictions, the suggested remedy almost always features an admonition to give up the problem: The drinker is advised to stop drinking; the gambler is to stay clear of gambling; and the binge eater is to avoid bingeing. There are additional, subsidiary paradoxes and tautologies involved. For example, alcoholics are not only urged to stop drinking; they are simultaneously asked to acknowledge their helplessness in the realm of alcohol. Thus, they are exhorted to show strength in an area of admitted weakness. It is a truism to tell people whose drinking is out of control that they ought to control their drinking (Efran, Heffner, & Lukens, 1987).

Surprisingly, such approaches sometimes work. A person goes to an AA meeting and really does stop drinking, or a gambler attends Gamblers Anonymous and starts a new and different life away from the casinos. In the paradoxical world of self-reference, tautologies can be effective. However, attempts to understand how such formulations work usually leave out the critical role of interaction—of context. Directives such as "don't drink," "don't gamble," or "don't wash your hands for three hours" are not uttered in a social vacuum. They form part of a social negotiation in which the individual is an active participant. Admonitions, per se, don't do the trick. What gives such admonitions potential usefulness is the conversation in which they are embedded. Clients and therapists—or members of self-help groups—converse in ways that help people generate options they were unable to *realize* by themselves or in other settings.

In therapy, these options are composed of interlocking participatory acts—each of which gives the others meaning. Paradoxically, in this enterprise, therapists are both essential and unnecessary. Think of a time when you felt a need to cry but were unable to "get yourself going." An old scrapbook picture or phonograph record wasn't enough of a stimulus. Interacting with another individual was required, and he or she had to say the right thing to trigger the flow of tears.

If interacting with one person isn't the answer, you might have to find someone else who will take a different tack. Often you have a sense of what is needed, although it cannot be articulated. Moreover, expressing it in words might spoil the effect. For example, you don't want to have to prompt someone to say "I love you."

Similarly, in therapy, things need to be said and done that require someone else's assistance. A therapist can be that someone. However, clients can also profit from other pairings, including relationships with friends, teachers, and acquaintances. Not everything therapeutic needs to happen in therapy.

Because of their technological objectivist bias, some therapists keep examining "interventions" as if they were concrete entities to be isolated, identified, refined, patented, and used as weapons in the war against psychological dysfunction. Thus, they keep missing the boat. The magic is not contained in isolated methods, techniques, or wordings. Of three people who attend an AA meeting—each ostensibly given the same message—one may quit drinking immediately, another may go away angry and disappointed, and a third may find value in something he heard there but only realize it three years later when his wife leaves him.

A woman who is a compulsive hand-washer may be unable to complete her behavior therapist's assignment at the time it is suggested, but wheels may have been set in motion that will later yield salubrious effects. One day, she stands in front of the sink and toys with the idea of leaving the water turned off. This leads into a series of self-experiments that begin to bear similarities to those she originally claimed she couldn't complete. As a result of these experiments, she later returns for formal treatment or makes significant progress on her own, without needing additional tutelage from a therapist.

Over the years, several of our clients have left as failures but returned as successes. We recall one woman who was furious about an "accusation" she thought we had made in an initial session. She refused to return. About a year and a half later she called to report that the session had been, in retrospect, the most valuable meeting of her life. She further shared the realization that *we* hadn't accused her of anything—*she* had done the accusing, using words she heard us say. In therapy, what counts isn't so much what's said as what's heard.

This may be the place to point out that we often take life—and therapy—too seriously. Therapists who think that what they are doing is vitally important have lost perspective. Clients have already lost touch with the big picture—the natural drift of living—and they do not need further reinforcement for the belief that they have "special" obligations and entitlements. As we have implied earlier, if a person contemplating suicide grasped the *unimportance* of it all, he or she might not consider suicide necessary.

Whatever you take seriously holds you in its grip and handicaps your ability to operate efficiently and think flexibly. For example, it is when you *don't* need a job that you do best at the interview. Likewise, you do your most creative and rapid work with clients whom you haven't come to view as "important."

Therapists might consider modeling ways in which clients can surmount the paradoxes of life's importance. (As Oscar Wilde put it, "Life is too important to be taken seriously.") The strategy is to recognize that projects are to be tackled with full commitment and energy, even though, on the cosmic scale, they are ultimately unimportant. Football players perform enthusiastically while the game is in progress—otherwise playing wouldn't be any fun. But when the game is over they are ready to move on to the next adventure. Likewise, clients need to play life's games full out, simultaneously recognizing that they are just games.

SUMMARY

In this chapter we described life as a structural drift without purpose or meaning. Using language, meanings are added and purposes are inferred. However, we have no choice about whether to participate in the drift—we are already doing so. Nor do we decide what to think about it. Our thoughts come to us, as if by magic, including thoughts like "I'd better think about this" or "I'd better not think about that." Terms like free will, choice, and self-control have currency in the linguistic domain. In that sense they enter the drift and affect our lives. However, they do not represent operational realities. Keeping semantics and operations separate in our explanations helps avoid confusions and conundrums.

The point of view we have presented—that life is a purposeless drift—is not intended to be grim or nihilistic. It is biologically sound. It doesn't remove from a person any properties he or she actually possesses. It does highlight the inaccuracies in people's concepts about how they function. Although initially disconcerted by the discovery that life isn't the way they had believed it to be, people eventually profit from being clearer about how life works.

Change is continuous and inevitable, although the vast majority of changes go unnoticed or are construed as insignificant. Therapists do not change clients, nor do clients change themselves. Clients and therapists interact, and their interaction yields outcomes that might not otherwise have occurred.[3]

Although we can use our experience to make rudimentary predictions about life and therapy, much of what happens is unexpected and occurs at unlikely times. Human beings are not like what cyberneticists call "trivial machines." As autopoietic entities, they are not fully predictable—either to themselves or to others.

This chapter has focused on the clinical relevance of autopoiesis and natural drift. In the next chapter we elaborate on the central postulate of Maturana's theory—that entities operate in accordance with their structures. We also introduce and explore the implications of two closely related concepts—***informational closure*** and the ***myth of instructive interaction***.

[3]This involves the crucial concept of orthogonal interaction, which we explain in more detail in later chapters.

CHAPTER 5

The Myth of Instructive Interaction

The simple but profound defining principle of structure determinism is that entities operate in accordance with their structures. Structures aren't static—they keep changing and evolving as the natural drift proceeds. The proposition that structure determines operation (which in turn affects structure) applies equally well to oak trees, daffodils, beer kegs, delinquents, movie producers, toasters, washing machines, and supportive therapy groups. Toasters toast and washing machines wash because of how they are constructed.

In understanding a phenomenon different levels of analysis are possible. For example, therapy groups operate the way they do both because of how groups are organized and *also* because of the structures of their constituent parts—clients and therapists. Although every structured system exists in a medium, it is the structure—not the medium—that determines how the system will respond to a given perturbation. The structure sets limits on what the system can do and become.

In other words, although you need to switch on the electric current to have your toaster work, the electric current does not need to "teach" the toaster about toasting. Nor can electricity turn the toaster into an appliance that does the dishes, grinds the coffee, or washes the clothes. The electricity is needed to *trigger* events in the toaster, but the rest is up to the toaster. Similarly, psychotherapy *triggers* changes in clients, but the kinds of changes that occur are a function of the structure of the client and the nature of the client-therapist coupling. The therapist does not unilaterally determine how, when, or if a particular client will change in a particular direction. Neither does the client.

When you are in a bad mood, someone might suggest that you plunk yourself in front of a TV set and cheer yourself up by watching a comedy. However, while in that mood, you may not find the show very amusing. In fact, it is possible that you will come away even more upset than you were before. Structure determinism is a warning to producers of sitcoms that they will be unable to ensure that their shows will have a given effect on any particular audience member. The producers and writers have to play the odds—they televise what makes them laugh and hope that a significant percentage of the viewers—since they have similar structures—will be similarly affected.

Holidays such as Thanksgiving, Christmas, and New Year's are, for most, occasions for celebration. However, as mental health statistics show, these are also times of severe depression for many. Furthermore, people are not always in a good position to predict what their reaction to the holidays will be or to change the reactions they don't like. Many insist to themselves that this year, no matter what, Thanksgiving dinner with the family will be a joyous occasion. Nevertheless, by the time the turkey is placed on the table, fights have broken out and no one feels much like eating.

Therapists sometimes suggest that moody clients get themselves into the holiday spirit by "going through the motions." Clients are instructed to wrap packages, go shopping for gifts, participate in the singing of Christmas carols, and so on. The theory is that if a person performs these "behaviors," the desired reaction will begin to occur. This is part of the behavior-generates-affect school of thought. The truth of the matter is that it doesn't *necessarily* work that way. Some people are unable to bring themselves to go through the motions. Others find that all that pretending backfires—they sink into a more profoundly depressed state: "I must be very sick. Even caroling didn't cheer me up. The others were having such a good time, and I stuck out like a sore thumb."

Two false beliefs underlie these simplistic behavioral methods. One is the belief that people are in charge of their behavior, even if they cannot control their thoughts and feelings directly. The second is the view that particular behaviors inevitably generate given meanings. These ideas, which are also common in our culture, are fortified by the traditional practice of construing thoughts, feelings, and behaviors as separate systems that interact and control one another. This tripartite categorization scheme—so often reified—creates more confusion than clarity. We discuss this issue further in Chapter 10.

Because most people can immediately move an arm or a leg at someone else's request—although without knowing exactly how they do it—they believe that behavior is more under their control than other aspects of functioning, such as mood or thought patterns. However, they forget that there are many behaviors that they would be unable to perform upon request, despite having the requisite skills and telling themselves that they would be desirable. For example, some encounter group members have been unable to take their clothes off even though they "wanted to" and others in the group were freely doing so. Similarly, when an emergency occurs, people often find themselves rooted to their seats, unable to move. Even trying to not look as one passes the scene of an auto accident may require more self-assertion than a person can muster. In other words, we are not as much in control of our actions as we like to believe. Being able to raise a hand when someone suggests it is not an adequate test of our ability to "do as we please" in the domain of action. Often there is a dramatic gap between what we do and what we say we'd like to do.

A depressed client we know was instructed by his behavioral therapist to "cheer himself up" by visiting certain friends and undertaking certain projects associated with his hobbies and interests. He was supposed to earn a certain number of "points" each week by carrying out these behavioral assignments between therapy sessions. Once, when he was complaining about feeling down, his friend—who knew about the assignments—suggested that he do more work on one of his hobbies. The client said he wasn't going to do that because he had already earned his points for that week. "But doesn't doing those assignments get you to feel better?" his friend asked. "Yes, sometimes, but who says I'm *in the mood* to feel better?" the client replied.

To the structure determinist, all changes are structural changes—even the small ones. Eating breakfast changes your structure, and so does reading the newspaper or drinking a vodka martini. Changes associated with therapy are changes in the structure of the organism, including those changes that seem temporary, inconsequential, or unplanned. The differences between men and women are structural, as are differences in their roles in the community. The potential mutability of such structures is what makes them interesting to scholars and scientists.

INFORMATION AND CLOSURE

We are living in the age of information, and terms like input, output, bits, and noise, originally developed in connection with telephones and computers, have become common parlance. Our familiarity with such words makes it all the more surprising to realize how recently they were invented.

For example, the use of the term "information" to denote data transmitted between senders and receivers dates back only to the late 1940s, when Claude Shannon was at work as a researcher at the Bell Telephone Laboratories (Gleick, 1987). Shannon was interested in mathematically quantifying the efficiency of electronic transmissions. "Bits" became his unit of measurement, and "noise" was the background electrical activity that potentially obscured the signal. Shannon set up simple information-transmission experiments in which "senders" chose items from a prepared list and telegraphed their choices to "receivers" at the other end, who attempted to decode them using their copy of the list. It is from these experiments that our contemporary model of communication—as the sending and receiving of bits of information—emerged. As we shall soon demonstrate, this model is misleading when applied to autopoietic entities.

It was not just Shannon's work that fixed telephonic images in the public mind, but also the work of neurologists, who found it appealing to portray actions of the nervous system in terms of "messages" scuttling along nerve fibers. It was an easy pictorial image for people to grasp—perhaps too easy. They began to think of the nervous system as a complex—albeit compact—telephone network. Of course, neurologists understood that this was merely an analogy—nerves didn't really "carry" information—they just fired. Moreover, the nervous system was, in many respects, totally unlike a telephone switchboard. Nevertheless, once the metaphor became popular, it began to have a life of its own. In people's minds—including many mental health professionals—the model had become a reality. It is now difficult to convince people that they do not operate like telephone systems or computers, and that communication isn't simply the transmission of bits of information from one person to another via the sense systems and the airways.

If you are looking for a way to represent human communication patterns, you might be well-advised to abandon the telephone model altogether and investigate instead the grooming behavior of chimps (Maturana & Varela, 1987). The grooming of chimps is coordinated behavior that helps establish and maintain a social order. Our conversations with each other serve similar functions. The fact that we are talking is sometimes more important than what is said. We intuitively appreciate this. We feel encouraged when members of a family continue talking to one another, even though their conversations may lack substance. Similarly, clients in individual and group psychotherapy settings often report being nourished simply by being there—linked in conversation—despite the fact that they didn't gain any particularly new or noteworthy insights.

Our emphasis on information transmittal has resulted in an underappreciation of the crucial value of gossip and chitchat in sustaining the well-being of people and communities. Being in communication with others is as much linguistic *massage* as the delivery of consequential news. We love to converse. Being placed in solitary confinement—or having your spouse read a newspaper at the breakfast table—deprives you of conversational grooming.

THE HAZARDS OF THE TELEPHONE METAPHOR

The telephone metaphor is further misleading because information is represented as coming from the outside, in the form of separate "inputs." However, the nervous system is a ***closed neuronal network***. It doesn't import information from elsewhere, it generates its own information. We therefore need to return to the earlier use of the term *in*formation, meaning "formed within" (Varela, 1979).

Even the sense systems do not sense anything except their own changes of state. Imagine a little girl sitting on the floor of a nursery school playroom, fully absorbed in her own fantasy game. Elements of the buzzing confusion going on around her find their way into her adventures, but only as aspects of the story *she* is weaving. Similarly, the nervous system plays only its own games. Perturbations on the outside provide the context in which those games unfold.

Let's use a slightly different analogy: Picture a toy submarine bobbling around in a bathtub of water. A person comes by and swishes the water around, creating a "typhoon." The behavior of the sub is affected, and the parts inside take a beating. However, different parts react differently to the perturbation. Delicate struts may break off as the model gets tossed around. Other parts weather the storm intact. Each part, because of its location and its structure, makes something different of the outside commotion. Likewise, the elements of the nervous system are differentially affected by environmental events. Furthermore, no part directly mirrors or maps the outside world (cf., Skinner, 1974). Nothing inside either the sub or the nervous system has been assigned the job of creating a replica of what happens outside. In fact, from the point of view of the nervous system, there *is* no outside. Concepts such as "inside" and "outside" are the inventions of observers who stand by the bathtub, watch the water being stirred up, and inspect the submarine for damage. The nervous system cannot get outside itself to make those kinds of observations, but words and symbols allow people to believe they can.

The point we are making is counterintuitive, and therefore difficult to grasp. People are brought up to believe they perceive the outside world.

The visual system, for example, appears to provide direct and immediate access to our surroundings. The eyes are said to be our windows on the world. However, although the eyelids open, the neurons of the retina do not. Energy waves bump up against the retinal surface—like the waves bumped up against the sub—but outside light cannot get in. Obviously, experiences we attribute to light—as well as all our other experiences—are created entirely within our own system. That system can produce magnificent light-shows, and with only a minimum of cooperation from the outside. This is evident in dreams, in response to sharp blows (when we "see" stars), when neurons are directly touched with electrical probes, and when chemical substances are ingested. At a fireworks display, there may be a lot going on outside, but nevertheless the sparkling colors we see are internal creations.

That we are fooled into believing that we "see" the world outside dramatizes how well coupled we are with our environment. Maturana and Varela (1980) use the analogy of a pilot making an instrument landing. He is enclosed in his cockpit, can see nothing through the windshield, and is concerned only with keeping some needles centered on their respective dials. After the plane is on the ground, his colleagues congratulate him on having done a superb job of landing. He protests that he was unaware of performing any navigational feats. He only turned some knobs in response to changing neon lights and moving pointers. Maturana's point is that our experiential lives take place entirely within the closed cockpits of our own nervous systems, but—because of our coupling with the environment—we usually manage to "land" safely enough.

Because the nervous system is closed, it is incapable of distinguishing between perception and illusion. The exact contributions of the environment to internal changes of state cannot be discerned. The meaning of terms like perception and illusion depends on the cross-comparisons of experience that language and communal living make possible. If a person were to grow up alone in the universe, he or she would treat all perceptual experiences as equivalent. Distinctions between reality and illusion are therefore social distinctions, not perceptual ones. Dreams, for example, are—while we are in them—as real as anything else. When we wake up, we have been persuaded to regard them as illusions. Thus, the person who described reality as the dream from which we have ***not yet*** awakened, was more correct than he or she might have suspected.

Very young children, incidentally, make few distinctions between dreams and reality. Gradually, they adopt the community tradition and begin considering their nighttime experiences illusory. When the son of one of the authors was a young child, he dreamt that he was at a circus, seated in the stands between his parents. He already understood that this hadn't really happened—it was just a dream. However, when his mother asked him to describe the circus acts he had seen in the dream, he looked puzzled and said, "But *you* know what they were—you were there!"

In some respects, individuals who are delusional or who hallucinate are not that different from children who haven't yet learned to label their dreams properly. Their perceptions may be socially awkward and nonconsensual, but they are perceptually vivid and they are valid. In conversing with such individuals, it might be helpful to keep in mind that the differences between their neurological processes and our own are minuscule compared to the similarities. As Claude Bernard (1865/1927) indicated more than a century ago, "There is nothing disturbed or abnormal in nature; everything happens according to laws which are absolute, i.e., always normal and determined. Effects vary with the conditions which bring them to pass, but laws do not vary" (p. 10). In other words, observable effects vary from case to case, but the underlying principles remain the same.

It is pointless (and disrespectful) to strong-arm delusioned individuals into giving up their reality in favor of our own. Such an approach just creates bitterness, suspicion, and alienation. It would be bad manners to go to a foreign culture and chastise the natives for doing things oddly. Instead, we would watch and listen, attempting to find meaning in their customs and commonalities between their experiences and our own. We would work to bridge the cultural gap. With individuals who are hallucinating or are delusional, we ought to proceed similarly.

With one actively delusional client—she thought others were inserting secret messages into her newspapers and broadcasting special thought-controlling signals over radio and television—we were able to make the "bridge" in an interesting way. Our discussions were really about putting "objectivity" in quotation marks, although we didn't explicitly label it that way. The client wanted her perspective validated (something we couldn't, in good conscience, do) and she was angry at those psychiatrists who had attempted to convince her that she was talking gibberish (which she wasn't). Fortunately, we had all seen a demonstration of the Ames room illusion at a local museum. The illusion is created by having a person peer through a window of a room at a person walking around inside. The person inside appears to change size as he or she walks back and forth. Observers looking down at the room from a catwalk overhead can see that the room isn't rectangular (as it appeared to be when viewed through the window), but is actually trapezoidal. The walls are set at odd angles, causing anyone seen against them to be shrinking or growing depending on his or her location.

Our client recognized that a person who only had access to the top view would not understand what the person looking through the window was reporting, and vice versa. Each would be convinced of the validity of the perceptions produced by his or her frame of reference. She also understood that there are times when life is just like that. (In fact, at some level, it's always like that.) Two people are unable to confirm each other's perceptions, because things look very different from each one's perspective. They disagree—not because they want to be surly or create trouble, but because they don't see any other options. In life, rarely is there a catwalk built above the "room" to help observers obtain a meta-view from which to mediate between the contradictory perspectives.

Although the discussions with this client were extended—and bumpy—she was able to grasp that even though her perceptions did not concur with what others believed, they were nevertheless legitimate. After that, she stopped fighting the suggestion that she take medication. She was also willing to read some material about schizophrenia. Up until that time, she had responded angrily to anyone who hinted that she was not "in her right mind." Yes, perhaps she sounded the way paranoid individuals sometimes do, but she had regarded that fact as an unfortunate coincidence—not proof that she was "mentally ill." Until that point in time, she astutely perceived that those who wanted to label her "mentally ill" were attempting to invalidate and delegitimize her perceptions.

INSTRUCTIVE INTERACTION

It follows from what we have been describing, including this example, that so-called instructive interaction, in which the nervous system is said to receive an intact "message" from the outside, is an impossibility. Yet the myth of instructive interaction persists and continues to permeate theories of education, psychotherapy, criminal justice, and child-rearing. If instructive interaction were possible, teaching would be simple. The teacher could tell students what they needed to know, and there would be no misunderstanding or loss in fidelity. Parents and children would truly understand each other completely, and clients could drop off their problems for therapists to solve, picking up the solutions a week later. Instructive interaction would make communication efficient—truly computer-like—but it would also create nightmares. What was put in would be, bit for bit, what came out. Disagreement would disappear. (Computers don't argue.) Education would become indoctrination with no room for creativity, invention, and interpretation. Each generation would learn and believe only what the previous generation knew. Thus, paradoxically, a process that eliminated mistakes and misunderstandings would also make it impossible for people and civilizations to grow and develop.

Nevertheless, the belief in the myth of instructive interaction leads to many of the perplexities of interpersonal relationships: How could she have done that to me? Why don't they care? Who do they think I am? Didn't he know how I felt? What's the matter with them? Where are their heads at? These are the kinds of questions that tumble out of people's mouths when communication doesn't follow a lock-step progression—when what is "received" isn't necessarily what was "sent." If we understood that in communication what is "heard" is *never* what was sent—that each person's hearing is unique—then we might begin to take these everyday misinterpretations less personally. Each person is marching to a very private drummer, but thinks the drumbeat is loud enough for everyone else to hear.

As authors, we may have written the words that you, as a reader, are now processing. However, you are not reading *our* book—you are using the words we wrote to create your own book—one that speaks to you. We control neither the way you interact with these pages—such as whether you go chapter by chapter or skip around (God forbid)—nor what you get out of what we have written. Readers who disagree with our thesis may have missed the point and so, too, might those who claim to agree completely. Writing and reading are conversations that include audience participation. This is why Umberto Eco (author of *The Name of the Rose* and *Foucault's Pendulum*) can say that "Reading is a cooperative action in which the reader is supposed to fill up a lot of empty space. . . . To communicate doesn't mean to tell everything." It takes a reader who is on the job to make a book grow (Weintraub, 1990, p. 8E).

In Alan Ayckbourn's comedy *How the Other Half Loves*, characters with interlocking lives participate in separate dinner parties portrayed concurrently on the same set. This is more like life than we generally realize. Picture a number of producer-director-actors who—by some odd quirk of fate—are required to mount their separate productions in the same theater space, at the same time, and using each other as cast members. Given this arrangement, there might be moments when, as in Ayckbourn's play, the scenarios fit well enough together to create the impression that only one coherent story is being told. However, since many divergent scripts are involved, sooner or later discrepancies in plot become painfully obvious. At this point, each producer-director-actor is apt to get huffy about how the others are sabotaging his or her masterpiece. Of course, that's not what they are doing. They are only trying to advance their own productions. Sometimes, bargains can be struck: Producer A agrees to incorporate part of B's third act, if producer B will reciprocate by amending his or her

Scene 2. However, when each performer keeps insisting that the other plays are of inferior quality or—worse yet—doesn't realize that there *are* any other plays, bedlam results. Moreover, in the realm of relationships, rarely is there a recognized representative from the producers' guild or Actors' Equity to mediate disputes.

Writing on a similar theme (and using a somewhat similar analogy), Stewart Emery (1977) reminds us, "Most of the time in life we are no more than extras in other people's soap operas" (p. 95). Sometimes, when we don't fit the role the other person has in mind for us, he or she is obliged to send for someone else from central casting. Being "fired" in this way isn't personal. In fact, events in relationships are never "personal." Each person is only trying to be faithful to his or her version of the script.

TRANSFERENCE

Freud, therefore, was correct in placing transference at the heart of his theory of treatment. Transference affects us all. It isn't just an affliction of the neurotic or a set of reactions specific to the psychotherapy setting. It isn't even necessarily a product of psychopathology or defense systems. It is an inevitable byproduct of how the nervous system is structured. *All* our reactions are tied to internal workings. When people react to us, they are really reacting to aspects of themselves. Because Freud was working within an objectivist framework, he conceptualized transference reactions as departures from reality. We prefer to think about transference in terms of the *relative* fit between a person's judgments and prevailing community standards. Reality is not the anchor—consensus is.

Therapists sometimes tell clients, "It's all up to you." Usually, that is taken to mean that the person has direct control over his or her existence and should use it to advantage. We have already argued that people don't have that kind of control. However, there is an alternative interpretation of the statement that seems valid to us and is in keeping with the current discussion: Since the nervous system is closed and instructive interaction is a biological impossibility, people's *conversations* with books, films, and other individuals—including their therapists—*do* belong entirely to them. A teacher in a classroom is giving as many different lectures as there are individuals in the room. (Those of us who have done some teaching know just how idiosyncratic some of those lectures can be.) Similarly, every person's therapy is an experience his or her own nervous system has put together, using the client-therapist interaction as the raw material.

Two individuals go to the movies. One is moved by the film, feeling that it effectively portrays the emptiness of contemporary urban life. The second person finds it boring and pretentious, and has a hard time figuring out what the director might have had in mind. It is customary to say that these two individuals saw the same film but had different reactions to it or hold different opinions with regard to it. But what is the "it" they are reacting to? A celluloid strip? A series of lights and shadows? We prefer to say that the two individuals saw *different* movies, each of which was contained—as a possibility—on the same reel of film. This phrasing emphasizes how much of the experience must be brought to (and taken from) the theater by the participants themselves.

In connection with a research project, one of the authors had occasion to sit in the auditorium of the George Eastman House in Rochester, New York, screening classic comedies from its extensive film collection. Only the projectionist and a few other people were present. In that context—an appraisal of film footage for a serious purpose in an empty auditorium—gems of comedy seemed strangely bland and devoid of content. The requisite "cooperation" between filmmaker and audience member was missing. The viewer wasn't, in that sense, pulling his weight.

When family members show up at a therapist's office, the therapist is apt to ask each of them for their opinions about what is happening in the family. Again, the traditional assumption is that these are many views of the same family. Our assumption, however, is that each individual has his or her own family, but that the cast memberships overlap. There are important differences in this way of saying it. The traditional view implies that there is a correct perception of the family that other perceptions will approximate to varying degrees. In fact, in the therapeutic context, it is often assumed that the therapist's appraisals define the "objective" standard against which other opinions are to be measured. (People talk about seeing a therapist to find out "who is really crazy in this family" or to settle "whose opinion is really correct.") Our phrasing makes it clear that there is no one standard against which the others can ultimately be judged. The therapist is hawking a particular point of view, just as is everyone else present. Questions such as "Was the sister really jealous of her brother's girlfriend?" "Is the father self-centered or merely hardworking?" "Does the wife's mother visit too often and intrude too much into family routines?" "Is the brother's schoolwork suffering because he hasn't been properly disciplined or because he is overly distressed by family fights?" are not objectively answerable.

Therapists have been a bit imperialistic in assuming that their terms should take precedence over and replace those that their clients use. Clients may decide to play in the therapist's ballpark for a while, but the new vocabulary (and the game it signals) is not necessarily a replacement for something else. A wife who is a "borderline" to her therapist remains a "nudnik" to her husband, and a worker with "oedipal strivings" is still just a troublemaker to his boss. The vocabulary of mental health professionals pathologizes and, in many instances, defames (Szasz, 1973). Ordinary idiosyncrasies and cultural distinctions are translated into afflictions.

When Salvador Minuchin began working with families, he coined the terms "enmeshment" and "disengagement" to characterize family subsystem boundaries (e.g., Minuchin, 1974; Minuchin & Fishman, 1981; Minuchin, Rosman, & Baker, 1978). It seemed to him that family pathology was related to overly fuzzy or rigid boundaries. Based on such theorizing, an instrument was designed to help measure such dimensions more objectively—the Family Adaptability and Cohesion Evaluation Scales (Olson, 1986; Olson, Bell, & Portner, 1978). The authors of the scale tried to establish norms that would categorize family functioning levels as being adaptive or maladaptive. However, they soon discovered that the pathological boundary characteristics of one culture (or subculture) were the normal practices of another (e.g., Skolnick, 1987). For example, American families appeared hopelessly disengaged by Chinese standards, and Chinese families seemed too enmeshed when judged by American norms. In the face of these cross-cultural differences, the investigators were forced to back off. They concluded that perhaps it wasn't the ***nature*** of the boundaries per se that mattered, but only whether family members agreed on their expectations of one another.

One wonders how family therapists, if they had been around at the time, would have reacted to the "enmeshment" in Gen. Douglas MacArthur's family. When Douggie went to West Point, his mother moved into a hotel near the campus. She took a room with a view of his dorm window, so that at night she could check up on whether or not he was studying properly (Atkinson, 1989). Visitors to West Point can still see the location from which she kept close tabs on her son. We are willing to bet that many family therapists, given the broad outline of this scenario (with the names removed to protect the guilty), would predict nothing but doom and gloom for the offspring of this family. Yet MacArthur went on to be an important and respected leader and appeared neither neurotic or indecisive to his colleagues.

Perusal of almost any of the biographies of the rich and famous will reveal patterns which, similarly, would have been considered bizarre by today's therapy standards. In the rush to pathologize, professionals underestimate just how parochial their opinions are. They consult with each other and with their clients but forget to check their predictions against wider community perspectives.

One of the reasons therapy can become a needlessly complex and lengthy procedure is that when people become "clients" their every quirk is scrutinized. The tendency of some therapists is to overanalyze idiosyncrasies, resulting in prolonged efforts to change patterns of behavior with which some of the rest of us live quite contentedly. Read the average psychological report and you come across description after description of behavior patterns that could characterize practically everyone, including the author of the report. In fact, if we paused to scrutinize daily life, it would "read" as bizarrely as most of what gets pathologized in such reports. After all, as author Jean Kerr reminds us, "the average, healthy, well-adjusted adult gets up at 7:30 in the morning feeling just plain terrible."

One Christmas, when Cabbage Patch dolls were the rage and were in short supply, it was average citizens—not mental health clients—who clawed each other in attempts to snag the few available dolls for their own children. Fights broke out and extra security guards had to be hired to restore law and order. This holiday mayhem was over a temporary interruption in toy supplies. Imagine if something truly important had been at stake!

When therapists talk glibly about unconscious defenses and maladaptive thought patterns, they also need to keep in mind that most of us, when we were younger, had no trouble believing that Santa Claus could make all those deliveries in just one night or that he could fit all those toys on his sleigh. He kept his lists straight without the aid of a Cray computer. Of course, that was easy compared to making simultaneous appearances at thousands of department stores throughout the land or sliding down—and *up*—chimneys with openings half his size. One of the authors grew up in an apartment that had a freestanding false decorative fireplace with no openings at all. Yet, since this piece of furniture was *called* a fireplace, and stockings were hung on it, he accepted it as the place where Santa made his yearly appearance.

We may be older now, but we have not outgrown our propensity to consider our own thinking *rational* when it is merely convenient: How many of us—when we are in pain—really want to think about where our internist finished in his or her medical school graduating class? Someone out there must be seeing a physician who nearly flunked out. Similarly, we like to believe that our particular surgeon is the best in the city—perhaps in the entire field. Listen in on your friends' conversations—even those who are therapists at work analyzing others' defenses—and you will have to conclude that the two or three "top" surgeons in the world are operating on practically everyone. They must locomote with the same sort of agility that Santa Claus displayed on Christmas Eve. They even find time to play an occasional game of golf.

OBJECTIVITY, SUBJECTIVITY, SOLIPSISM, AND PARTICIPATION

To some, the notion of an informationally closed nervous system raises the specter of solipsism. Also, they worry that such a view treats subjectivity as a special virtue—something to be celebrated. These concerns derive from several misunderstandings. First, the reader will note that we do not applaud subjectivity. In fact, we rarely use the term. Since, in structure determinism, objectivity (without quotation marks) is not a possibility—subjectivity doesn't exist either. The terms objective and subjective, like "up" and "down," are defined in relation to each other (Keeney, 1983). When you take away one, you lose the other. In structure determinism there is the recognition that "everything said is said from a tradition" (Varela, 1979, p. 268) and that knowledge, therefore, is neither objective nor subjective, but participatory.

Second, we do not operate as social isolates. We participate in communities, and what we think and believe is a byproduct of that participation. The sciences and the humanities are the collective outgrowths of millions of acts of observer-participancy (Overbye, 1981). Truths don't simply spring out of our heads as arbitrary inventions. They grow out of, and are constrained by, communal practices. Distinctions recap a history of interactions. How we think, believe, and act is the story of who we are. Although we own that history, we have not been granted a license to choose another. That is what keeps the position we have been describing from being solipsistic.

THE "MIGHT HAVE BEENS"

Specifically because life *isn't* solipsistic those lengthy therapy conversations about the "might have beens" are usually ineffective. They are conversations about a person who doesn't exist. Sure, it is likely that if the person was "less jealous," "more reasonable," "less stubborn," "more tolerant," "less dependent," "more adventuresome," then things would be different. But life is not lived hypothetically, and we have already asserted that people do not have the power to change their attributes at will. If they did, therapy would indeed be easy.

Therapy thrives on breaking up patterns that are encouraged elsewhere. Therefore, it doesn't go well if it consists of allowing the client to continue to do the two things he or she does best—complain and make New Year's resolutions: "There I go again, being jealous." "From here on in, I'm going to start doing what *I* want." "I keep seeing him, but I *know* he's no good for me." "I keep wanting approval." "My self-esteem is too low." Most troubled individuals have been trying to improve themselves their whole lives. They frequently sermonize or present themselves as "damaged goods." Conversations of the sort we describe above perpetuate that trend. At best, they lead to what Watzlawick, Weakland, and Fisch (1974) characterize as first-order change—more of the same. Although the vocabulary a client and therapist use may be more sophisticated, the process is not much different from what presumably went on in the person's family when he or she was nagged to be more considerate, more communicative, less moody, and so on.

New Year's resolutions—in therapy or not—are subtle requests to be less true to oneself. But satisfaction requires being *more* true to oneself, not less. For example, a client had spent considerable amounts of time and money with previous therapists trying to learn to be "less sensitive." He had been told all his life that he had a thin skin. Finally, he gave up. He realized that in certain domains he was going to be more temperamental than others and that was all there was to it. Instead of attempting further "repair" work, he accepted that this would be a characteristic of his, and he would have to find ways to use it to his advantage or to work around it. It would be going too far to say that he became proud of it; however, he did stop making massive attempts to hide his reactions from others. Once, during an argument, he yelled at a friend, "Okay—so I'm sensitive—so what of it!"

Actually, once he had accepted who he was in this domain, there were some unexpected changes in his reactions. He found that his upsets were less frequent and less severe. Paradoxically, he changed more in the three months following his acknowledgment of who he was than during the previous two years of daily, weekly, and monthly attempts to reform. It was okay to be levelheaded and okay to have an outburst. In fact, he found that he *liked* having a good old-fashioned tantrum from time to time. Where necessary, he apologized to others for causing a bit of a commotion. That was a lot better than constantly monitoring and suppressing who he was, in the interests of appearing even-tempered. He found it was true that when you have permission to be who you are, changing becomes easier.

WHATEVER CLIENTS WANT, CLIENTS GET

Psychotherapy isn't a "treatment" applied like a mud pack to a passive organism, and clients do not wait until they get to the therapist's office to start changing. They have been changing all along. The visit to the therapist's office is just the next step in an argument they have been having with themselves. When people seek therapeutic services, they are not stepping "outside" their tradition—they are attempting to preserve some aspect of it. A person is always *continuing* his or her argument, although, in the process of dialogue and debate, the terms of the argument keep shifting.

As Maturana points out, the whole story of life is conservative. Therefore, the statement that therapists hear often, "I want to be different," cannot be taken literally. Clients want to be different only in the sense that they want equilibrium restored. Something in which they have an investment has been threatened, and they want that threat diminished or eliminated. It behooves the therapist to find out exactly what the threat is. Perhaps, after a period of relative peace at home, war has broken out again. Despite studying hard, a student is not meeting his school's minimum grade-point requirements. A spouse has stopped complaining and started packing. The boss has scheduled a special conference for Monday morning, and the news isn't going to be good. The person not only was drunk again, but this time was arrested for drunk driving. A daughter won't stop seeing her unemployed boyfriend, and now she has become pregnant. And so on.

The person's attempts to conserve are not proceeding satisfactorily through just talking to in-laws, marital partners, children, or friends. Something more drastic is needed. Otherwise, there would be no motivation to seek out a therapist. Furthermore, if seeing a therapist doesn't result in sufficiently rapid improvement in the ongoing "conversation," the client may leave and seek some other form of relief. Autopoietic customers are always right. If they don't get what they are looking for in one store, they shop elsewhere. From the perspective of the client, therapy is one of a number of possible mediums in which to pursue life's conversation.

Structure determinism means taking the organization of the organism seriously. It can't be overemphasized that, as informationally closed entities, people do not "take direction" from the outside. They participate in conversations and change accordingly. As therapists, we are invited to co-drift with our clients. However, whenever the resulting dialogue isn't effective in preserving that which the client cherishes, we are apt to be dismissed. Although clients allow us to play a role in their evolving worlds, we do not have the power to directly change or control their lives.

SUMMARY

People do what they do because of how they are put together, and they do it in connection with (but not on direct instruction from) the medium in which they exist, which includes other people. Unlike views that emphasize input-output relations or simple reinforcement contingencies, structure determinism leads us to more fully appreciate the organism as an organizationally closed, self-determining entity. The person conserves an identity and does not simply "take in" information from the outside. Shedding what Maturana has labeled the "myth of instructive interaction" forces us to give up the notion that we directly instruct, treat, or cure. The wisdom of this realization is obvious to anyone who has conducted a detailed investigation of the nervous system or has lived with a teenager.

Now that some of the basics of Maturana's theory have been covered—natural drift, informational closure, distinction-making, structure determinism, the role of language, and "objectivity" in quotation marks—we can further discuss the distinctly human propensity to tell stories and construct explanations. And we will be able to zero in on the particular stories people call "problems."

CHAPTER 6

Stories, Explanations, and Problems

Human beings are inveterate and skillful storytellers—and they have a habit of becoming the stories they tell. With repetition, stories harden into realities, sometimes trapping the storytellers within the boundaries that the storytellers themselves have helped to create (Bruner, 1986). When a client arrives at a therapist's office, he or she comes armed, not just with raw experience, but with a set of fables to share. (The client even has stories about the therapist whom he or she hasn't met yet.) His or her problems, as we shall see, take the form of glitches in a dramatic narrative (Spence, 1982).

Beginning therapists often take clients' narratives too seriously—as factual accounts of past events. These therapists and their clients spend too much time tracking down the details of events that presumably took place years ago. This kind of historical emphasis is usually wasteful of everyone's time and energy. Even Freud was unsure about how to regard his clients' reminiscences about childhood events. Were they recollections of actual happenings or fantasy constructions? Alleged discrepancies between Freud's private beliefs and public pronouncements about this issue have recently become the subject of heated debate (see, e.g., Malcolm, 1984; Masson, 1984). Whatever Freud may have actually believed, one thing is now clear—recollections can never depict objective truth, even under the best of circumstances. Memories are not veridical transcriptions of actual events, retrieved from some mental file cabinet. They are *performances* enacted by people in the present, under specific circumstances and in connection with particular goals (Jenkins, 1974).

RECOLLECTIONS ARE PERFORMANCES

It is easy to demonstrate that what a person claims to remember is largely manufactured for a particular purpose. For example, when you recall having done something–skating, swimming, standing in a supermarket line–you typically envision yourself the way an *observer* would have seen you rather than the way things would have looked through your own eyes. You tend to see yourself from a position *outside* yourself–over your shoulder, so to speak. In other words, in your mind's eye, you "watch" yourself swim or skate as if you had been a photographer recording the event. Therefore, the visual image you think you recall is mainly a construction that you are now piecing together. Jaynes (1976) describes it this way: "Looking back into memory, then, is a great deal invention, seeing yourself as others see you. Memory is the medium of the must-have-been. Though I have no doubt that . . . you could by inference invent a subjective view of the experience, even with the conviction that it was the actual memory" (p. 30).

Studies have shown that even when people are utterly convinced that particular images are direct portrayals of actual happenings, the images often turn out to be confabulations containing portions of events widely separated in time and place (Loftus, 1980; Loftus & Loftus, 1980). For example, a man recalls that, as a child, he leapt over a fence and then entered a phone booth a few yards away. However, investigation reveals that the fence he remembers was in one state but the phone booth was in another, hundreds of miles away. The family had moved during his youth, and he inadvertently combined aspects of two incidents into a single image. The incident, as recalled, never took place, despite the fact that the image is vivid, detailed, and utterly compelling. As Ashleigh Brilliant writes, "Some of the things that will live longest in my memory never really happened" (1979, p. 36).

Recently, two siblings comparing notes about childhood incidents were startled to discover that they had been telling contradictory versions of the same anecdote. Each brother distinctly remembered himself as having been the person who took the family dog to the vet's to be put to sleep. One recalled lifting the dog onto the doctor's examining table and talking with him about what was to be done. The other recalled the dog's "last look" as he said goodbye to him and "knows" that the dog was lying on the floor of the vet's office–not on an examining table. Neither recalls the other brother's having been present. Discrepant recollections of presumably the same incident are not at all unusual, and, if we bothered to make the relevant comparisons, we would be aware of many more of them.

Even if the mind were able to operate like an unobtrusive or hidden camera, positioned behind the person, it would still not be capable of producing a comprehensive rendering of an unfolding event. Cameras cannot be everywhere at once. Moreover, they have to be stocked with film of selected sensitivity, fitted with particular lenses and filters, run at a given speed, and started and stopped according to a particular schedule. Furthermore, high-speed cameras, infrared cameras, and polarized-light cameras all capture elements not seen through ordinary lenses. Finally, any film footage produced must eventually be developed, viewed, and—most important of all—interpreted by human beings who bring to those several tasks all their usual biases and blindspots. Therefore, only nominal, highly edited aspects of what took place find their way onto film.

If film recordings are unable to tell the full story of an event, certainly human recollections, told and retold through the filters of language, experience, and context, are even more suspect. In short, people cannot neutrally or objectively report on happenings—their depictions are always arguments for something.

Therapists who operate with the objectivist belief that a person's account of past circumstances can be made accurate are kidding themselves. Even the sudden vivid flashes and "ah-ha's" are of questionable validity. Some theories of therapy, such as primal scream (Janov, 1970), operate with a related erroneous belief—that clients will be freed from internal distress once the truth about their past is revealed. However, there is no one-to-one correlation between the correctness of a recollection and the level of mastery it yields. Woody Allen—the quintessential neurotic—touches on this point when he quips that despite all the elaborate and exciting recollections unearthed in his therapy sessions, he has no real intention of changing anytime soon.

Lately, psychoanalysts have begun to agree that the *truthfulness* of what is recollected is less important than its *effect* on the patient's current view of life. Clients' recollections are being recognized as active reconstructions rather than literal truths (e.g., Schafer, 1983; Spence, 1982).

EXPLANATIONS ARE REFORMULATIONS

Recollections and other forms of explanation are simply reformulations of events in alternative conversational domains. They do not, by themselves, supplant or change that which is being recalled or explained. Knowing that water consists of hydrogen and oxygen molecules does not make it any less wet! Many of us can recall when we first developed a particular food aversion. We "understand" where the aversion came from. Nevertheless, we may still be unable to taste that bite of Brussels sprout, lima bean, Jell-O, or whatever else we find too repulsive to contemplate ingesting. Likewise, a psychotherapeutic account of fear, even if "accurate," does not *necessarily* render a person any less afraid.

Explanation is simply activity. Its relationship to accomplishing a particular goal varies from "A" to "Z." At one point in his career, George Kelly (1969) intentionally gave his clients bogus and preposterous psychological explanations of their symptoms. He reported that these "fake" explanations worked about as well as any of the more popular or acceptable ones. All that seemed necessary was that the explanations he invented "account for the crucial facts as the client saw them and that . . . [they] carry implications for approaching the future in a different way" (p. 52).

Another psychologist recalled having been given a test of mechanical aptitude early in his career, before he had personally studied test construction. Encouraged by the unusually high score he earned on the test, he proceeded to immerse himself in various handicraft hobbies. Later, when he had learned more about issues of test validity, he realized that his score on the aptitude test had probably been meaningless. By that time, however, he had already trained himself to be a skilled craftsman. The information on which he had based his avocational pursuits was almost certainly false, but the life-path to which it led was transformative nevertheless.

Many of the explanations that today's therapists and clients believe in will later turn out to have been sheer nonsense, just as past theories and beliefs now seem like hogwash to us. For instance, even though Anton Mesmer's patients reported being cured, none of us today would want to attribute the effects of his treatments to "animal magnetism," as Mesmer did.

The changing, language-dependent nature of problems can be illustrated by examining recent shifts in sexual mores. These changes have occurred with enough rapidity that one can readily trace the creation and demise of particular problem categories. For example, not long ago oral sex was considered perverse. Many individuals were therefore deeply distressed to find themselves drawn to such practices, and some sought relief through psychotherapy. Their therapists were equally convinced that these practices were pathological. They had little difficulty finding evidence of deep disturbances—superego lacunae, arrested egos, primitive oral fixations, and unresolved oedipal complexes. Now that oral sex is more accepted, the situation is different. These days, sex therapists are more likely to see people who are *unable* to enjoy these previously "perverse" practices. The cultural conversation about oral sex has taken a new turn, and—with that change—a slew of impulse control and sexual displacement problems have simply vanished into thin air.

Similarly, as homosexuality has begun to be languaged differently in the culture, and the term "gay" has become part of everyday parlance, psychiatric appraisals of the mental health of individuals with same-sex sexual preferences have been tempered (Bayer, 1990). New facts have come to light and old ones have been reappraised. The notion of homosexuality as arrested or distorted development has given way to the concept of an alternative, constitutionally determined, developmental pathway. At the same time, bisexuality—once thought to be nonexistent—is increasingly recognized as a distinct sexual pattern. (Woody Allen considers it an ideal way to double your chances of getting a Saturday-night date.) Commenting on all these changing trends, psychiatrist Thomas Szasz (1980) notes that our most prevalent sexual practice—masturbation—started out as a sin, graduated to the status of illness, and is now being proffered by sex therapists as a form of treatment.

It is easy to provide multiple examples of former "pathologies" that are currently viewed as signs of good health and previously acceptable practices that have become causes for alarm. Sunbathing and eating large quantities of red meat and dairy products used to be signs of good living but are now "no-no's." Placing personal ads to find romance or living together without being married are no longer considered scandalous. Now that smoking has proven to be "hazardous to your health," a cigarette isn't the same old smoke anymore.

At one time or another, foot-binding, lip-stretching, wig-powdering, harem-keeping, and heretic-burning have all been considered business as usual. In England, during the Middle Ages, mothers rolled over on their unwanted infants, suffocating them to death "accidentally on purpose" (Kellum, 1974). Even through the early decades of the 20th century, parents in many parts of the world practiced female infanticide (Panati, 1989). Members of a culture routinely invent, change, and resolve problems by making and putting into practice new and different distinctions. As conversation drifts in different directions, problems change complexion.

Some of these changes are aided by advances in technology, but, on the other hand, some technological advances have been made possible by changes in language practice. Often it is a "chicken-or-egg" situation. For example, we now talk more openly about sexually transmitted diseases, partly because these disorders are better understood and therefore less frightening. Years ago, however, people's reluctance to even mention the word syphilis was one factor that prevented them from getting effective, timely treatment. Similar situations have prevailed more recently with regard to other disorders, such as breast cancer, the addictions, and various mental illnesses. On the other hand, Betty Ford and other celebrities have gone public with their personal stories as part of an attempt to reduce our word-shyness (Johnson, 1946) in these matters.

There are fads in medicine and in mental health that can be almost as mercurial as styles in fashion. Individuals identifying themselves as having certain problems and symptoms find themselves moving from the offices of one group of specialists to the waiting rooms of another group. A person who several decades ago would have visited a minister might today seek the advice of a family physician, a chiropractor, or a nutritionist. Years ago, anorexia was considered so rare and exotic a condition that when a case turned up in a hospital the entire staff wanted to have a look. Today, anorexic and bulimic clients are commonplace, as are agoraphobics and the panic-disordered. Chronic fatigue syndrome and the Epstein-Barr virus (the so-called yuppie disease) are being proposed as explanations for a wide variety of complaints and deficiencies, along with seasonal affective disorders, hypoglycemia, pollen allergies, and work-shift disruptions. There is nothing wrong with any of this, provided we remain clear that there are more stories than things to tell stories about.

STORIES AS PRACTICES

As we have indicated, a story is part of—and justifies—a set of practices. For instance, as sociologist Erving Goffman (1961) reports, psychiatric patients typically develop a "sad tale" to legitimize their presence in the hospital. To professionals, the face-saving narratives of inpatients all begin to sound alike: People attribute their situation to overwork, mistreatment by a spouse, a miserable childhood, drugs and drink, and so on.

Because a story forms a constituent element in a person's life, it is virtually impossible for the person to behave differently while telling the exact same tale. People are obliged to update their stories to keep pace with changing programs of action. If they have taken a sharp turn in one direction or another, they are expected to be ready to explain how and why that change in direction came about. Even positive changes must be properly accounted for. New directions require appropriate transitional "face-work" (Goffman, 1959).

An individual who has built a reputation for being antisocial cannot simply "have a good time at a party" without providing a plausible account of how this event was different from similar events that the person previously attended. The viability of a culture is based on assuring a certain reliability of interaction by keeping people in set roles. Anyone who steps out of character too far or too often threatens to bring down the entire social house of cards. Cultures (and the individuals they comprise) have a stake in maintaining moment-to-moment interactional consistency.

We recall a former client who awoke one day and realized that he had exhausted his usual stock of complaints. At least for the moment he found himself feeling "content." However, his usual self-descriptions were all of the "poor me" variety, and he thus found himself deprived of his customary conversational gambits. As a "complainer" he was not used to managing interactions with others from the point of view of cheerfulness. Complaining was a long-standing, cherished pastime—one at which he had become quite adept. Letting go of grousing was, for him, "unnatural." We suggested that he might complain a little about being so cheerful—just to stay in character.

Clients who report they are having trouble "breaking an ingrained habit" often really mean that they are unable to figure out a way to smoothly switch roles. They have anchored their life routines to a particular persona: addict, phobic, depressive, or ne'er-do-well. Maturana argues that leaving any cognitive domain can be a painful operation, particularly when you are not yet sure what another domain will bring (Simon, 1985).

We once worked with a mute catatonic individual who hadn't spoken to anyone in years. Picture his situation: Regardless of how it started, silence had, over time, become the hallmark of his existence. If he were to suddenly begin talking about the weather, the status of the local baseball team, or the new nurse on the ward, this abrupt change in behavior would have constituted an unbearably awkward break in his established social role. What would his years of being silent mean if he began speaking for no particular reason?

Therefore, if he was to speak, a suitable opportunity for making the transition would have to be created. It took a month of daily, consistent, and often painful visits for us to create such a setting. For the most part, our visits with him were brief—after all, there wasn't yet much to talk about. They were held off the ward, out of the public eye. During these meetings, the wisdom and legitimacy of his long-standing silence were never called into question, nor was it assumed that he would definitely begin speaking. In fact, speech per se was never discussed. Instead, we indicated by our presence, our persistence, our regularity, and our demeanor that we could be trusted and that we were willing to "converse" via any medium of exchange that was then available or might become available. We were not put off by his silence. We believed that, with or without speaking, he had useful things to say about himself, the world, and his place in it.

Eventually he did speak. At first he did so with his head tucked down and in a low tone of voice. That made his first words less startling both to him and to us. He edged his way into talking, the way a person tentatively enters cold water. However, once he began speaking he was quite articulate. He railed in anger about the way he had been treated over the years. In his opinion, most people were little more than uncivilized animals. They had betrayed him repeatedly, and thus weren't worth communicating with. The content of his speech provided a strong justification for his silence, as well as for his resuming direct communication at this point—he wanted to be transferred to a hospital nearer his home town, so that family members could visit him if they so desired. He thought we might help him make his wish come true.

We dealt mainly with the content of what he had said, and not the fact that he had said it. We agreed to make his request for transfer known to the proper authorities. To have fussed over the fact that he was now speaking would have embarrassed everyone, and was to be avoided. Also, asking him to explain exactly why he had chosen to speak to us at this particular juncture would have been asking for trouble. The less said about his speaking, the better.

He soon began talking to others on the ward—making specific requests and regaling anyone who would listen with angry diatribes about the scurrilous nature of human civilization. (By a few weeks later, some of the staff members wondered if they hadn't been better off when he was pursuing a policy of silence.) A few months later, the authorities did grant his request for a transfer, and he was moved to an inpatient facility in his home state.

Years ago, Skinnerian researchers experimented with retraining speech sounds in mute schizophrenics, rewarding speech with simple reinforcers such as cigarettes and chewing gum (Isaacs, Thomas, & Goldiamond, 1960). In retrospect, we wonder if this was really the "operant conditioning" of speech sounds, as these investigators believed, or whether they had inadvertently provided these individuals with a convenient excuse to resume speaking. The patients were presumably being "taught" to speak again, and were being paid off with tangible (nonsocial) rewards. Thus, they could begin speaking without being untrue to any previous stance they had taken vis-à-vis participating in ordinary social interaction. The situation was no longer defined as conversation but as verbalizing for profit.

Every parent knows that youngsters who have for years steadfastly refused to try certain foods may develop a liking for them while they are away from home (perhaps at a summer camp or while staying at a friend's house). Similarly, those who work with children know that tantrums are most readily brought to a successful conclusion if the child can be isolated from those who witnessed the tantrum develop. In other words, the probability that a modification in role will occur is increased when a person can abandon his or her old "self" without incurring a loss of face.

Therapy may be an ideal opportunity for a person to escape the grip of reputations that have outlived their usefulness. The rubric "psychotherapy" facilitates modes of interaction that might otherwise be difficult to arrange or justify. Other useful contexts for change include self-help groups (such as Alcoholics Anonymous and Gamblers Anonymous), religious revivals, and encounter marathons. Some individuals have cleverly arranged their own opportunities to be different by starting a diet or an exercise program, getting a new hairstyle, switching to contact lenses, or buying a radically different wardrobe. "Marker" life events—such as deaths, births, marriages, divorces, graduations, relocations, and promotions—can also be pressed into service, as can special birthdays, such as turning 30 or 40 (Nichols, 1986).

It may sound strange to talk about having to use various legitimization devices to bring about changes for the better. However, we must keep in mind that—as social creatures—we *are* our stories and definitions, and we are obliged to keep them in good working order. Therefore, definitional shifts of any sort require expository clarification.

GETTING STUCK IN STORIES

Explanations and stories shape and sustain traditions; they orient and organize action. However, no matter how compelling they seem, they are still just stories. The trick is to use them without getting overly attached to them. There are always other stories that might be told. If you don't like today's stories, more are coming.

We have been arguing that since problems are established by definition and by mutual agreement, they are language phenomena. This does not imply that they are unimportant, ephemeral, or unreal. Problems in language hurt, and they persist. (Our parents were wrong when they told us, "Sticks and stones can break your bones, but names can never hurt you.") However, to be kept alive, problems must be talked about. Perhaps this is why young children—with only rudimentary language functions—have a reputation for getting over problems pronto. They can be in tears one moment and laughing about something else the next. Adults are more apt to linger over their problems, conversing with themselves repeatedly about every conceivable possibility and outcome until their entire conversational existence is problem-dominated.

Problems can also disappear even though the circumstances associated with them remain essentially intact. People wake up one morning and the troubles that weighed heavily upon them the night before now seem unimportant, although nothing has really changed. In arguments, a person is willing to fight "to the death" over some principle that, within a few moments, he or she can barely remember. The fight is declared over, although nothing concrete has actually been resolved. A slight repositioning of the "observer" generates wholly different sets of distinctions and leads to drastically different ways of reacting. Tripp (1987), for example, in describing sexual interaction, points out that not only do individuals have a certain disdain or repugnancy for the sexual practices of others, but that "even recalling one's own practices out of context may cause a person to shun the thought, if not to bridle at it" (p. 118).

LABELS AS OBSTACLES

There is another good reason to avoid taking a particular formulation at face value. Sometimes we work hard to solve a problem that would have disappeared by itself if the conversation had merely moved on into other channels. Unfortunately, some therapists tend to encase problems in a rigid language structure. In their quest to be precise—to pin problems down in objective, concrete terms—people are labeled, problems are named, and flexibility is lost. Problem definitions need to be allowed to float and drift a bit. When problems are given undue attention, they become weightier and are less likely to clear up on their own.

Likewise, case notes and agency records can saddle people with "histories" they might be better off without. We were on the phone with a gentleman who wanted to know if we treated "borderlines"—his wife was one, and they both had problems. We tried to indicate that we didn't treat borderlines, we treated *people*, some of whom might have been given that label. Talking to him, and later to his wife, was like chopping one's way through a thicket of verbal misunderstandings. Her father had been an alcoholic—didn't that complicate the prognosis? What was the overall success rate for adult children of alcoholics? Sometimes she didn't sleep well—didn't that mean something? These two people were buried under so many layerings of mental health jargon that digging them out threatened to be a major undertaking. Underneath all that verbiage were two frightened, confused, and hurting individuals. However, it was difficult to determine where they began and where the fallout of their last mental health contact ended.

Our first—and most important—intervention was to say "stop," "wait a minute," "hold on," "whoa." It seemed apparent that to make effective contact with them we needed to get back to some live questions that had been buried beneath the conceptual clutter. Their situation—when we finally returned to plain English—wasn't actually that complex. There had been shifts in their lives—kids moving away, deaths of some relatives and friends, an automobile accident (with some legal loose ends), and some unexpected house repair bills. In the final analysis, the designation "borderline," which started out as something they had read about in a magazine article, wasn't the least bit appropriate. It had been latched onto as an attempt to explain what was happening to them, both individually and as a couple.

As handy as words or labels can be, they short-circuit observation. They preclude detailed examination of the phenomena to which they refer. This is why some artists have refused to attach titles to their paintings or have given them nondescript names such as "Work #112" and "Study in Blue and Green." They know that a name can prevent you from seeing the canvas. Playwright Samuel Beckett steadfastly refused to discuss the meaning of his plays. He argued that if he could explain them, he wouldn't have needed to write them.

Words are equally blinding, whether their connotations are positive or negative. Neither a person labeled attractive nor one considered unattractive is seen for who he or she actually is. Neither an "expensive" nor a "cheap" wine can be truly tasted. That's why most wine-tasting sessions are conducted sans labels or telltale bottles. The moment people *become* binge eaters, anorectics, obsessive-compulsives, agoraphobics, addicts, depressives, or what have you, much of their behavior gets swept into a category and is no longer available for alternate appraisals. Recently, for example, we had occasion to remind an agoraphobic client that *everyone*—agoraphobic or not—has trepidations about being admitted to the hospital for an appendectomy.

There is a subtle, related point worth mentioning. Diagnostic terms such as "bulimia," as well as everyday personality descriptors such as "worrier," "hothead," and "snob," are appellations applied from an *outside* perspective. People only use such terms in describing others or when they are describing themselves from someone else's viewpoint. After an evening of reading the newspaper, snacking, and talking on the telephone, a man looks back at what he has or hasn't accomplished and labels himself a procrastinator—perhaps beating others to the punch. However, these were not acts of procrastination at the time they occurred. Even if, while reaching for another magazine, the man "knows" he is postponing work, it is only during that instant of self-appraisal that procrastination is born.

People can shuffle back and forth rapidly between acting and observing their actions. Talking on the telephone is in one domain, and chastising yourself for wasting time is in another. A diet is broken before and after chewing that extra bite of cake. The cake tastes good—the ingestion is language-free—but the self-evaluation that immediately follows may create a bitter aftertaste. In other words, there's playing the game and there's keeping score, and although these two may be closely linked, they are separate operations.

Because of the potential confusion of domains, both clients and therapists are likely to make the mistake of construing the bulimic as having an eating problem; the alcoholic, a drinking problem; or the phobic, a fear problem. The problem is not in eating, drinking, or reacting fearfully. Those are the domains in which everything is just as things should be. It is in the realm of appraisals and comparisons that the difficulties lie. For instance, a person with a fear of heights is not responding peculiarly—he or she is responding the way any of us would (and have) when under severe threat. One of the authors once found himself paralyzed at the top of a ski slope. Suddenly, all the supportive encouragement he remembered having given phobic clients seemed embarrassingly naive and vacuous—he couldn't "float with the fear," "take a risk," "let go," or "jump into action." He could neither head down nor back up. Fears only seem disproportionate to danger when they belong to another person or are evaluated from another perspective. To better skiers, the author's reactions might have seemed silly and excessive—he was worrying over nothing. The author felt similarly, once he was safely back at the lodge. The next time you glibly advise a "phobic" person to take a risk, picture yourself attempting to let go of the airplane for your first parachute jump.

What would be genuinely helpful would be a *full* acknowledgment of the legitimacy of the person's fear. With "objectivity" in quotation marks, that kind of empathy becomes easier. In that framework, there is no such thing as an "irrational" fear. After all, the system doesn't bother to sound the alarm unless it is under survival threat. Acknowledging the legitimacy of the person's fear reduces two potential problems to one. Instead of having to deal with both the feared object and its associated reputational issues (like "Why am I such a coward?"), all resources can be focused on the former. When the objective frame (i.e., objectivity without quotation marks) is used, clients often get a bad rap, first from themselves and their associates, and then from mental health professionals as well.

As self-observers, people say they are depressed or that they are anxious. But words like "depression" and "anxiety" are summary labels that do not allow us to get to the heart of the matter. We encourage such individuals to report more of the truth of their experiences. The depressed person might confess, "I ache because I let someone down." The anxious person might beg, "Quick, hide me—they're catching up (and catching on)." When we get close enough to our experience, distinctions between "thinking," "feeling," "acting," and "being" dissolve. We will have more to say about this in Chapter 10, which concerns the emotions.

OVEREMPHASIZING "SIGNIFICANCE"

Explanations are like words, only more so. Just as words serve as shorthand expressions for aspects of experience, explanations attempt to condense and encapsulate still larger living patterns. In the mental health field, such condensations erroneously amplify the determinative importance of particular incidents over everyday drift. They yield a false picture. In life as it is lived, all successive moments "count"—not just the special few that are embroidered into our narrative tapestry. By not taking into account those presumably insignificant intervening "points," the meanings of the few moments we do highlight are distorted. To the extent that we base our advice to one another on literal interpretations of these stories, everyone is misled. A father tells his son how he settled on a particular career, when in fact that isn't at all how it happened. It becomes a false guide that the son strives, in vain, to emulate. Similarly, those who tell others how to kick a habit, how to make a marriage work, how to get ahead in a career, how to study, and how to find happiness are all peddling tales that they themselves may fervently believe but which cannot be trusted.

Note the willingness of many former whatevers—addicts, phobics, insomniacs, school dropouts, convicts—to pass out advice to others based on "what worked for them." Unfortunately, they don't know what worked for them—they only know the story of it. Moreover, such stories are subject to change without notice. A local newscaster who was overweight trumpeted the method by which she finally lost weight and "kept it off," advising her listeners to try the same route. By a year or so later, she had put back every pound she had lost and fell silent about the matter—until one night when she announced that she was "full-figured," proud of it, and had no plans to change. We're waiting to see what she will suggest next.

A number of years ago, a client who was serving a brief stint in prison for a drug-related offense confided to his fellow inmates that the experience had "scared him straight." He was ready to recommend the experience to others who needed a jolt of reality. A more savvy prisoner, hearing him go on and on about his having seen the light, said genially: "Your first time in, eh? It'll last about 48 hours."[1]

---

[1]As the reader may know, various "scared straight" programs, in which long-term convicts confront young offenders about what lies ahead, have not had a good track record (Carpenter, 1990). Even some of the cons doing the lecturing have been prosecuted for further crimes, either while incarcerated or after their release. Similarly, experiments here and abroad with boot-camp style programs for delinquents have had statistically disappointing outcomes.

A psychologist we know, who authored a respected text on "how to study," confided that he had never really used the method he presents in the book. In fact, all through his highly successful academic career, he hardly ever worked at his desk with the window ajar and a light source coming over his left shoulder. Like most of the rest of us, he slouched on a bed, had the TV going full blast, and crammed like crazy before exams and deadlines.

Therapists, too, give advice that they either have never tried or that they themselves have been unable to follow. A client with relationship difficulties saw a psychiatrist for the first time and was delighted that this therapist—unlike others he had seen—admitted frankly that his own love life hadn't always been anything to write home about. To the great relief of the client, they were able to chuckle together about some of the compromising positions they had each gotten themselves into over the years. The session started out being about medication—it ended up with the client feeling like a "person" once again.

SPECIALIZED LANGUAGE FRAMEWORKS

People tend to award "ownership" over phenomena to members of particular speciality fields. Diabetes gets assigned to physicians, free will to philosophers, subatomic particles to physicists, salvation to theologians, ions to chemists, inflation to economists, and corruption, influence-peddling, and votes to politicians. A field is a specialized language approach—an explanatory scheme. But an explanation neither replaces nor takes possession of the phenomenon it is explaining. The same territory is always available to be mapped in many different ways, and each map may serve a distinct, useful function. High blood pressure is usually mapped medically, but it can also be mapped using the framework of hydraulics, economics, sociology, psychology, education, and so on.

Consider ulcers. Since biochemical and behavioral interventions have both proven helpful to ulcer patients, there has been a tendency to award "joint custody" of ulcers to physiology and psychology. That's why they are referred to as psychophysiological or, in the older terminology, psychosomatic. Sometimes ulcers are described as representing an interaction between physiology and behavior (as if that characterization weren't just as applicable to every other aspect of life). However, the cooperation isn't between physiology and psychology—it is between physiologists and psychologists. Members of those fields agree to bring their respective perspectives and vocabularies to bear on a common phenomenon. The confusion between the phenomenon itself and the explanatory schemes applied to it is widespread. We notice our students making pronouncements such as:

"Sports are 80 percent physical and 20 percent mental." (On this particular topic, of course, they have been bested by Danny Ozark's well-known proclamation: "Half of baseball is 95 percent mental.") In any event, the mental health field is riddled with needless debates about whether a particular disorder is *really* biochemical, genetic, emotional, and so on. This takes objectivity out of quotation marks.

The world—unlike the stories we tell about it—is not parceled out into separate compartments or interacting elements that match the departments of a university or medical school. Our approaches (and vocabularies) are divided—not the events themselves. Use of a term like "insomnia" appears to put falling asleep (or not falling asleep) into the province of medicine or psychiatry. This impression is reinforced when sleep preparations are used to induce sleep. However, a person who isn't sleeping soundly might also be aided by behavioral training, a conversation with a religious advisor, a conciliatory phone call from a child away at college, the purchase of a new mattress, the promise of a better job, or a glass of warm milk—all available without prescription. Neither falling asleep nor any other aspect of life's processes owes exclusive allegiance to a particular discipline.

We regard it as inadvisable to draw impermeable boundaries between events and assign them to particular fields. Subject-matter divisions are to be taken lightly; they only provide starting conceptual handles for investigatory projects. When we confuse explanations with the phenomena being explained, we are tempted to expect some critical piece of information—perhaps from an especially large-scale NIMH study—to come along and settle questions about what fields get jurisdiction over which disorders.

Lately, this sort of false expectation has been raised with regard to a number of conditions, including alcohol abuse, schizophrenia, and manic-depression. Can these disorders be traced simply to inherited distinctions in body chemistry? Of course not—no more than detailed studies of the visual system can fully explain art or obviate the need for artists. Granted, genetic and biochemical investigations are highly useful. They contribute to our understanding of structure from particular vantage points. With regard to the ingestion of a substance such as alcohol, for example, reaction differences related to body chemistry certainly are to be expected. Similarly, there is no doubt that individual differences in nervous system structure affect how environmental perturbations will be processed. However, patterns of alcoholism in a given country are not reducible to the language of chemistry, the study of family lineages, or the economics of the liquor industry. Again, no conversational mode appropriates its subject matter or exhausts the explanatory possibilities.

SHIFTING FOCUS

It is useful to have the freedom to change "lenses" from time to time, first using one level of analysis and then shifting to a larger, smaller, or different unit of study. Each analysis opens up fresh possibilities for intervention. Some of the great discoveries of science and medicine were simply a matter of widening or changing the boundary definitions of a phenomenon. The breakthrough in unravelling the mysteries of typhoid fever occurred when the quality of nearby river water was included as an investigatory focus. Similarly, the study of malaria surged forward once the definition of the problem was widened to include the life cycle of the anopheles mosquito. In each of these instances, a change in focus resulted in the rapid availability of new facts, the emergence of new patterns of observation, and shifts in the locus of potential programs of remediation and prevention.

In psychotherapy, there are equivalent phenomena, in which changes in the definition of events modify what can be seen and which interventions become possible. For example, a man comes into treatment complaining of a bout of anxiety. The particular therapist he visits happens to think in family systems terms, and redraws the symbolic boundary of his complaint to include patterns of relating in the family. Suddenly, anxiety has become "disappointing mother." Had he visited a behaviorist, the client's anxiety might have turned into "lack of assertiveness." Each way of "chunking" events leads to different investigatory pathways and, potentially, to different discoveries, conclusions, and interventions.

The individual, the couple, the family, the extended family, the client-therapist team, the community, and the ecosystem are all potentially productive investigatory units. So, too, is the unit suggested by Goolishian and Anderson (1987)—the problem-determined system. It comprises all those who "language" an issue in similar terms. It has the advantage of cutting across traditional boundaries of kinship and location. When we are not objectivists, we can examine phenomena using a floating-point rather than a fixed-point logic (Durkin, 1981). Like a calculator that shifts its decimal point to accommodate to different scales, we can shift our viewing window as necessary for a given project.

SUMMARY

Problems are spin-offs of human conversation. We become the stories we tell each other and ourselves, producing effects that range from the ridiculous to the sublime. Words and explanations can be both friends and foes. Although they are needed as organizational tools, they limit and obscure what can be apprehended, compressing experience into fixed channels. Whatever doesn't fit escapes notice.

When we fail to keep "objectivity" where it belongs—in quotation marks—we confuse our explanatory schemes with the phenomena they were created to explain. This confusion of "logical types" leads to unproductive debates about whether given disorders *are* biochemical, genetic, mental, sociological or some combination thereof. It also results in therapists' taking explanations overly seriously and spending too much of their time polishing them.

Professional jargon has encouraged therapists to reify and treat abstract concepts rather than clients. As a result, their clients lose touch with the detailed texture of their lives, and their attempt to discern more productive life pathways is hampered.

Concepts like *cause*, *purpose*, and *blame* complicate the conversations of life. In the next chapter, we discuss how therapists and clients can avoid the philosophical confusions connected with these words and the stories in which they are embedded.

CHAPTER 7

The Confusing World of Cause, Purpose, and Blame

Give people a sequence—any sequence—and they automatically make "sense" of it in terms of a series of purposes. Show people a short film of two geometric shapes—one approaching another, the second beginning to move away—and the audience *sees* one form purposefully launching the other into space. Such interpretations of purpose are virtually impossible to avoid. Just as the chaser lights on a movie marquee really do seem to be moving, the shapes in the film seem to be engaging in purposeful action. It is difficult to keep in mind that the purposes we infer belong to us, not to the shapes (Bruner, 1986).

All our stories—even those that are barely more than fragmentary observations—incorporate a sense of purpose (Efran & Lukens, 1986). Almost as soon as children learn to speak, they turn into "Why?" machines. Why do the clouds move? Why does the wind blow? The whys become more sophisticated with increasing age, but they never go away. Once language enters the picture, our lives are filled with causes, purposes, and blame. Thus, there is a paradox: Life is a purposeless drift into which each speaker scatters a seemingly inexhaustible supply of causal inferences.

Planets go around and around without expecting to get anywhere in particular; so do electrons. In fact, physicists tell us that all the atomic and subatomic particles of which we are presumably made manage quite nicely without the kinds of purposes and causes we attribute to everyday phenomena. Purposes and causes are not to be found in nature—they are organizational tools people use to give meaning to a past and a future, in the context of a "now."

Purposes are *constructions* that help us make sense of the world we think we know. Except in the human imagination, concepts such as "progress" – implying a multitude of purposes gradually coming to fruition – have little meaning (Sarason, 1981).[1] In matters of intent, motive, and direction, nature is silent; people are noisy. Throughout human history, people have imagined a succession of morals and meanings in the universe around us. In all instances, more sophisticated inquiry revealed that these were themes we invented and projected onto our surroundings. Camus (1946) reminds us that everywhere there is the *benign indifference* of the universe.

If this were a philosophical treatise solely devoted to causal inference, we might take our time exploring the four meanings of the term *cause* proposed by Aristotle or examining the distinction between the notions of proximal and distal causation. It would be time well spent. However, we will have to settle for a whirlwind tour, leaving aside some of those niceties in favor of a rough-and-ready description of how people fill their worlds with a plethora of confusing purposes and causes, mostly of the billiard-ball variety (Aristotle's "efficient" causation). Then we will suggest steps that clients and therapists need to take to avoid the logical quagmire that this overlay of causal explanations can create.

INVENTING CAUSES AND PURPOSES

Basically, people begin to "create" cause and purpose by subdividing phenomena into parts. Obviously, unless something has at least two parts – an "A" and a "B" – there is no "thing" to blame for the state of some other "thing." The more parts you separate out, the more purposes and causes you can invent. For example, if you chunk a person's life along traditional lines, into the activities of eating, sleeping, procreating, studying, working, playing, and so on, then each part can be said to cause one or more of the others. Working hard can be said to cause sleepiness, and sleep can be said to rejuvenate the motivation to work. As it turns out, most of our causal chains have this kind of circular quality – you can start anywhere and get back to where you came from. Consider the familiar adage: We eat to live, and live to eat.

Wherever you have causes, you can, if you like, also postulate purposes: "The purpose of working hard is to be able to relax." "The purpose of having children is to keep the species going." Using language, any cycle can

[1] James Thurber wrote, "Progress was all right. Only it went on too long."

be broken up into causes or purposes. For example, a person gets married, has sex, and spawns offspring (if anyone still does it in that order). Thus, we surmise that the purpose of sex and marriage is to have children. Those children then can have children of their own, and on and on—giving everyone at least one solid purpose. Since we are all in the world together, it is hard to find individuals who are willing to stand up and assert that that purpose—the propagation of the species—isn't, by itself, a worthy goal. (Every once in a while, members of an "overpopulation" group protest feebly.)

Note that inventing purposes—and they are invented—is usually an exercise in creating tautologies. A description is turned into a purpose that is then asked to account for the description. The example we just gave starts with the defining characteristic of life—self-perpetuation—and states that it is the purpose for which the characteristic exists. Such circular renamings aren't illegal, but they don't advance the cause (no pun intended).

Imagine that you have just arrived from another galaxy. Your spaceship happens to land in a yard with a picket fence. A cat is pacing back and forth behind the fence. Knowing nothing about such creatures, you peer intently (with all three eyes) through one of the openings between the slats. First you notice some whiskers. Then a cat's head appears, and finally you see a cat's body and a tail. Since the cat is pacing, that sequence is repeated over and over again—whiskers, head, body, tail. Putting two and two together, you come to recognize a pattern: Whiskers come first, and regularly *cause* a head to appear, which in turn *causes* the appearance of a body and a tail. You are comfortable with this cause-and-effect theory because you haven't yet realized that the cat is a *unity*. We don't usually attribute causes to unities. Although earthlings would not be fooled by the cat, Alan Watts (1966)—using essentially the same analogy—points out that we are fooled practically everywhere else. We split integrated phenomena into arbitrary pieces and claim that one piece causes another or is the purpose for which the other exists. For example, instead of thinking of the human race as continually evolving, we break it up into a succession of individual histories, giving each person the "purpose" of contributing to the next generation.

We do the same thing at many other levels of analysis: "I'm stuffed because I ate too much" separates eating from stuffing, and makes one the cause of the other. Similarly, "I fell asleep because I was tired" divides a single fluid process into two separate units. People, to their own confusion, trade simple and not-so-simple pseudo-explanations all day long. Consider the following assortment of nominal fallacies: "She acts that way because she's neurotic." "My laziness prevents me from getting anything done." "I wouldn't be so depressed if my life wasn't filled with sadness." "I'm a nervous wreck because I worry so much." "I wouldn't hate him if he weren't obnoxious." "I can't get up in the morning because I'm a late riser." "We keep fighting because she refuses to listen to my side of things." "I don't speak up because I'm not very outgoing." "I'd meet more people if I weren't so shy." "She hurts people because she's a sadist." "He can't help cleaning—he's compulsive." "Her dependency needs make her vulnerable to the wishes of others." "She turns me on because she's so sexy." "He lashes out at others because of his strong aggressive drive." "My insomnia keeps me up at night." "He gets the problems done faster because he's more intelligent than I am." "I react strongly to blood because I have a weak stomach." In all of these cases what is being said is less than meets the eye.

Applying a stock causal formula (Ossorio, 1978) isn't as useful as people have grown up believing it is. Unless people are careful about how they attribute causes, they end up with an indiscriminate mishmash of descriptions, interpretations, explanations, and tautologies. Causal statements do not necessarily identify unique processes or structures, and they do not necessarily increase explanatory power.

Even Freud became trapped in this game. In one of his more controversial pronouncements, he described death ("quiescence") as the final aim or purpose of life (1920/1959). To say what he said in jauntier terms, "Life is a terminal illness." This statement is true to the basic causal formula; it attributes something *later* to segments of a phenomenon that come earlier. Freud's phrasing wasn't very helpful, and neither is the more contemporary version.

LINEAL, CIRCULAR, AND RECIPROCAL

Family therapists, systems thinkers, cyberneticists, ecologists, and cognitive-behavioral workers, among others, have lately recognized the limitations of construing life (or parts thereof) as a string of cause-and-effect sequences. They point out that even the operation of a lowly thermostat cannot be adequately described in lineal[2] cause-effect terms. For example, while the temperature is busy causing the thermostat to change, the thermostat, through its connection to the furnace, is at work affecting the temperature. Thus, instead of one thing causing another, there is an endless feedback loop, without any clear beginnings or ends. Living, breathing, conversing

[2]The words *linear* and *lineal* are often confused. Linear describes a relationship between two variables—they produce a straight line when plotted against one another. A lineal sequence (unlike a recursive or circular sequence) does not return to its starting point (Bateson, 1979).

human beings are at least as complex as thermostats, and therefore they cannot be described in strictly lineal terms either. Some sort of reciprocal or circular determinism model seems called for (Bandura, 1978; Bateson, 1979). However, even reciprocal determinism models do not successfully head off the convolutions that undisciplined causal thinking can bring about (Dell, 1982a).

In fact, the only way out of such quandaries is the way we came in: being clear that causal analyses are part of our semantic world and are not intrinsic to the phenomena we are observing. Causal formulas—lineal *or* circular—have their uses, but to avoid mischief they must always be selected carefully, with full knowledge of the observer biases they represent. Ascribing causes and purposes sometimes leads nowhere except to other, similar ascriptions. Ultimately, in an interconnected universe, there is no true, single "cause" of anything—not of the "big bang" that presumably started it all, the big collapse that might end it once and for all, or any of the goings-on in between to which we are so attached.

We were all brought up to repeatedly ask "Why?" However, in a purposeless universe, it is sometimes better to restrain ourselves and ask "What?" instead. "*Why* are you crying?" becomes something like "*What* is the thought that helped you cry?" "*Why* are you afraid of going home?" is translated into "*What* happens if you go home?" Instead of "*Why* did you leave so impulsively?" we ask, "*What* were you thinking as you were leaving?" "*Why* do you get so angry?" becomes "*What* would you like to do to him?" Rather than "*Why* can't you and your father get along better?" the question is "*What* would you like to say to your father?" or perhaps "*What* do you need to do to complete this phase of your relationship with him?"

Obviously, details of phrasing can vary. There is nothing sacred about the words why and what. In fact, a person can ask one question using the wording of the other. What's more important is to get free of the semantic cycle of false causes. Establishing cause or purpose can be an unproductive mental game.

Often we don't need to traffic in causal attributions at all. We know *what* we like even when we don't know why we like it. We know that when our brother was late, we got upset. We also know that when he apologized in a particular way, our distress vanished. That much we can be certain of, and it is important. The rest is often idle inference.

Therapists get themselves and their clients into difficulty when they take causal formulations too seriously. Those with a functionalist bent are among the most frequent offenders. They apparently have no shame in reasoning backward from presumed *effect* to presumed *cause*, glibly inferring purposes along the route. Sometimes they state causal hypotheses as if they were observed facts. The following is an example:

> One way the young person can stabilize the family is to develop some incapacitating problem that makes him or her a failure, so that he or she continues to need the parents. The *function* [italics added] of the failure is to let the parents continue to communicate through and about the young person, with the organization remaining the same. . . . The "child" can be forty years old, and the parents in their seventies, still taking their crazy son or daughter from hospital to hospital and doctor to doctor. (Haley, 1980, p. 31)

At a time when autism was still considered a psychic (as opposed to organic) dysfunction, parents of autistic youngsters were regularly "accused" by many clinicians of wanting (obviously for unconscious reasons) to keep their children in an infantile state. No wonder advocates for the mentally ill and their families have responded with bitterness to some of the therapeutic interventions to which they have been subjected over the years. Functionalist interpretations are easy to come by, hard to get rid of, and often inflammatory.

Children who are sick usually get extra attention from their parents. Should we therefore assume that children catch the flu for the purpose of coercing attention from their parents? Parodying all this, Bogdan (1986) writes, "Suppose I win the New Jersey lottery and embark on a major transformation of my life-style. My wife doesn't like the new me and files for divorce. Should we say that the function of my not having previously won the lottery was to protect my marriage?" (p. 33).

A woman embarks on a series of romances, none of which work out. Is it reasonable for her therapist to infer that she is sabotaging her own love life? Is she unconsciously playing out her mother's injunction that she's a failure? Is she unwilling to let another man take her father's place? Unfortunately, clients are all too ready to buy into such unsubstantiated interpretations. Many such individuals are not any less lucky in love than countless others, although they may want an official psychiatric "reason" for their failures. Other such clients do indeed have more difficulty than the average person establishing a long-term romantic "fit," but not necessarily because their purpose is to fail. Many simpler hypotheses ought to be checked out before we accept causal inferences based on circumstantial evidence. Not everyone is equally desirable as a partner. People differ along many dimensions of attractiveness, interpersonal skill, and tangible assets. Even the place a person lives and works is apt to affect the shape of his or her social life.

Milton Erikson sometimes felt that clients having trouble finding a mate needed a makeover at a competent beauty parlor, some advice on buying clothing, and some tips on where and how to meet potential dates, rather than more psychologizing about self-destructive impulses and self-fulfilling prophecies (e.g., Haley, 1973). Behaviorist Nathan Azrin (Dannenberg, 1976) succeeded in helping out-of-work clients get jobs mainly through his straightforward coaching about who to call, what to ask, and how many "no's" to expect. One of the authors was once involved in a university counseling-center project on dating anxiety. The staff noticed that there was a major difference between students who seemed to be going out and those who weren't getting dates. It wasn't that the successful students were never turned down—they were. But they got right back on the phone and extended an invitation to someone else. However, those students who were more concerned about their popularity took every rejection personally. If someone said "no," they might wait weeks, or even months, before approaching someone else. Ironically, the actual ratio of acceptances to rejections was about the same for both groups. If the "less popular" students had learned about those statistics, they might have been less prone to take the rejections so personally. Fancier interpretations would not necessarily be needed.

Sometimes, therapists claim that because a client's behavior pattern keeps being repeated, it must be neurotic or maladaptive. However, human beings are fundamentally conservative systems—they easily repeat what they have already done, even if it was only partially or sporadically successful. Picture a person who loses his or her keys. The hunt consists of going through the same motions over and over again, looking in the same places more than once until the keys are found or someone comes up with a fresh idea about where they might be. When the plausible options have been exhausted, the person returns to doing whatever worked the last time his or her keys were lost, even if it isn't that sensible. Some perfectly sane individuals find themselves searching the same pockets five and six times over. They empty the top dresser drawer of all its contents—sometimes more than once—and, if that doesn't yield results, they run their hand all around the inside of the empty drawer, as if they expected a secret panel to open up and reveal the keys. This isn't repetition compulsion. It isn't self-sabotage. It isn't attention-getting. It is the conservative system at work.

In human affairs, repetition is the rule, not the exception. Therefore, it is novelty of approach that requires explaining. It startles us to realize that we are so set in our ways. We like to think of ourselves as rational creatures. However, viewed close up, we are creatures of habit pretending to be more sensible and cerebral than we are.

We have argued that the flu is, in most cases, just the flu—not a plea for attention. But suppose a child became so fond of the affection she got while sick that, after she recovered, she ingested various substances in an attempt to make herself ill again. Wouldn't that be acting on a purpose—conscious or unconscious? Descriptively, yes; operationally, no. Fundamentally, her behavior would be no different from that of a thirsty animal returning to the place where it last found water or a pet nuzzling up under your hand to be petted. These behaviors are not produced by mechanisms of purpose. The fact that the girl speaks and can give a running description of her own actions yields, in language, a sense of purpose. It also adds to the potential adaptability—some might call it *cleverness*—of her behavior. She has more subtle options than most other creatures. However, that doesn't alter the basic fact that her mechanisms (attention-seeking, eating, sleeping, studying, playing or any of the other activities to which we have bothered to affix names) proceed without intentionality. Intentions remain ascriptions by an observer, even when that observer is the girl herself.

INDIVIDUALITY AND BLAME

We recall one winter day when a particularly large pothole on a nearby street was causing problems for passing cars. Drivers got out of their cars, chased after their dislodged hubcaps, checked their vehicles for damage, and did a bit of gratuitous cursing. Undoubtedly, these motorists framed the event as individual misfortunes. (When we later spoke to someone at the highway department, she claimed that none of them had bothered to call to report the situation.)

If people had been accustomed to viewing their lives in communal rather than individualistic terms, the event would have been immediately seen as an occasion for collective action. However, in our culture, each motorist considered his or her plight a personal matter. These drivers were not intentionally shirking their civic duty. In taking their cars to their own particular service stations for repairs, they were just doing what came naturally. They were being 20th-century Americans (Sarason, 1981; Slater, 1970). In some other cultures, the opposite response would have been just as automatic—and just as difficult to modify.

A society can be defined partly in terms of how its citizens assign attributions and affix blame. In our culture, it is usual for people to describe themselves as free-standing units, battling problems that originated outside themselves and for which they can blame external factors: "My mother's impossible." "I can't shake this depression." "I have had agoraphobia since I was 18." "My husband gambles." "I have a stressful job."

Each person sees himself or herself individually "facing life" (as in the old radio serial, "Portia Faces Life"). Ironically, our current individualistic, as opposed to tribal, mentality is almost wholly a product of relatively recent developments in *communal* language patterns (Jaynes, 1976; Sampson, 1978, 1981). Industrialization fostered ways of talking commensurate with the notion that people are sovereign—albeit replaceable—units (Campbell, 1949).

Each pattern—the communal and the individualistic—has advantages and disadvantages, and each specifies a way of living and talking. We tend to take such styles of living for granted. A virtue of a trip abroad is that the contrast effect provides an opportunity to view your own cultural practices anew. You begin to see the way you live as one option among many. Psychotherapy provides similar opportunities. In dialogue with the therapist, clients can appreciate elements of their lives from an alternative perspective.

Our culture's prescription for depicting problems in individualistic and external terms is not entirely consistent. On the one hand, people are encouraged to consider themselves "rugged individualists," playing an active solo role in shaping their destinies. On the other hand, people are allowed—sometimes required—to "plead the fifth" when accounting for their failures. On these occasions, they are invited to slip into the role of innocent bystander, victim of fate, or powerless pawn. The rules for successes are different from the rules for failures. As essayist C. S. Lewis put it, "It is only our bad temper that we put down to being tired or worried or hungry; we put our good temper down to ourselves."

Many therapists operate with an inconsistent philosophy, which they inherited from the culture around them. Like everyone else, they want to have it both ways. They want clients to act with courageous self-determination, but they account for client shortcomings in terms of external causes. Inconsistencies in assigning cause and blame combine with misuses of the concepts of change and control (as we suggested in earlier chapters) to produce a semantic fog. For example, therapists frequently tell alcoholics that they alone are in charge of their lives, and only they have the power to change. At the same time, they are quick to agree that drinking and associated problems are the result of corruptive family scripting, potent addictive forces, and unlucky hereditary legacies—in short, everything *but* self-determination. Similarly, a feminist therapist might stress the need for women to control their own destiny, while explaining a particular client's inability to sustain relationships with men as the inevitable outcome of a father's emotional absence.

In other words, therapists routinely apply a deterministic theory to the past but apply a theory of autonomous action ("willpower") to the present and the future. The verbal formulas that result aren't theoretically clean; therefore they ultimately fail as explanatory tools. Unfortunately, the client's life can become a battleground on which injunctions derived from incompatible world views are pitted against one another.

Consider the embarrassing complications that sometimes arise when mental health professionals testify in court. They are asked to certify whether a criminal act is due to inadequate parenting, poverty, poor impulse control, symptoms of mental illness, or personal malevolence. How much of what the person did was "bad," and how much was "mad"? Which aspects of the crime were the person's own responsibility, and which are attributable to having grown up in a particular subculture? In other words, who caused what, and who, exactly, is to be blamed? Because we operate with contradictory theoretical assumptions about human motivation and functioning, this is precisely the kind of adjudication that is impossible for the professional to make. Moreover, gathering additional facts does not make the situation any clearer. New facts—like the old ones—can be interpreted within any of the conflicting causal models. The tendency of professionals, placed in this strange situation, is to vacillate wildly between philosophical positions, depending primarily upon whose ox is being gored.

For example, when it is *our* house that has been burglarized, or *our* neighbor who has been brutally raped, we want to hold the criminal personally and individually responsible—we want justice done, and perhaps we wouldn't mind a bit of revenge, to boot. However, when these events occur at a distance, we are more willing to invoke psychological and sociological perspectives. Shouldn't we provide the perpetrator, who was himself sexually abused, with treatment, a second chance, job training, and so on?

INCONSISTENCIES IN WORLD VIEW

Virtually all social science theories are deterministic—they leave no room for free will. Yet, in the courtroom, professionals act as if they could discriminate between instances in which behavior follows those principles and instances in which it does not. In therapy, also, they operate with changing standards. The more they get to know (and like) the client, the more the client is exonerated of blame.

Historically, there has always been a problem reconciling scientific doctrine with moral, religious, and humanistic viewpoints. Mental health workers operate at the cusp of these conflicting traditions. Most of the time, professionals simply forge ahead, pretending that such inconsistencies do not exist or are unimportant. They like to think that such abstract matters need only concern the professional philosopher or scholastic theologian. However, once a person starts paying attention to the "glitches" that arise in attributions of cause, blame, and purpose, they seem to crop up everywhere.

For instance, we often honor individuals for scholastic or athletic achievement when the abilities that allow them to rise above others are largely a matter of native endowment—aptitudes the person did nothing in particular to earn. Conversely, we sometimes rebuke them for "not living up to their potential." (As a result, some talented individuals wish they were more ordinary.) On the other hand, we sometimes give people extra credit for being highly motivated or working hard. However, motivation, like talent, is something one either has or doesn't have. Is the person "motivated for treatment" somehow more respect-worthy than the person who finds that he or she has no particular desire to change? The rules aren't very fair or consistent. The pattern of rewards represents a clumsy and confusing reflection of the community's vested interest in eliciting particular performances.

The first step in freeing ourselves from the grip of these confusions is to notice that they arise from an inadvertent intermingling of world views. We have available to us multiple explanatory options, each of which comes equipped with a characteristic vocabulary. Nature never dictates which scheme to use. When several models are unwittingly applied at once or grafted together in ad hoc combinations, confusion arises. To paraphrase Shakespeare, the inconsistencies are not in the stars, but in ourselves.

A client and therapist are puzzling over the causes of an impending divorce. When did the divorce start, who is to blame, and what purposes does it serve? Perhaps it was when the husband turned 40, realized he was unhappy, and blamed the wife? Maybe it was when he hired a new and attractive secretary? Could it date back to their courtship, when his obvious flirtatiousness was noticed but never openly discussed? Perhaps her friend's having paved the way by getting her own divorce had something to do with it? Or could it have been the stresses and strains connected with raising two rambunctious children?

Divorce as a domain of issues has no automatic boundaries—no predetermined causes or purposes. Since a problem and its solution are a matched set—like a question and its answer—where the boundaries are drawn is of considerable importance. Boundaries fix the way the problem is viewed, the feelings it generates, the variables thrust into the spotlight, and the outcomes likely to be accepted as solutions. Moreover, since the boundaries are not objectively given and cannot be established by an appeal to facts, they must be decided on by the participants, as a function of conversational negotiation.

Simple cause-effect formulas may appear to work well in narrowly circumscribed segments of our world, such as when a glass of milk has been spilled and we have to decide who should mop it up. Even in those limited instances, our causal analyses may go astray unless everyone involved accepts the same set of initial premises and boundary conditions. For example, the child whose arm bumped the milk glass claims it was because his brother was fighting with him (and shouldn't have been) or was rocking the table after he had been told to stop. In such cases, a potentially endless discussion about "who started" and "who's to blame" will erupt. As any playground worker can tell you, such debates are unproductive. Each participant can propose a cause-effect sequence that invalidates the other kid's claims, using many of the same facts: "Yes, I hit him, but that's because he wouldn't give me back my ball." And so on.

In the divorce courts, family therapy, and other such potential battlegrounds, these bids for causal supremacy are anything but trivial or funny. Paradoxically, once one is involved in that sort of cross-complaining, the playground worker's solution is about as good as any: "You're all to blame." Better yet is an education that helps people recognize the logical lunacy that these sorts of conversations engender. Clients need to understand how attributions of false cause keep them in a rut. Instead of attempting to arbitrate such disputes, therapists must play a leadership role in moving clients out of them entirely. They must avoid lending weight to their clients' attributional suppositions. In addition, as we implied in earlier examples, they need to reexamine their professional vocabulary and root out constructs that perpetuate limited causal notions.

In our culture, the concepts of blame and responsibility have unfortunately come to be used interchangeably. People say, "I hold you responsible for such and so," when they mean, "I blame you for it." Blame and responsibility are very different from one another. But blame is an accusation or judgment drawn from an outside perspective. The "observer"—perhaps the person himself or herself—says, "You did this one way and should have done it another." Responsibility does not have a pejorative connotation, and it doesn't necessarily imply choice. It reflects a simple acceptance or acknowledgment of who one is and what one does. It is not (as some think) the dutiful enactment of obligations assigned by others—as in being a responsible citizen. People who are being true to self are responsible, even if their behavior strikes others or themselves as reprehensible or blameworthy. We have talked to a few individuals in prison who committed homicide "responsibly"—that is, they accepted that they had killed someone and didn't claim to be "victims" of bad parenting, booze, the devil, or powerful outside forces.

You can be exonerated of blame, but not of responsibility. Recognizing that you are being yourself is being responsible. "Paradoxically, the experience of helplessness or dominance results from the attempt to locate responsibility outside of self and sets up a closed system out of which it is sometimes very difficult to extricate a valid experience of self; since the self which might otherwise be responsible has been excluded in the attempt to protect it from guilt, shame, blame, burden and fault" (Erhard & Gioscia, 1977, p. 121).

DESCRIPTION IS PRESCRIPTION

Examine practically any case report from this perspective and you will discover attributional inconsistencies of the sort we have been discussing. Psychiatric case histories are not just collections of facts about patients; they are "briefs" aimed at justifying particular plans and causal formulations (Rabkin, 1970). The way purposes and causes are described in the case history presages the mode of interaction the staff and patient will have. In these reports, some patients are portrayed as pitiful victims of circumstance, while others are characterized as ruthless manipulators, selfish children, or brutish animals. Accordingly, some are patronized, some outmaneuvered, some chastised, some disciplined, some befriended, some proselytized, and some ignored. All patients may be entitled to their symptoms, but some are a little more entitled than others.

Given that we are all human beings, certain inconsistencies in patient-staff relations are to be expected. In all areas of medicine, patients' personalities affect, to some degree, how hospital staff members respond to them. However, in the arena of mental illness, the differences are much more extreme. The situation is aggravated by the objectivist veil that blankets diagnostic and therapeutic practices. Philosophical and moral assumptions and practices are buried beneath pseudo-objective jargon.

The terms and descriptions in the official psychiatric nomenclature are, as others have indicated, an inconsistent mix of value judgments, causal and characterological attributions, loose metaphors, and observational criteria of varying degrees of specificity (e.g., Tischler, 1987). Virtually every diagnostic category contains loaded terms such as "exploitative," "indecisiveness," "cruel," "touchy," "impulsive," "overconscientious," and "spiteful." Szasz (1973), who considers the psychiatric vocabulary a "language of loathing" (p. 27), describes mental health diagnoses as "stigmatizing labels phrased to resemble medical diagnoses" (p. 26). He notes:

> The problem with psychiatric diagnoses is not that they are meaningless, but that they may be, and often are, swung as semantic blackjacks: cracking the

subject's dignity and respectability destroys him just as effectively as cracking his skull. The difference is that the man who wields a blackjack is recognized by everyone as a thug, but one who wields a psychiatric diagnosis is not. (p. 71)

Carson (1990), in calmer but equally stern tones, warns that unless the system is totally overhauled, mental health professionals run the risk of perpetuating an "ultimately unproductive illusion." The issue isn't that value judgments are involved or that causes and purposes are proposed. The problem is that they are disguised as objective assessments that then cannot be debated as philosophical choices.

TRUTH IN ADVERTISING

We have been suggesting that the way an event is construed and *narratized* becomes virtually inseparable from how it is experienced. Changes in description are therefore integral aspects of experiential changes. However, this does not mean that therapist and client can toy with established meanings without consequence. We said earlier that chairs ought not be called tables. Our linguistic agreements with one another—even those to which we personally object—demand that we maintain certain definitional consistencies and that we arrange smooth transitions between one definitional set and another. Definitional breaches are not to be taken lightly; perpetrators may be persecuted, or prosecuted, or both. A person who announces that he or she is a plastic surgeon had better have a diploma from a medical school to back up the claim. Playing fast and loose with definitional truths creates an Alice-in-Wonderland world that a culture cannot condone. A willy-nilly changing of meanings undermines necessary social continuity.

In our approach to therapy, words and definitions are recognized as powerful tools. Like anything powerful, they should be considered potentially hazardous and used with care. A surgeon's scalpel must be wielded judiciously if it is to prove helpful to the patient rather than destructive. Because of the importance we place on language, we take issue with therapists who trifle too readily with established words and meanings. For example, some strategic and family therapists attempt to put a happy face on virtually anything a client does, no matter how egregious. They freely dispense expedient reinterpretations—"positive connotations" and "reframes"—for clients' activities. Although we understand (and agree with) the notion that meanings are social constructions, that does not imply that they can or should be modified at whim. Participating in a culture is a commitment to abide by established language conventions. Capricious renaming of actions for short-term gain may entail unexpected, hidden, long-term risks. If you cheapen the verbal coin of the realm now, it is hard to escape the inflationary effects later.

As therapists who emphasize language, we want to establish ourselves—first and foremost—as being reliable players in the verbal community. We express our objections openly, and we stand behind what we say and do. Therefore, we do not positively connote or reframe client actions just for immediate effect. We say what we mean and mean what we say, and we invite clients to do the same. We sometimes refer to this as Horton's rule, from the classic *Horton Hatches the Egg*, by Dr. Seuss: "I meant what I said and I said what I meant. . . . An elephant's faithful one hundred percent!" (Geisel, 1940, p. 16).

Although we frequently encourage clients to see the world from alternative perspectives, that is not the same as engaging in verbal sleight of hand. The methods we use are not strategic ploys—they are honest proposals for alternative ways of looking at life. For example, a few years back, a new game called "wallyball" was invented. (It is similar to volleyball, but uses an enclosed four-wall court.) The name wallyball respects the established meanings of its component terms (wall and volleyball). Wallyball is a creative alternative—it provides additional ways for people to spend time together. However, no hypocrisy is involved—no lies are being told. On the other hand, when a strategic therapist "reframes" the failures of an underachiever as a heroic attempt to draw attention away from a conflict her parents are having, a lie *is* being told and hypocrisy *is* involved. Worse yet, some strategic therapists tend to state such interpretations as facts even though they themselves do not necessarily believe in them.

Nichols (1987), in a careful discussion of the pros and cons of reframing, notes the overemphasis of some reframers on the power of verbal magic. He warns, "It matters less what the therapist is selling than what the patient is buying. In the long run, people buy what is true and what works. It is a mistake to think that the right reframing statement transforms experience—not for long it doesn't" (pp. 239-240). We would add that it can be difficult to recoup the trust and good will that is lost when clients later discover that their therapists have been selling them a bill of goods.

A therapist we know makes a practice of "positively connoting" everything his clients do. He thinks he is helping. We think he is kidding himself. His clients are more savvy than he realizes. Clients may be initially buoyed by these platitudes, but they soon long for something more authentic. One of his clients put it this way: "I lie enough to myself. I don't need someone else doing it for me."

THE PURSUIT OF CANDOR

Reporting *experience* faithfully is fundamental to psychotherapy as we practice it. Of course, part of the candor we respect consists of keeping things in their proper compartments—stories need to be labeled stories, and opinions should be put forth as opinions. "Objectivity" must be kept in quotation marks. Psychiatrist Ron Smothermon reminds us that opinions, given as opinions, can make an enormous contribution to our lives. However, those same views when "offered as the truth are pure venom" (Smothermon, 1979, p. 220).

Naive realism, the tradition in which most of us have been brought up, teaches us to disparage personal desires and beliefs as trivial and to base important decisions on objective facts alone. This bias often leads people to mistake their opinions for facts and to duck responsibility for the actions they take and the priorities they establish. They attribute to natural laws or external authority deeds that they themselves enact.

For example, over the years, a war has been waged against Dutch elm disease ("Made for the Shade," 1990). It has been fought with an arsenal of man-made poisons. When we save a tree using these chemicals and declare a victory for Mother Nature, we engage in a sort of verbal ventriloquism. Of course "Nature" is not interested in wiping out Dutch elm disease or, for that matter, in preserving Dutch elm trees from extinction. *We* are. In fact, calling a poor fungus trying to eke out a simple living a "disease" prejudices matters at the outset. There is nothing wrong with protecting elm trees. However, languaging it as an act of "maintaining ecological balance" is duplicitous. *We* decide what the proper balance should be, and we do so in terms of our preferences. For example, many people who advocate extreme measures to save the Dutch elm as a species would be quite content to see "killer bees" exterminated, despite the resulting loss in *that* species' representation.

When applied to human relationships, the practice of stating preferences as objective givens is particularly pernicious. People who take unpopular actions (whether in families, hospitals, or other organizations) virtually always defend their actions as objective necessities rather than as personal penchants. Outright fabrications are generally not necessary, nor are they as effective as facts skillfully selected and strung together. A plethora of economic statistics can be found to support lowering taxes, leaving them alone, or raising them still further. The death penalty has repeatedly been "proven" ineffective by the facts, yet it is frequently resurrected by groups seeking to curb crime. The truth is that these groups *like* the death penalty and want to use it, whether it works or not.

SUMMARY

Typically, clients portray themselves as innocents marching through life, more or less minding their own business, until they stumble upon one of life's booby traps. They rarely construe such obstacles as being of their own making. Instead, they see themselves as the victims of circumstances—being at the wrong place at the wrong time. But problems are spin-offs of human conversation. People create problems for themselves by the things they believe and the way they talk with one another. In those conversations, terms like "cause," "blame," and "purpose" can represent trouble spots—places where people confuse semantic formulas with system operations. Professionals, too, rely on concepts that reify causal explanations.

In a purposeless drift, declarations of cause, purpose, and blame are linguistic inventions. They are biased, partial views seen from particular observational perches. They are always arguments for something—they attempt to give the speaker a competitive edge over others. If someone else *caused* the milk to spill, he or she is the one who is going to have to clean it up. However, there are as many possible causal ascriptions as there are candidates to mop up the milk, leading to a stalemate of sorts. Since these attributions do not depict operational realities, they cannot be proven or disproved. They can only lead to a labyrinth of endless debate and confusion. Therapists must resist entering into such debates and must help clients extricate themselves from the predicaments to which these typical language habits dispose them.

There are inconsistencies in the causal implications of the philosophies that guide our lives. We want to be given credit for our accomplishments but be absolved of blame for our shortcomings. Science (including social science) advocates strict determinism, but more humanitarian enterprises emphasize free will and self-determination. Mental health professionals are forced to practice on the cusp of these conflicting traditions, and they sometimes veer in one direction and sometimes in the other. Moreover, by construing mental health in objectivist terms, they shield themselves from a thorough recognition of the value-laden nature of their practices.

One of the most important qualities a therapist can offer his or her clients is trustworthiness—in essence, "truth in advertising" (Ryder, 1987). Therapists need to respect language and use it wisely, since it is a powerful tool. Therapists who employ verbal tricks and manipulations for immediate effect may end up losing their most valuable commodity—their reputation as a reliable "player" in the language community. Entertaining fresh alternatives and exploring other explanatory frameworks does not require the use of verbal subterfuge. Helping people talk straight is at the heart of the therapeutic venture; the therapist should set a good example.

Problems and solutions go together like questions and answers. The phrasing of one dictates the phrasing of the other. The boundaries we draw around events determine which problem/solution sets will occupy our attention. Boundaries are not dictated by external facts—they are negotiated by members of the community. It helps if participants are clear about their role in establishing or modifying particular boundary definitions.

In earlier chapters our focus has been on the basics of individual functioning. The connections between people—couplings—have been mentioned, but not explored in detail. The next two chapters remedy that situation, focusing on the effect of one person on another. In Chapter 8, we begin this consideration with a discussion of the contractual obligations and expectations that weave our lives together into a common fabric. Also, in this context, we give specifics about how we handle issues of fee, scheduling, and some other logistics of the clinical contract.

CHAPTER 8

Contractual Understandings

In earlier chapters, when we described life as a natural drift in a medium, perhaps the reader pictured a world that was amorphous and disorganized. However, drifts, including those that take place on an evolutionary scale, produce definite structures and organizations. Sand dunes drift, but at any given point in time they have a definite shape. Clearly, human communities—although everchanging—are not chaotic and formless. People generally lead orderly lives and play their assigned roles in the social structure.

Language supports the structure of the community. In this chapter, we maintain that this structure is a fabric woven of contractual obligations and agreements. Just as the structure of our bodies sets certain limits on what we can accomplish, our contractual arrangements, maintained in language, solidify additional parameters.

People have contracts about which side of the highway to drive on—the left in Britain, the right in the United States—and for how to behave when a favorite uncle dies. Contractual rules govern how to tell jokes, hold silverware, run garage sales, and endorse checks. We even maintain contract-like arrangements with inanimate objects, although obviously the objects in question are not given much say in the matter. Glass tumblers, for instance, are expected to contain liquids and stay where we put them. They are not supposed to leak on one day and hold water the next, nor are they supposed to rise mysteriously into the air without any visible means of support (Proffitt, 1977).

Some of our contractual rules provide guidelines for what to do when ordinary rules are broken—that is, they are contracts about contracts. If a tumbler started levitating on its own, a person nearby, noticing that the usual rules of operation had been violated, might interpret the event as a practical joke or as part of a performance by illusionist David Copperfield.[1] If such levitations persisted, he or she might seek religious or psychiatric counsel or have the drinking water tested for traces of LSD. We never say: "Oh, well, the glass is rising today. How nice." In other words, when our expectations are violated, we invoke back-up devices to protect us from concluding that the world is simply chaotic and unpredictable. Many Californians, for example, attempted to make sense of the World Series earthquake of 1989 by construing it as God's way of punishing them or teaching them some important lesson. This was preferable to believing that events of that magnitude happen capriciously.

Even our most routine, commonplace interactions are guided by a complex web of contractual arrangements, many of which operate more or less automatically, outside of focal awareness. For example, a bird's-eye view of patrons' interactions at a fast-food restaurant would reveal an exquisitely choreographed ballet of beings, who, through multiple unspoken understandings, skillfully manage to avoid bumping into one another. They don't sit at each other's tables and only rarely do they break into fist fights over the use of the ketchup dispenser. The rules that guide such interaction are notoriously difficult to explicate because they are woven so completely and seamlessly into the fabric of everyday living (Goffman, 1971). That is why travelers can usually be spotted as foreigners despite their ardent attempts to dress and behave the way natives do. It is probably also why it has proven so difficult to tutor individuals with social deficits to perform more than passably well in interpersonal contexts. Even after considerable instruction and many role-playing practice sessions, their behavior still seems odd, although it is hard to put your finger on exactly what it is that they are doing wrong.

It is useful to describe the orchestrated patterns of living in contractual terms rather than simply in terms of expectations, understandings, belief systems, or assumptive structures. The language of contracts conveys the active, urgent nature of these arrangements. It isn't just that people casually "expect" a cup to remain on the table, or even that they just "believe" that it

---

[1] Magic, of the David Copperfield sort, is dependent on an understanding of usual contractual arrangements. Young children sometimes fail to appreciate a magician's tricks precisely because they do not yet grasp the nature of these agreements. Therefore, they do not see what is so special about objects suddenly appearing or disappearing, changing color, or speaking with human voices.

will—they virtually *demand* that it do so, and remonstrate loudly if it behaves otherwise. Cup manufacturers know how surly customers can get when the cups they buy do not perform to standards. Therefore, they go to considerable lengths to ensure reliable performance. In the face of even minor contractual violations, people are apt to bare their fangs, breaking through the thin veneer of civilization that keeps our usual interactions running smoothly and amicably. The strong reactions that occur in response to even minor breaches of contract reveal the extent to which we rely on such patterning to sustain the social order.

BROKEN AGREEMENTS

An agreement broken or left incomplete creates a "pathology"—a mess which, if allowed to persist, invalidates the perpetrator and blemishes the lives of all those involved in the perpetration. Every contractual transgression is a personal and communal liability. Even transgressions that others agree to overlook or politely excuse as unimportant extract a price—they accumulate and gradually erode the quality of life. This is the complaint of many city-dwellers who find that nobody seems to give a damn—neither salesclerks, city workers, government officials, repair people, contractors, landlords, nor pet owners.

In the conversation of living, completed agreements are sources of self-satisfaction, but incomplete or broken agreements shackle self-esteem and drain vitality. Transgressions become more convoluted as avoidance and hypocrisy are laid on top of the original infraction. The transgressions in people's lives seem conceptually linked to one another, producing a cumulative haze through which people view their existence.

Because broken agreements simultaneously weaken the social fabric and tarnish self-image, a good rule of thumb in life—for both clients and therapists—is to keep every agreement you make, including those that are only implicit. For many people, following this rule will mean exercising more restraint in making promises. These individuals have usually been quick to promise but slow to make good on their word. However, in life, all a person really has is his or her word. To the extent that it doesn't mean anything, then, by the process of logical deduction, he or she doesn't mean anything either. Keeping your word makes you *significant*, both in your own experience and in the experience of others. Not keeping your word has the reverse effect. The key to self-satisfaction, then, is being true to self, which includes, as a crucial component, meaning what you say and saying what you mean (our "Horton" rule). On this issue Richard Bach (1977) writes: "Your only obligation in any lifetime is to be true to yourself. Being true to anyone else or anything else is not only impossible, but the mark of a fake messiah" (p. 59).

Practically speaking, of course, being true to self is an ideal none of us can fully achieve. However, the principle of not making any agreements you do not intend to keep serves as a useful guide to the diagnosis of what is wrong when things don't seem to be on track. In order to repair the damage created whenever you are unable to successfully fulfill contractual obligations, you need to acknowledge the lapse and renegotiate the relevant contracts, taking into account the interests of all concerned parties.

STALE AGREEMENTS

Contracts that were once valid and relevant can obviously become outdated. These, too, need to be reexamined and renegotiated. Otherwise, we may find ourselves pursuing goals that were once experientially meaningful but have now devolved into a series of empty slogans. For instance, at one time we wanted to make a lot of money, become a movie star, or swim in the Olympics. These dead goals, "out of sync" with present desires and values, no longer define the self. Any goal not being actively pursued in some form or another is a dead goal. The debris of dead goals chokes off life. Outmoded goals need to be acknowledged as such and clearly abandoned, so that current goals can be plainly articulated and vigorously pursued.

Take, for example, a person who grew up wanting to become a doctor. Now he or she is struggling to get through medical school and wondering whether the effort is worth it. More than likely, this person is operating with an outmoded attachment—a stale concept of being a physician that no longer fits who he or she is. If such is the case, this individual should seriously consider dropping out of medical school, although doing so will involve renegotiating contracts with parents, spouses, fiancés, or others who were anticipating that the person would become a doctor.

Agreements that have been allowed to slide must be rehabilitated, and any damage done (to self and others) needs to be repaired. This is not very mysterious. If, in the business world, a shipment is not delivered on time, a member of the firm would be wise to (a) acknowledge the problem, (b) ascertain if the goods are still wanted, (c) arrange for a new delivery date, and (d) compensate the affected customers for inconveniences or losses they have suffered as a result of the foul-up. If those steps are not taken, the ill will generated may very well result in a loss of future business. Customers who become sufficiently unhappy may go a step further—doing their best to sully the firm's reputation with friends and acquaintances. Irate customers have been known to resort to extreme measures, such as dynamiting a company's offices or renting a billboard to tell the world their side of the story. Recently, we passed a van on the highway sporting a large sign on its roof. The sign warned other consumers to steer clear of the auto agency from which the van had been bought—they had presumably ignored the owner's complaints and left him to fend for himself with what the sign labeled "a lemon."

In interpersonal relations, the principles underlying contractual dealings are exactly the same as in the business world, including the possibility of generating extraordinary wrath when contracts are in default. Everyone knows Congreve's warning that "heav'n has no rage like love to hatred turn'd, nor hell a fury like a woman scorn'd." Jilted men aren't especially pleasant either. People involved in broken agreements understandably rail against themselves, others, and the world at large.

A student tells her parents she will definitely earn an A, but gets a B instead. She is in contractual "default" even if she claims—legitimately—that this particular teacher "doesn't give A's." Paradoxically, offering the excuse verifies the fact that a contract was indeed in force and has been violated. Moreover, unlike some courtroom scenarios, legalese cannot really be used to duck the implications of a broken agreement. Even implicit contracts, in which the "i's" were never dotted and the "t's" were never crossed, exert an inexorable pull on the individuals involved. Perhaps a woman never *explicitly* promised to remember her mother's birthday, but when she forgets there may be hell to pay in terms of guilt, hurt, and recrimination.

Everyone understands when such transgressions have occurred, including the individual who may now be attempting to weasel out of the consequences. However, in some families, the fallout of a denied transgression continues to haunt the individual's thoughts and dreams. Recriminations can be passed from generation to generation, sometimes beyond the grave. In one striking case, a son found a way to "get even" with his domineering father after the father had died. Although the father had clearly expressed the desire to have a traditional religious burial, the son had him unceremoniously cremated, without the services of a religious official—violating the precepts of the father's religion as well as his last wishes.

CYCLES OF COMPLETION

As we have suggested, even small, everyday transgressions—forgetting to buy a birthday card or neglecting a phone call—have a way of adding up. Even those private promises made to oneself—never announced to anyone else—can affect one's self-worth. When you are not meeting your own standards, it is difficult to get yourself off your back. Arguing with yourself is like trying to win an arm-wrestling contest between your right and left arms. It is a fight that cannot be won.

Logically speaking, agreements, once made, can end in one of only three ways—they must be honored, breached, or renegotiated. The effects of these three outcomes are distinct from one another. It doesn't matter whether the contract in question is, by some outside standard, wise or foolish, realistic or fanciful. A contract—even a foolhardy one—is a contract nevertheless. When it is abrogated, the losses really exist (i.e., have been distinguished). Depressed people actually *are* in default in some domain, anxious individuals *are* being chased by something, and suspicious individuals *have* been repeatedly betrayed. Perhaps this is what prompts David Shapiro, in his description of neuroses, to claim that people come by their problems honestly (1965). Sometimes the nature of the loss, the attack, or the betrayal isn't readily apparent, particularly to outsiders. However, in each case, a contract with some aspect of the world, as experienced by the individual, has been violated. Some personal "cup" didn't stay where it was supposed to.

Labels such as "neurotic" allude only to the difficulty others have in appreciating the significance of the contracts the person negotiated. Sometimes the neurotic individual has a similar difficulty, when he or she takes the observer's position. Nevertheless, in the person's experiential world, a contractual glitch exists, is consequential, and needs to be identified and repaired. People who are depressed, anxious, or suspicious are not going to "get better" or "feel better" until they find ways to fulfill or renegotiate the contracts that are "disordered." Used in this way and freed of medical connotations, the word "disorder" becomes singularly appropriate. Something or someone isn't performing in accordance with expectations.

Cleaning up the mess created by improperly constituted or broken agreements is sometimes as easy as offering someone a simple acknowledgment—bearing witness to the fact that you didn't do what you had promised. At other times, more extensive repair work is needed. Restorative actions can include saying particular things to particular individuals—such as "I was mistaken" or "I recognize that I'm the one who did that." They can also include taking very concrete corrective actions, such as modifying bank accounts, rewriting wills, changing job titles, visiting distant relatives, giving up child-custody claims, completing college, raking leaves, and taking out the trash. (Remember, we do not make sharp distinctions between actions that are purely verbal and those that involve other elements. Life is all action.)

Once contracts have been successfully completed, they disappear—they cease to be psychologically relevant. After contracts that have been abrogated are successfully repaired, the involved parties experience completion. They are freed to move on to other matters. Notice that in cleaning up the mess that incomplete contractual arrangements entail, issues of "fault" or "blame," as we usually use those terms, are not particularly germane. Department stores issue rainchecks for out-of-stock sale items even if "it wasn't the store's fault." People find themselves frustrated and angry when an aging parent contracts Alzheimer's disease, even though clearly no one is to blame. A missed appointment creates distress for all the participants concerned, even if it can be "justified" as having been "caused" by an unexpected traffic jam.

In fact, contractual failures easily justified by circumstances are often more difficult for participants to handle, since they are deprived of what they might consider to be a legitimate outlet for their frustration. When fault can be established, someone or something becomes a handy target for retribution. Note the public frustration that occurs when a person commits a heinous crime and then takes his or her own life immediately thereafter. The first sin is compounded by the fact that he or she deprived us of a mechanism with which to properly rebalance the books.

In discussions of contractual violation, two terms—apology and acknowledgment—are often used interchangeably. However, it is important to preserve the distinction between them. When a contractual breach occurs, acknowledgment is necessary, but not apology. The person isn't required to "feel sorry." Moreover, his or her sorrow or guilt doesn't rectify the breach. In fact, it often constitutes a subtle plea to be excused from the consequences of having committed the transgression in the first place. A person who feels sufficiently "sorry" expects to be let off the hook. As one slightly perplexed youngster put it, "I don't know why my teacher made me go to the back of the room—I said I was sorry, didn't I?" The emphasis needs to be on the reparative process, which includes acknowledgment and remediation but can do very nicely without guilt or sorrow.

CONTRACTING TO DO THERAPY

Thus far we have been speaking about contracts as they might apply to living in general. We now turn our attention more directly to contracts that govern psychotherapy. Such contracts begin to be formulated even before particular clients and their therapists meet. Cultural understandings underpin arrangements made by clients and therapists and provide the authorization for therapy to occur. A therapist would not (and could not), for example, just walk up to someone on a park bench and interact therapeutically. There is no cultural mold that would render such an interaction understandable, and it would thus be perceived as odd and intrusive. Under those circumstances, the advice of even the most "brilliant" of therapists would probably be summarily rejected. (Many therapists have been burned in their attempts to provide their own family members with "therapeutic" advice. Here, too, their counsel is apt to be cavalierly dismissed, since in the family context they are sons, daughters, fathers, or mothers—not mental health experts.)

In an interesting study of phobias in children (Rosenfarb & Hayes, 1984), a learning-theory-based procedure was found to be effective only when it had been labeled a "treatment" and the subjects had therefore been led to expect that they would profit from it. When they engaged in exactly the same procedure but without the contractual understanding that it was supposed to be curative, the status of their phobias remained unchanged. To put it glibly but succinctly, therapy is only therapy when it is (contractually) therapy.

The therapy contract includes criteria against which progress can be monitored and outcomes evaluated. It sets *acceptable* and *expectable* payoffs and costs. A contract that is poorly framed or easily misunderstood creates a good deal of mischief, some of which may not be immediately traceable to initial contractual inadequacies. Horace's adage, "Well begun is half done," applies here. A clear contract makes it possible to accomplish near miracles, but an ambiguous contract can be a profound impediment—making it difficult to achieve even minimal progress.

The contract is what puts the teeth into therapeutic work. The objectivist can always assert that a therapist's activities are determined and justified by objective facts or social necessities. However, we do not have that liberty. We accept personal responsibility for the projects in which we engage, and it is the contract that clarifies in everyone's mind what those responsibilities are. The activities of therapist and client are seen as a series of personal preferences, coordinated by social agreement. Although clients and their therapists are the primary "signatories" to the therapy contract, the contract is negotiated against a background of cultural and professional norms and understandings. Something similar happens when a customer visits a hairstylist. Together, they decide on the right "look." However, the lotions used in producing the look must meet certain governmental safety standards, and the styles considered will undoubtedly reflect current cultural trends as pictured in magazines, on TV, or in the movies.

There is another parallel between hair styling and therapy—in both, the person may go in with only a vague idea of what he or she wants to have happen and may not be able to express, in words, exactly what is wanted.

In therapy the client presumably cannot fully articulate what is required. By its very nature, the beginning of an inquiry is characterized by uncertainty. Adventurers begin with a general direction in mind. However, the details of the voyage are discovered as the trip unfolds.

Over the years, psychotherapists have attempted to devise specific rules of operation for every aspect of their interaction with clients—how to dress, how to say hello, where to hold sessions, and what kind of furniture to use (Sharma, 1986). There are written and unwritten rules about physical contact, self-disclosure, maintaining confidences, taking notes, releasing records to insurance companies, answering the phone during sessions, discussing fees, and offering food or drink. Some of these rules have, over time, attained functional autonomy. A particular rule that may have made sense in a particular culture or under specific circumstances is now followed rigidly and routinely, despite changes in theory, in people, and in life. The atmosphere of experimentation in which methods were originally created is easily lost, and thus the novel ideas of one decade become the rigid constraints of the next.

A psychologist consulting to a large state prison learned firsthand how rules take on a life of their own. He noticed that at a certain time each afternoon all activities were interrupted and the men returned to their cells to be counted. Puzzled over the need for this—especially since it usually came in the middle of his group therapy sessions—he asked the warden about the purpose of the mid-afternoon lock-up. The warden explained that a count was needed whenever there was a changing of the guard. This made sense to the psychologist until he realized that the shift change didn't occur until several hours later. "Ah," said the warden, "but that's when it used to happen."

In some instances, individuals who abide by rules invented earlier are entirely unaware of how those rules came into being or the purpose for which they were originally invented.[2] In a few cases, the personal quirks of pioneers inadvertently became templates for the practices of others. It is said, for example, that Freud's practice of sitting behind patients—out of their line of vision—mainly represented his personal discomfort with more direct and prolonged eye contact. Since that time, the practice of having the therapist seated behind the client has become, in the public mind, the sine qua non of "real" therapy. It is so embedded in our cultural consciousness

---

[2]Similarly, several generations of women in a family always cut a ham in half before they put it into the oven. One day, a daughter asked her mother to explain this custom. The mother wasn't sure, but promised to ask *her* mother. It turned out that when the grandmother was first married, her oven had been too small to hold a whole ham, and so she cut it up in order to make Sunday dinner.

that cartoonists use it to identify psychotherapeutic interaction the same way they might use an icon of the Eiffel Tower to represent France.

In our culture, client-therapist contracts usually ride piggyback on the model of relations established between a physician and his or her patient. One of the authors recalls being startled when, during a case that seemed to be going well, a client suddenly dropped out of sight. The therapist was concerned that something had gone drastically wrong. He searched his mind in an attempt to locate the factor to which the client might have had such a powerful, adverse reaction. Later, he discovered that, in fact, nothing had gone wrong. The client was fine and had actually been delighted with the "service" she had been rendered. (She was actively recommending the therapist to her friends and relatives.) However, she viewed the therapy relationship as parallel to the one she had with her internist—when her "fever" disappeared, she simply stopped communicating with her doctor. Had there been another "flareup," she would surely have been back in touch. Therapists have to take into account the specific model clients are apt to initially invoke, and clarify with them aspects of the relationship that might be different from what they are expecting.

Mental health workers in an urban hospital that was situated near a rural community frequently found themselves dealing with very puzzled farmers. The farmers had no idea why they were being asked to talk more about their problems rather than being given a prescription or sent for additional blood-work. Nobody had bothered to offer them an explanation about "psychotherapy," and they assumed that their sessions were leading to some more discernible, concrete intervention.

TIME MANAGEMENT

Time arrangements, which are among the most basic contractual elements for therapy, have been the focus of many bitter client-therapist misunderstandings. We want to discuss time and scheduling in some detail, since our own approach to these subjects is distinctly untraditional. In our view, the ordinary arrangements have become split off from their historical contexts. For example, when clients were seen almost daily, relatively short sessions (the "therapeutic hour") made good sense. However, clients are now seen at less frequent intervals, and it isn't always clear that the 50-minute hour (which, in some cases, has been further decreased to 45 minutes) is the most sensible arrangement.

Not only has the 45- or 50-minute hour become de rigueur for many forms of therapy, but practitioners often feel obliged to end sessions at precisely the appointed time, regardless of what might be happening in a particular session. This policy has been defended as necessary for establishing a safe and stable therapeutic framework of operation for clients and therapists (see, e.g., Langs, 1989). Langs and other such theorists argue that without such strict limit-setting clients will succeed in manipulating the therapy and that, furthermore, their manipulative strategies will not stand out in sufficiently sharp relief to be properly analyzed. We do not dismiss this argument lightly. Consistency has its value, and structure can be both reassuring and instructive. On the other hand, rigid time rules create problems of their own. For one thing, life simply does not fit neatly into 45- or 50-minute chunks; different therapeutic tasks may require different amounts of time to accomplish. Surgical operations are not all the same length, and Broadway plays are not required to end precisely two hours after they begin. Thus, there is a structure and a schedule, but also provision for the fact that some stories take longer to unfold than others.

Under strict time-limit rules, sessions have been ended abruptly while the client is in the middle of tearfully reliving a crucial experience of loss or enacting a full-blown tantrum. Such strictures fail to provide clients with the opportunity to complete an important cycle of experience and to restore an appropriate public "face" before departing. Thus, this may result in *less* safety, rather than more. The entire burden of accommodating to these time strictures is usually placed on the clients. Their complaints, protests, or reactions become just more grist for the interpretive mill. There is no way to call a neutral "time out" to discuss the matter, person to person.

We prefer a different operational mode. We want our clients to understand that once certain processes have been allowed to begin, we will assume an obligation to see them through to completion, even if it takes more time than expected. If logistics require that the process be segmented, we will take some responsibility for helping the person temporarily "cap" the experience.

Our model of therapy is therefore more akin to that of the surgeon (or the internist) than to that of the psychiatrist. A surgical procedure isn't over until it's over, and internists rarely tell their patients to put their clothes back on and return the following week because an examination or procedure took longer than expected. Similarly, we like to end sessions at junctures that feel like natural stopping points, not when the clock hands reach a particular point. We confess that, under this plan, some of our sessions have gone on for two, three, or even four hours. The shortest session on record lasted only 15 minutes, of which five minutes or so was clearly social padding; the task at hand just didn't require any more time than that. For complex tasks, we have sometimes arranged marathon meetings, agreeing to work all day or all night if necessary. It helps in such situations if everyone involved understands that there is a willingness to stay on the job until the assignment has been completed. That arrangement can successfully undercut a client's fear-related motivation to stall for time. In ordinary sessions, clients can too readily postpone crucial moments for some later meeting, the way a person preparing to parachute-jump for the first time might pray for inclement weather.

We do not enslave ourselves to the clock or the appointment book. We use time-keeping devices only as aids, not absolute masters. In our work, the task is primary, and other considerations, such as time, place, tradition, or convenience, are, of necessity, relegated to positions of secondary importance. We set up our therapy so that the logistics of sessions maximally support the project at hand, even if this means stepping outside of the routines of practice. Different therapy projects or different aspects of the same project require different time arrangements. We see no particular reason to use the exact same format throughout.

FEES

We normally charge clients by the *session* rather than by the clock—it de-emphasizes clock watching. We would actually prefer to charge by the "job" or the "procedure," the way surgeons and contractors do. We have, in fact, experimented with just such arrangements. When we first suggested such ideas, they seemed radical. These days, therapists have become more accustomed to novel fee arrangements because of the widespread acceptance of capitation plans in managed health care systems and employee assistance programs. It is ironic that we have had to wait for the push—more like a shove—from insurance companies to launch new experiments in offering services.

In several instances we offered clients money-back guarantees—they would get a full or partial refund if a designated goal could not be satisfactorily achieved in a reasonable amount of time. For the therapist to collect a full fee, both client and therapist would have to agree that the desired goal was indeed reached. Should *either* client or therapist be disappointed with the outcome, the therapist would collect only a small consolation prize for being able to say "we tried." In this atypical arrangement, each participant purposely risks something. The client risks not getting what he or she reputedly wants, and the therapist risks the loss of income and status. On the other side, there is something enjoyable and desirable about living at risk—it rewards working arduously and creatively on a project and behaving as if producing the outcome really mattered. Playing full-out is satisfying. It is living dangerously—the opposite of going through the motions. Projects that run on automatic, using stock formulas, cease to be much fun. Ultimately they lead to burnout—and profit no one.

Years ago we consulted on a similar "money-back" basis to a manufacturing firm that was having internal personnel problems. We didn't do it to live "at risk." We were in competition with a well-known consulting firm. We were inexperienced and had no reputation in that area at all. We made the offer in order to have at least some competitive advantage over the other company. We wanted to be able to say "try us—you have nothing to lose." What started as a "marketing ploy" turned out to be highly advantageous. We weren't being paid big bucks for a job we weren't sure we'd be able to do. No pretense was involved; everything was free and clear. We had a lot of operating freedom. We went in to get the job done, and we proved our worth to the firm each and every day we were there. It was a gratifying arrangement that worked for everyone.

In working with people, surprises have great impact. (We will have more to say about this on a theoretical level when we talk about orthogonal interaction in the next chapter.) One of the authors saw a woman who had been hospitalized a number of times and had had traffic with a variety of psychiatrists and mental health workers. She had an elaborate tale of woe to share, including the fact that her husband had run off with another woman and even her own daughter—by a previous marriage—had abandoned her. She had lost her job in the midst of her hospitalizations and was struggling to make ends meet. She claimed that relatives had betrayed her and cheated her out of money she deserved, and doctors, too, seemed more interested in collecting fees than in being of help.

Although the author had come highly recommended to her, she was doubtful that she could pay anything close to his private fee since she was so down on her luck. She already owed money to repairmen, lawyers, and physicians; besides that, her car was about to be repossessed. The author said that there would be no problem—there wouldn't be a fee at all. The services would be free of charge. That was the one response for which she was unprepared. She sat in stunned silence, as if she hadn't heard correctly. She had been ready to launch into a prolonged, contentious negotiation over money—a process, incidentally, at which she was no amateur. Moreover, she would have then added the author to her long list of professionals who were mainly out to "make a buck."

It was clear to the author that haggling with this person over monetary arrangements would be a mistake. He was either going to take the case—in which case he might just as well forgo the small fees that might result—or he would have to recommend that she seek low-cost services elsewhere. He decided to take the first route. It was the right decision. It put the arrangement on a different footing than anything she had experienced elsewhere. Of course, money figured heavily into the therapy discussions, and because of the nature of the contract it was an issue on which the therapist could claim to be "clean." The author was very happy to be of service and the lost fees were somewhat recouped later because of the many other people she recommended for treatment. However, in one case, the author did have to correct an impression of one of the recommendees, who came in saying, "I understand you don't charge fees."

At least in private settings, the client's fee is one of the contractual elements that is easiest to control, and novel arrangements can be used to advantage. Even in clinics, therapists have sometimes cleverly managed to work out flexible arrangements with regard to fees and other logistic details. Any aspect of the contract should be considered malleable, so that the circumstances can be shaped to support the project at hand.

Clinicians sometimes protest that they are given little say over their working conditions. They claim they could not, even if they wanted to, operate in the way we have been describing. However, just as surgeons must insist on a certain level of antisepsis as a precondition for operating, therapists must insist on having at least minimal control over their working conditions if they are to be effective. For example, we deplore the common practice in many of today's psychiatric hospitals of allowing insurance policies or bureaucratic rules to dictate the way therapy is done or which kind of treatment is to be offered. To us, it seems unethical to first determine the length of stay an inpatient's insurance coverage allows and then permit that figure to shape the treatment recommendation. Yet many mental health professionals seem to have become accustomed to that way of proceeding. There ought to be an outcry about it, but in some settings barely a whimper has been heard.

SCHEDULING

Like most therapists, we *tend* to see clients once a week, but we don't have a rule about it. Some clients are seen biweekly, at monthly intervals, or on odder schedules. There are times—fortunately not many—when it is useful and necessary to see a person every few hours or to maintain virtually constant phone contact, even if each telephone conversation lasts only a minute or two. Again, the scheduling is asked to play second fiddle to the nature of the task to be accomplished.

We usually schedule a next appointment at the conclusion of the previous one, rather than designating a set time as "belonging" to a particular client. Sometimes it would be pointless to meet again before a particular event took place or before the outcome of a given assignment was known. In these cases, a meeting isn't scheduled until the person calls in to say "mission accomplished" or indicates that a snag has developed that requires further face-to-face discussion. Like the internist, we schedule sessions only when something particular needs to be accomplished, rather than on the assumption that meetings should occur at fixed or regular intervals.

We have indicated that we like to continue a session until we reach a natural juncture point. When the press of other obligations (for therapist or client) make this impossible, we acknowledge the incompletion and make plans to pick up where we left off at the earliest opportunity. This is analogous to a surgeon's having discovered more pathology than expected during the course of an operation and being forced to leave some procedures for another day. It isn't desirable, but sometimes it is necessary.

There is nothing sacred about an office. Sometimes there are other locations that provide more suitable environments for moving an inquiry forward. We have no hesitation about leaving the office when necessary. For instance, we have taken a number of phobic clients to a nearby amusement park—Six Flags' *Great Adventure*. It is a phobic's nightmare. There are giant Ferris wheels, sky rides, roller coasters and "free-fall" machines—and it's all safety-checked and well-insured. Our aim in going there is *not* to extinguish fears or systematically desensitize clients, but rather to make available to phobic clients the adult equivalent of monkey bars. There are opportunities to test and challenge oneself—to conduct mini-experiments in reactivity and survival methods. A person can confront his or her belief systems and study the strategies by which they were formed and sustained. We think of it as an elaborate outdoor laboratory facility with sophisticated equipment. Best of all, it has been made available to us at low cost—the price of admission.

Of course, not all phobias take the same form, and there are other locations for specialized "field work." A young man with concerns about his body, particularly the size of his genitals, got great value by visiting the showers and locker room of a nearby health club. In the past he had gone to great lengths to avoid undressing or showering in public. Initially, even the possibility of a trip to a physician's office caused him to cringe with embarrassment. We sent him to the health club to conduct a series of self-experiments with "seeing" and "being seen." He learned a lot, although others at the club would not have been able to guess that he was on "secret assignment." Particularly useful was the fact that he could go back as often as he wanted and set the pace of self-discovery.

WHO ATTENDS?

We have no ironclad rules about who should, or should not, attend therapy sessions. We have consulted with individuals, spouses, families, friends, and work groups. We rarely insist that an entire family appear or that members of multiple generations be seen together. In work with couples, we usually want to meet with each individual alone for at least part of the time. Sometimes we have announced that we will work with whoever chooses to show up; on other occasions we have expressed a strong preference for meeting with a particular subgrouping of the individuals involved. Again, different tasks require different groupings. In our opinion, it is a liability to adopt a rigid, one-size-fits-all mentality.

A divorced wife wanted to bring her whole family in for another round of family therapy—they had seen a family therapist before the divorce. The immediate problem was a 13-year-old daughter who wasn't doing well in school and was said to have an "attitude" problem. The mother would get calls at work to help settle disputes that had broken out between her and her older sister. This seemed to be a family in which it was hard for anyone to take a clear stance. Everyone felt obliged to go along, half-heartedly, with whatever others said. For example, the daughter would be willing to "come" to family sessions if they were held, but she didn't really see what purpose they would serve. The therapist agreed. He, too, didn't think they would serve any particular purpose. He indicated that, in this instance, he had no desire to see the family together. In fact, he wanted only to talk to the daughter—privately—and only if she wanted to talk to him. She could determine the agenda for the meeting. Members of the family had complained that nobody knew where this girl stood—that she wasn't being communicative. Of course, it's hard to be communicative if you're not allowed to be in disagreement. In a private session that "belonged" to her, she had plenty to say. The right to say "no"—it doesn't matter much what the issue is—is fundamental to being yourself. This was a case in which the *form* of the meeting—an invitation to a solo session—symbolized the need for privacy and autonomy that had been missing in family interactions.

MANIPULATION AND RESPONSIBILITY

Professionals who are accustomed to operating with more standard boundaries of time and grouping generally worry that our way of working encourages clients to be manipulative. However, a paradox seems to be at work: The more a therapist guards against being manipulated, the more he or she seems susceptible to it. We are quite relaxed about therapy. We don't make a fuss over the issue of being manipulated, and therefore we rarely experience what the client does in those terms. Since we never suggest that clients are entitled to a set amount of time, they have little need to wheedle *additional* time. Since we do not meet at predetermined intervals, they do not need to use suicidal threats or other dramatic gestures to coerce extra meetings between regular sessions—there are no regular sessions. Or, to put it conversely, every session is a special session. We welcome client suggestions concerning what to do next, and when, but we always give ourselves a clear vote in the proceedings. Because we are task-oriented, we are in an ideal position to repeatedly pose the question: "How will what you are suggesting help get the job done?"

Some therapists seem almost to be afraid of their clients. They seem to go overboard protecting themselves against real or imagined intrusions. They have unlisted phone numbers and scrupulously guard information about their private lives. They refuse to disclose whether or not they are married, have children, play tennis, or enjoy going to the movies. This virtually forces inquisitive clients to engage in extensive (and sometimes bizarre) detective work. Clients have been known to look up birth, death, and marriage records at City Hall, to stake out the therapist's home, and to call under assumed names to ferret out additional information. Some have even been able to enlist the help of friends in these clandestine activities. (A client who is able to get a friend to ring the therapist's doorbell under the guise of selling magazine subscriptions deserves credit for superior powers of persuasion and industriousness.)

These excessive attempts on the part of clients to gather information are the reciprocal of therapists' excessive attempts to maintain privacy. The two strategies dovetail perfectly, mutually stimulating and reinforcing each other. Therapists who consider it essential to keep the therapy relationship entirely separate from the rest of life invite the kind of escalating client curiosity that becomes increasingly difficult to manage. A self-fulfilling prophecy is created: The more such walls are reinforced, the more they invite being breached. It is the gifts you aren't allowed to open until Christmas morning that you most desperately want to know about. After the boxes have been opened, the contents turn out to be fairly ordinary "stuff," not worth all the fuss and anticipation. Therapists might want to pick up on the paradox that many celebrities intuitively understand—that wearing dark glasses and traveling in limousines excites the very notoriety they *claim* to want to avoid. As learning theorists argue, deprivation gives stimuli potency (Goldiamond, 1972).

We don't construe ourselves as victims of the actions of others, including clients. We know how to say "yes" and how to say "no." We work with clients because we choose to, and we work with them in particular ways by mutual agreement and consent. Under these circumstances, we rarely find terms like "manipulation" and "pressure" applicable. Manipulation only exists in a language framework in which individuals—including therapists—wish to deny responsibility for what they do. We are not at war with our clients and do not feel the need for a stock of elaborate rules and regulations to block powerful client intentions.

PHYSICAL CONTACT

Physical contact between client and therapist is perhaps the area in which therapists have most frequently and fervently attempted to substitute rigid rules for individual judgments. However, few of the guidelines suggested really work, and none of them ensures responsible behavior. We are reminded of the foolish regulations instituted over the years at college dormitories, when college administrators attempted to control sexual contact between male and female students. There were all sorts of peculiarly worded rules—doors were to remain ajar a certain distance, lights of given wattages were to be left lit, and so on. Interestingly, the rules almost never stated directly "no intercourse," "don't get pregnant," or "avoid contracting venereal disease." Students have always managed to successfully skirt all these regulations, sometimes exercising great cleverness in abiding by the letter of the law. They leave the door ajar the required number of inches, but cover the resulting gap with a cloth. They leave a 60-watt lamp burning, but have painted the bulb black. A number of years ago, at a well-known university, male students protested an unpopular rule requiring them to "dress" for dinner by showing up wearing *only* the requisite ties and jackets, and nothing else.

Touching—sensual, sexual, or generic—is a topic that stirs up intense reactions and multiple associations in clients and therapists alike. Yet touching isn't a "thing" that can be pinned down, given fixed meanings, and satisfactorily regulated. As prostitutes frequently report, the "sexual" fondling of their clients may be anything but sexual to them—it is an impersonal business transaction. On the other hand, the touch of a physician conducting a routine examination may be highly erotic for a particular patient, all the more so because of the secret and taboo fantasies the patient weaves into the experience.

Even in the absence of any actual physical contact, interpersonal situations can come to have intense sexual meanings and undercurrents. For example, Yalom (1989) recounts a session with a female client during which the two of them inventoried the contents of her purse. Although there was no physical contact whatsoever, he describes this as having been an intensely intimate interaction for both of them.

The mistake we repeatedly make in adopting an objectivist stance toward human behavior is to confuse concrete actions with experienced meaning. We attempt to regulate the former under the false belief that in doing so we ensure the successful management of the latter. There are clients who should be hugged from time to time, and others who should rarely, if ever, be touched. Nude group marathons, with or without the obligatory California hot tub, can advance some kinds of personal inquiry. In other instances, being naked—with or without the hot tub—adds nothing useful to the proceedings. No form of touching—not even the sensual and sexual varieties—can, without detailed considerations of context and meaning, be finally and objectively determined to be good or bad, wholesome or unwholesome. This is as unfortunate as it is true, since life would be so much simpler if it could be successfully run according to standard rules that were always applicable.

We are not endorsing explicit sexual contact with clients—there is little reason to suppose that something of that sort would serve a useful purpose in this day and age. On the other hand, on issues of mores and morals, most of us have regrettably short cultural memories. We overinterpret current standards as correct and stable, and become smugly self-satisfied that no sane individual would argue for alternative possibilities. That is a dangerous stance. In a culture, practices and standards change rapidly—and in both restrictive and permissive directions.

For example, it ought to be remembered that there were Jewish religious practices in the First Temple period (ending with the Babylonian exile) that included "male and female sacred prostitution (fees donated to the Temple as a means of absolution), the introduction of young men to the sexual-religious exaltations of orgasm within the Temple, and ceremonial mouth-genital contacts between priests and worshipers" (Tripp, 1987, p. 5). At the other extreme are cultures that encourage or demand lengthy periods of sexual abstinence—up to several years—between married individuals (Greer, 1984).

When taking current conventions as "objective" frames of reference, we conveniently forget how much variety there is in human practices throughout the world and across time periods. We need to be careful about concluding that given practices, even those that seem bizarre and drastic to us, are "pathological" or ill-advised, leading directly and inevitably to negative outcomes. In fact, the ill effects of many deviations in pattern are probably more due to the effects of social labeling and related ostracism than to the practices themselves. We recall a father and daughter from small-town America who, it was discovered, had been having an incestuous relationship for a number of years following the death of the mother. When they found out about it, the social workers were aghast, but, frankly, the father and daughter weren't sure what all the fuss was about. The father had sexual needs, and the daughter was willing to cooperate. As he naively but sincerely explained to the social workers, he thought it would be better "just to keep it all in the family rather than bothering outsiders about it."

PROFESSIONAL ETHICS

Ethical and unethical behavior cannot be reliably separated simply by determining whether individuals are complying with regulations. Being ethical sometimes *necessitates* a violation of commonly accepted canons of practice. According to newspaper and magazine reports, therapists often fail to notify the authorities about certain instances of suspected child abuse, even though the law clearly requires it, because they recognize that reporting the situation would cause everyone, including the child, more harm than good. A recent *60 Minutes* episode documented cases in which Florida child-welfare authorities mistakenly removed children from their homes, creating unnecessary trauma for all concerned. (Sometimes, of course, caseworkers err in the opposite direction, waiting too long to bring suspected abuse to the attention of the authorities.)

Note that ethical standards, as defined by rules and the outcomes of judicial proceedings, keep changing. In the famous Tarasoff decision (Tarasoff v. Regents of the University of California, 1976) establishing the so-called "duty to warn," the clinician had not done anything "wrong," until *after* the legal decision was rendered. In fact, he took a series of steps most of us would have considered responsible and adequate. What was ethical until that time suddenly became unethical because the case went the other way. The situation is now more complex because other court decisions appear to partially conflict with the conclusions reached in the Tarasoff case. Our point is that a clinician faced with a given set of circumstances must ultimately draw his or her own conclusions about which pathway is ethical to pursue. Just as judges must render decisions when such matters come before them in the courts, clinicians must make tough decisions as circumstances arise in their practice. These decisions can be made in the context of legal precedents and prevailing professional opinion. However, in specific situations, general precedents never substitute for individual judgment. If we all simply followed the rules literally—an impossibility in the real world—psychotherapeutic innovation would grind to a halt. By definition, new theorizing and experimentation must inevitably stretch the limits of accepted practice. This is true in every field. In the 1880s people were arrested and fined for manufacturing and distributing prophylactics. In the early 1900s people were so sensitive about purchasing *deodorants* in drugstores that they felt obliged to ask the pharmacist for them in hushed tones, blushing with embarrassment (Panati, 1987). Times change.

Therapists find themselves in a situation no different from that of the television producer, the writer, the sports hero, or the corporation executive. They make decisions and take risks. Giftshop managers had to decide whether it was right to sell Freddy Kruger dolls, complete with plastic replicas of lethal steel fingernails. Bookstore managers had to decide whether to display copies of Salman Rushdie's novels in the wake of death threats and bombings. Producers and directors continually decide how much violence, nudity, obscenity, or sexuality is acceptable in a given movie or TV script, and they sometimes produce different versions for home and foreign markets. In all these areas, absolute rules cannot be formulated. Often the courageous act of a single producer or advertising executive shifts a previously accepted limit. For example, Otto Preminger, in releasing the film *The Man with the Golden Arm* (1955), ignored the Hollywood code against explicitly portraying the deleterious effects of heroin use. At the time, he was criticized severely for having taken that step; later he was applauded for breaking important ground.

In an interview, Bill Cosby was once asked to talk about the secret of success. He said that he had no formula for being successful, but that he did have one for being unsuccessful: Do nothing that might offend someone. The biographies and autobiographies of virtually all the people we admire, from Freud to Galileo—individuals whom parents seem eager for their children to emulate—are filled with instances of chances being taken and rules being violated. Our best-known inventors, artists, explorers, producers, actors, architects, statesmen, and scientists have stubbornly refused to accept and be confined by the conventional wisdom of the day or the advice of their critics. It is only with hindsight that their efforts are fully appreciated—in some cases, only posthumously. Paradoxically, parents want their children to do great things but simultaneously to play it safe and avoid trouble. Therapists, to be effective, must avoid having their therapy become the dispensing of a series of culturally-accepted bromides that are neither valid nor truly useful. There is a necessary uncertainty in living—in all domains of experience—and it is difficult for many clients and their therapists to appreciate that fact. They want rules, assurances, and formulas. We all like the idea that "being good" and sticking to the rules leads to a predictable, fulfilling, and risk-free life.

The entire therapeutic venture is fundamentally an exercise in ethics because it involves the inventing, shaping, and reformulating of codes for living together. Ethical concerns therefore go beyond obvious professional considerations, such as whether or not therapists should have sexual intercourse with present or former clients. (Ironically, some therapists who scrupulously avoid any hint of professional impropriety appear to have few qualms about wasting years of their client's time and money by stringing them along and encouraging false hopes.) Objectivist terms—"treatment," "healthy adjustment," and "cure"—disguise the intrinsically moral nature of the therapy enterprise. As Szasz (1973) has long argued, therapy at its best is a contractual arrangement between consenting parties, each of whom takes personal responsibility for participating. Success is judged by whether or not the participants feel their contracts with one another have been fulfilled.

SUMMARY

Only occasionally do we find it useful to concretize contractual terms by committing them to paper. A therapy contract is a living, changing document—not something that is negotiated once and then tucked out of sight. It would not be an exaggeration to say that the entire process of therapy is fundamentally an ongoing contractual negotiation. Even more generally, the life of the client can be usefully construed as being a process of keeping, breaking, revising, and repairing contracts with self and others. Marriage is, of course, a contract, and so are the other milestones of civilized living—parenthood, career, family ties. We have already suggested that psychological depression seems connected to an individual's failure to live up to his or her experienced contractual obligations. People with alcohol problems often seem to be buying time before they have to face up to contractual obligations that they have placed on "hold." Thus, issues surrounding the handling of agreements are central to a wide variety of mental health concerns, and therefore, central to psychotherapeutic dialogue. To be healthy, wealthy, and wise, clients (and therapists) need to keep their contracts in order.

In this chapter we dealt with some practical aspects of contracts and agreements. In the next chapter, we need to talk a bit more theoretically about the nature of relationships between people—particularly the concept of structural coupling and the nature of the "orthogonal interactions" that help generate new possibilities in people's lives.

CHAPTER 9

Coupling, Orthogonality, and Problem-Solving

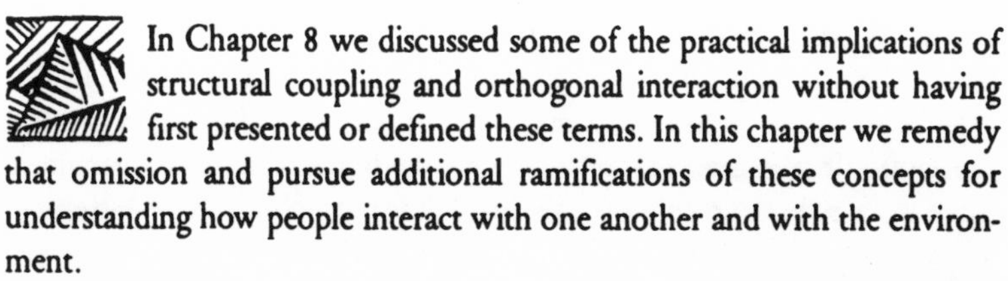

In Chapter 8 we discussed some of the practical implications of structural coupling and orthogonal interaction without having first presented or defined these terms. In this chapter we remedy that omission and pursue additional ramifications of these concepts for understanding how people interact with one another and with the environment.

People and their surroundings are constantly changing. Yet, throughout all these changes, certain aspects of a person's organization must remain stable; otherwise he or she would not be able to have an identity. Bill changes careers, gets divorced, loses 20 pounds, and moves to California—something which, by the way, he vowed he would *never* do—yet he remains Bill. Over time, he will be involved in a series of integrations and disintegrations—as a student, a client, a husband, a baseball enthusiast, a job candidate, or a colleague. However, at all times he stays sufficiently coupled with his environment to stay alive and remain a person.

People, as autopoietic entities, do not operate in a vacuum. They occupy an everchanging niche in a medium. That medium consists of more than just atmosphere and inanimate objects. It includes other living organisms—most significantly, other people. In an earlier chapter we used the analogy of multiple playlets being enacted side-by-side in the same performance space. For this to work out, each performer must find ways to arrange a peaceful—or not so peaceful—coexistence with fellow actors. To put it more formally, we become structurally coupled to our surroundings and each other.

Person-to-person couplings are similar to any other couplings in nature, although they are more crucial to human beings and are usually at the heart of the difficulties that clients bring to therapy. All couplings adhere to the same fundamental principle: Whenever entities coexist in proximity for any length of time and for any reason, they undergo progressive modifications of their structure so that the fit between them *improves*. As you continue to wear a shoe, it begins more and more to resemble your foot and vice versa. In fact, bring any two objects together—sandpaper and wood, for example—and they grow more and more alike. (Some swear this is even true of people and their pets.) Put a teenager into a room and, in short order, that room begins to resemble any other room he or she has ever been in. The longer the stay, the more striking the resemblance. Visitors to the Grand Canyon can witness this principle of ever-increasing fit on a much larger scale. The river and rock have been mutually adapting to each other over many millennia.

A similar process occurs in a family after a baby is born. The infant is shaped by the practices of that family, yet at the same time the new member of the family intrudes on established routines, insisting noisily that they be modified to accommodate to his or her needs. In certain respects, the family that existed before the baby was born exists no longer. In its place is a newly constituted family with changed priorities and patterns of allegiance.

We often focus on one side of an accommodatory equation rather than the other. For example, we readily observe the ways in which a piece of driftwood is changed by the ocean. However, because of the enormous differences in scale, we neglect to notice the changes the wood brings about in the ocean. Similarly, when you "break in" a pair of shoes, you are initially aware of how the shoe changes. When a painful corn or bunion develops, you become more aware that it has been a two-way process.

Living is a series of structural couplings with accompanying "rubs." Your quiet picnic in the woods perturbs nearby insects, and they, in turn, perturb you. No matter where you go, you cannot get away from the impact of others. Even alone on an island, you still talk to yourself in the language of your culture and evaluate your circumstances using culturally derived concepts. Thus, the life of any human being is thoroughly social, even when it includes lengthy periods of physical isolation or involves so-called antisocial or asocial behavior. A hermit's silent protest against civilization and a mass murderer's noisier one are both socially shaped.

Most of us harbor the illusion that, if we wanted to, we could pack up our possessions and head off into the hills, leaving some of our troubles behind. Moreover, as we said earlier, we think about our lives in terms of individual accomplishments and failures, private thoughts, and unique personality characteristics. But our moods, talents, goals, and evaluations are inextricably and intricately linked to the collectivities of which we are a part (Sampson, 1989). If you should decide to go off into the hills (equipped only with your Swiss Army knife) you would therefore be well-advised to adopt the Robinson Crusoe strategy of keeping up the practices of the culture and locating some Man (or Woman) Friday to help you. Otherwise, you may be surprised to find that the personality you wanted to get back in touch with on the trip is slipping ever further away from you. People know themselves in terms of the "clubs" in which they are active participants.

DISRUPTIONS AND NOTICINGS

As couplings become smooth, fewer adjustments need to be made, and the effects of the pairing become less apparent. When a couple first gets married—provided they haven't previously lived with one another—a lot of *noticing* happens. It's all the little things. She never makes the bed in the morning. He likes his toast burnt. She sleeps with two pillows. He doesn't use a bathrobe. She puts ketchup on her eggs. He doesn't eat eggs. She wants the toilet seat down. He wants it up. And so on. There are apt to be lots of fights and unpleasant discoveries "after the honeymoon is over." Individuals who thought they were "so much alike" find that they have overestimated the degree of "fit" and have begun to trip over their many differences. That's what makes the first year or two of marriage precarious (Arond & Pauker, 1987). However, if the spouses stay together, their routines begin to grow together. This can later lead to another kind of loss, expressed in complaints such as "He takes me for granted," "We never do anything anymore," or "We've become two old stick-in-the-muds."

It isn't exactly a question of whether people are happy or unhappy together. It is more that they have undergone a process of figuratively and literally *becoming* one another. If and when they should separate, a hole will have been created in each of their lives proportionate to their degree of mutual involvement. For this reason, many individuals who had claimed to be driving each other crazy nevertheless date each other all over again after a separation or a divorce. In part, the void they are each attempting to fill fits almost exactly the shape of the person they left. Such individuals are often taken aback to discover how much comfort they find in each other's presence and how alienated they feel when with others. We know more than one couple who have, under such circumstances, divorced, remarried, and then divorced again, giving a literal meaning to the expression, "Can't live with 'em and can't live without 'em." When death separates a couple, the emptiness experienced derives from the fact that a well-honed coupling has been wrenched apart.

The grief phenomenon occurs, although with less intensity, in many other life settings. Even students who genuinely hated school may feel somewhat "hollow" following graduation. At the end of the celebrating, they are not sure what to do with themselves. At that time, reunions and "staying in touch" seem like good ideas, although by a year later, when a class reunion is actually held, there may be less enthusiasm for it than there was initially.

A client-therapist coupling is, in most respects, like any other. The individuals grow together and form a bond. Even if they don't particularly like each other, they get used to being together. They adapt to each other's presence and style. If they remain together long enough, they will have trouble separating, just as a married couple would, and for exactly the same reasons. Therapists talk about clients' struggling with "termination" issues. For the most part, therapists themselves create these issues by expecting a long-term affiliation to end with a short-term finale. It is a basic design problem. All of us—not just clients—are built to react strongly when couplings on which we have relied are disrupted. Goodbyes are always painful.

Our own practice is to steer clear of the concept of termination entirely. As we indicated in the previous chapter, we change the details of our association all along the way as client needs change. Paradoxically, this is an instance in which we follow the medical model more closely than some of our colleagues do. A physician doesn't *terminate* his or her patient. However, the frequency and nature of visits are adjusted in accordance with the patient's health status. At any time, the patient can call for an appointment, consult on a problem, or come in for a checkup. We have cases in various stages of activity, but none of them are, in our minds, "closed." In that sense, the term "former client" is a misnomer. A son or daughter grows up and becomes increasingly independent, but never becomes a "former child." Similarly, our graduate students go their own way and move on in their careers, but they remain our students, and many stay in touch. Even students and clients we haven't seen or heard from in a long while are in our thoughts, from time to time, and we assume that we are in theirs. The concept of "termination" has a flavor of finality we want to avoid. It is an unwelcome byproduct of another practice we consider inadvisable—namely, setting up the expectation that therapy consists of meeting week after week for long periods of time.

FAMILIARITY BREEDS COMPLACENCY

In fact, generally speaking, the longer a client and therapist meet together, and the more they follow a set routine, the less good they can do for one another. The value of the client-therapist pairing lies in the differences in the lenses through which client and therapist see the world. The longer they spend with one another, the more their points of view condense into a single perspective. After you have studied long enough with one teacher, it may be time to move on to another (while nevertheless acknowledging the contributions of the first). A widely held view in graduate education is that students who have done their undergraduate work at one institution should move on to graduate studies at another. This gives the student a second set of perspectives and also forces faculty members continually to field questions from students with different backgrounds. A similar principle is applicable to therapy pairings. What is initially fresh and useful about a particular coupling becomes stale and limiting after a period of time.

Researchers, too, have found that most therapy progress occurs within the early stages—the first six to eight sessions—with less dramatic movement later (Dell, 1982a; Green & Herget, 1989). It has long been understood that nothing in life is knowable unless there is an interruption in ordinary activity, a rearrangement of what William James (1890) called the kaleidoscopic flux. In other words, "when the shoe fits, the foot is forgotten" (Merton, 1965, p. 112). Therapy, like any other educational endeavor, has to continually break up patterns of thinking and acting to be effective. Only an "outsider"—a foreigner—can successfully do that. Clients and therapists start out strangers but gradually become "neighbors" who unwittingly share the same blind spots and ensnare themselves in a common conceptual thicket. This doesn't represent a personal deficiency on the part of the therapist or a devious or manipulative move on the part of the client. It is an inevitable aspect of the coupling process. It is also a strong argument for not settling into routines.

Many devices can help prevent stagnation. Even bringing in others from time to time—supervisors, consultants, family members—can reinvigorate the proceedings. Directors, rehearsing a play, sometimes notice that the cast is progressively "going to sleep" as the actors become familiar with each other's rhythms and as rehearsals drag on. However, when the director invites a few friends in to watch, the energy of the cast and the level of inventiveness in the hall pick up again. A balance needs to be struck between the disorienting effects of too much novelty and the numbing effects of complacency. Therapy, to remain effective, must continually be *reinvented* as it goes along. Set formulas—even good ones—don't work for long.

A particularly lethal, but common, formula is to begin sessions with stock phrases such as "How have things been going?" or "How has the week been?" These questions, more appropriate to social settings than to therapy, usually steer the proceedings into barren conversational channels. They are an invitation to the client to complain, to recount circumstances, and to slip into the familiar but unproductive role of victim. They rarely help the client or therapist focus on a therapeutic question.

ARE METHODS NECESSARY?

It's easy to give specific formulas and prescribe particular techniques for this situation or that. Treatment manuals that present lists of methods apparently sell well and how-to sessions draw large crowds at psychotherapy conventions. Many practitioners keep searching for those magical, sure-fire recipes. However, like a meal of empty calories, the techniques found only constitute a short-term fix, and one has to keep going back for more. Catering to this endless craving, authors have compiled anthologies of ready-made metaphors, analogies, stories, and anecdotes (see, e.g., Mills & Crowley, 1986). A number of therapy books advise therapists about where they should sit, how they should answer the door, and what personality styles they ought to adopt. Some advise "using humor"—as if humor were a commodity that could be purchased at a local supply house.

We have eschewed prescribing standard methods because we think taking that route provides a solution to the wrong problem. From our perspective, every therapist already has access to all the methods he or she will ever need. Additional or fancier techniques are unnecessary. In fact, in some ways, therapists would do better if they could drop some of their preconceived notions about particular techniques and formats, along with the sense that therapy need be "serious" business (Rotter, 1972).

Most methods evolved out of particular client-therapist couplings. In the setting in which they were invented, they were relevant and effective. However, the belief that they can be abstracted and patented for generic use is an instance of falling prey to the myth of instructive interaction we discussed earlier. It is the same fallacy that has plagued so-called "methods" courses in teacher-education programs. The magic of education is in the coupling, not the method. Varela (1989) notes that we have to learn to live on the shaky ground of our own developing interaction, "abandoning the hope to arrive at . . . an explicit, fixed approach to therapeutic practice" (p. 23).

Slavish adherence to methods devised by others creates an illusion of competence that retards the development of an individual style of functioning. We hope that through our discussion of principles and through the examples we give, we are able to convey a flavor of what therapy can be. However, these are not "authorized" pathways that guarantee particular therapeutic outcomes.

Effective therapists are experimentalists—they don't need to be armed with stock formulas and anecdotes. They invent new strategies as they go along, on the spur of the moment. If one gambit doesn't get the point across, they devise another. They keep going until they get it right—for that particular person, at that particular juncture in the relationship. Therapy happens in the moment. Precommitments make it hard to keep attention on the question at hand. They give the meeting a canned feeling—just the opposite of what's needed.

We are reminded of some of the graduate students in our training program. They are bright, enthusiastic, and sensitive. Many of them entered the field because they were the sort of people friends sought out for counsel. However, as soon as they try to "do therapy," everything falls apart. The effectiveness they had before they became therapists-in-training evaporates. It takes many of them years to recover, and some probably never do. Before they began training, they were willing to take chances and make mistakes. They had a good intuitive grasp of what was needed, and they listened well. Now, in trying so hard to be professional and to impress, they take everything too seriously; they are frightened and tight, grabbing onto one technique after another. When they get into sessions, their thinking and hearing go on the fritz.

In some instances, the mask of professionalism becomes so complete that the client is deprived of the opportunity to come in contact with the genuinely caring person behind the mask. In our center, there have been occasions when the clients, who have often been around the mental health system for a while, have ended up having to take care of and nurture their student-therapists, rather than the other way around. One client, who couldn't help noticing the pressure her therapist seemed to be under, felt moved to lend her a book on how to manage anxiety.

THE CONSERVATISM OF SYSTEMS

As we said in an earlier chapter, human beings are conservative systems. Even organisms that *appear* to be seeking "something new" are actually attempting to restore what has been, but in a new form. The old form has stopped working. For instance, as the quality of life for peasants in a country decreases, there may be talk of revolt. Although the rhetoric of revolutions emphasizes the "new," revolutions are primarily driven by an erosion of the old. Revolutions—political, scientific, and personal—have conservative aims (Kuhn, 1970; Marris, 1974). In science, theories that were working well begin to creak as more and more anomalies come to light. The proposal of a new theory is an attempt to restore the smoothness that had begun to be lost in connection with the old one.

On the interpersonal front, clients who claim they "want to change" are only attempting to decrease the costliness of their current adjustment. When a client talks about wanting to be new and different, we know that something in that person's life is pushing a bearable situation over the edge into intolerability. (We always inquire into what that factor is, since, at least for that moment, that is what the session will be about.) As an analyst we know once put it, people seek therapy when the pain of changing seems less than the pain of continuing, just as people typically visit their physicians only when they are suffering enough to make the expense and inconvenience of arranging an appointment worthwhile.

Although clients are never eager to be different, despite their rhetoric, they are destined to be shaped or molded in some way by their interaction with the therapist. Even if a client leaves within the first five minutes of the initial session, never to return, it is too late for the client to avoid being affected in some way by the association. Walking out, complaining to others about what happened, trying to put it out of his or her mind—these are all system adaptations to the coupling. Moreover, if the person leaves, his or her next therapist (or previous therapists) will be judged in relation to the context this interaction created. Just as the communication theorists argue that a person cannot *not* communicate (Watzlawick, Beavin, & Jackson, 1967), it can be argued that a coupling is an inevitable and irreversible alteration of the drift.

ORTHOGONAL INTERACTION

Think of every coupling as a kind of "club" in which the person holds membership. However, club rules, activities, and membership requirements differ. Being involved in one form of interaction elicits different responses than being in another. For example, a person who is shy and retiring at a social gathering may turn into a tiger on the ballfield. Since people are members of more than one club at a time, they run into logistical problems keeping their different "selves" sorted out. Teenagers, for example, have to move the telephone into the next room when they talk to their confidants. The persona they use with their parents is different from the one that "plays well" with their friends. Goffman (1959) has eloquently described the kinds of devices people employ to keep their various social worlds separate. For example, salespeople are polite and deferential with customers "out front." Then they go "backstage" into the stockroom, where, with other employees, they mimic, curse, and ridicule the customers. Similarly, conversation at a nurses' station or in a hospital staff room often has an entirely different tone from that of staff-patient bedside repartee.

In all these instances, we stumble across the phenomenon of ***orthogonal interaction***. A person interacts with someone ***outside*** a particular club in a way that is different (i.e., orthogonal) from what the club rules specify. Changed in some respects by this interaction, the person returns to the club and participates somewhat differently in it. This, in turn, leads to new developments in the organization and the operation of the club. For example, a person makes a trip abroad and is impressed with French cooking. After returning, he or she tries out some new recipes, and thereby gradually changes the eating habits of the entire family. In other words, club rules are modified not just by strictly internal happenings but also by the fact that members engage in a variety of orthogonal interactions outside the club boundaries.

The multiple changes that orthogonal interaction instigates can be automatic and irresistible in operation. For example, George Burns was having lunch with Jack Benny and decided to play a practical joke on him. Throughout the meal, Burns kept reminding Benny that later, when they would both be at Jeanette MacDonald's house for dinner, it would be very ***rude*** of him to laugh if she should offer to sing for her guests, as she usually did. Burns stressed repeatedly that Benny was, at all costs, to behave himself at dinner and to avoid cracking up. That evening, when MacDonald did offer to sing, Benny found himself uncontrollably convulsed with laughter. MacDonald's invitation immediately conjured up an image of Burns' earlier admonition, and he couldn't prevent himself from laughing. The first orthogonal interaction modified Benny's "structure" so that his behavior in another domain was irrevocably affected (Randall & Mindlin, 1989).

A college student is sent off to get educated—not to change the family. However, he or she returns home with "crazy new ideas" that bother other family members and affect family structure. Being educated means becoming someone different—not just adding "information" to a preexisting structure. It also means that the old ways of "fitting" can no longer be expected to work smoothly and new forms of adjustment must be found.

Governments have sometimes learned this lesson the hard way. They send their intelligentsia abroad on expensive grants to learn about medicine, or physics, or some other modern technology. However, when these individuals return, they may stir up discontent among their compatriots. Ironically, a regime may eventually be toppled by the actions of the very individuals it supported most handsomely.

Because of the phenomenon of orthogonal interaction, new pairings are always potentially disruptive to the status quo. It is no wonder, therefore, that relatives and friends often view a person's seeking therapy with mixed emotions. On the one hand, they want the person to "get help." They hope that he or she will emerge from treatment a more fulfilled individual (and one who is easier to live with). They may also be tired of bearing the burden of caring for the person alone.

On the other hand, they are at least vaguely aware that clients and therapists will have private meetings that constitute a kind of conspiracy. Cozy, long-standing arrangements are apt to be "evaluated" and disrupted by an outsider. In the process, the client inevitably becomes a sort of double agent, required to betray confidences and report on intimate details of his or her relationships. Both clubs have a strong lien on the person's loyalty. The client and therapist collude to design and initiate actions that will affect the lives of others, whether they like it or not. You can't go home again, and you cannot return from a client-therapist coupling unaffected.

THE ORIGIN OF PROBLEMS

Clients have problems because they operate, as does everyone else, in multiple domains—different clubs. The rules of one coupling run counter to the rules of another. The clients live, therefore, in "emotional contradiction" (Mendez, Coddou, & Maturana, 1988). There is a problem in packaging; what they want comes along with something they don't want. People don't know how to keep the one while getting rid of the other. They want the security of marriage, but hate to be tied down; they want children, but don't like changing diapers; they want a degree, but don't like schoolwork. There is something they want to conserve and something that seems attached to it that they wish they could "disintegrate." Psychologist Israel Goldiamond often gives the example of an old car that burns oil, guzzles gas, breaks down frequently, and rattles like crazy. On the other hand, it gets you where you are going without your having to sink money you don't have into a new one. Symptoms, he says, are like that. They get you something you want—but at very high cost.

People want to continue getting that which they desire, but they hope they can somehow reduce the overhead. They also hope that this can be done with as little personal change as possible, because, as Maturana notes, change is always dangerous. It "entails a jump into an unknown . . . cognitive domain" (Simon, 1985, p. 43).

To accomplish this change, therapists have to help the client view the situation anew, invoking a broader frame of reference than the one the client was using. Unfortunately, those who *language* problems similarly come to have the same problems and can only envision the same solutions (Goolishian & Anderson, 1987). Therefore, to be helpful, a therapist must have the ability to transcend the language framework in which the client is trapped. He or she must be able to induce the client to step outside the original, constraining frame. "The solution, like all solutions to apparent contradictions, lies in moving away from the opposition and changing the nature of the question, to embrace a broader context" (Maturana & Varela, 1987, p. 135).

Sometimes a therapist is unable to see beyond the client's frame. Then it is time to refer the client elsewhere, to employ the services of a supervisor or consultant, or to set in motion other perspective-widening processes, such as rereading a Tolstoy novel or going to see an escapist science fiction movie.

One of the authors, when he was a beginning graduate student, was asked to counsel an undergraduate student who was flunking out of school. The student talked about how academics were meaningless to him, how he would rather be out in the "real world" building houses, fixing sinks, or running machinery. This was at a time when the author and fellow graduate students were also having trouble seeing the relevance of some of their academic assignments. It all seemed rather far removed from the desire to "help people" that originally motivated applying for graduate training. As the sessions went on, the author found himself agreeing silently, more and more, with the complaints the student was voicing. The degree of overlap between their perspectives was high, and increasing daily. The author got more and more depressed and could entertain fewer and fewer "helpful" options. Finally, a supervisor, listening to tapes of the case, had to step in and come to the rescue of *two* individuals—the client and the therapist—who could perceive nothing but bleakness ahead.

The need to explore the client's terrain from a novel perspective creates a paradox: If a therapist is too much an outsider, he or she will not be able to appreciate the dilemma the client is struggling with. (Tourists may enjoy watching a native ritual, but they are in no position to appreciate the nuances of meaning contained in each dance step and gesture.) On the other hand, if the therapist is too much an insider, the client's and therapist's shared biases will militate against achieving the necessary overview.

This paradox—the need to be both inside and outside—has led master therapist Carl Whitaker to suggest that therapists take up a position near the border of the client's community (Neill & Kniskern, 1982). In fact, Whitaker thinks social outliers or mavericks make the best therapists. In his opinion, they should be individuals who are neither situated so far outside the fold that they can be written off as alien or bizarre nor situated so close at hand that they merely replicate the culture in which the client is already enmeshed.

THERAPIST AS JESTER

Szasz (1973), in dealing with the same paradox, chooses a more picturesque metaphor—the court jester. He argues that the court jester, like the therapist, has the delicate role of confronting his client—in this case the king—with painful truths that might otherwise be ignored or misconstrued. He does so in the friendliest possible way. To this end, members of the court allow the jester to take certain liberties with court rules—in effect, to occupy a unique role as insider and outsider, simultaneously. The role is not without its hazards. At any moment, the jester may give offense. For this reason, a career as a court jester—or as a psychotherapist—is not for the faint of heart.

As we have suggested, every culture contains friction-producing discontinuities (Dollard & Miller, 1950)—jagged edges between one subset of expectations and another. Friends want you to try cocaine, and television ads are urging you to "just say no" and become an active participant in the war on drugs. Your boss expects you to be loyal to the firm's interests, and your shop steward is expecting you to spearhead an unfair labor practices complaint. Your spouse wants you to attend your child's class play, and you want to go on a skiing trip with your friends.

Therapists help clients engineer creative solutions to these "interface" disturbances (Rabkin, 1970). However, they simultaneously sow the seeds of societal change (Orlinsky, 1989). In the past, jesters, in attempting to preserve the court's integrity, inevitably stretched its boundaries. Similarly, today, therapists who help clients negotiate exceptions to social rules thereby call into question the rules themselves. When one exception is allowed, additional exceptions become more likely.

By absorbing some of the shock of interface clashes, therapists help sustain the cultural illusion that all's right with the world. At the same time, they serve as undercover agents who help "dissidents" work out more harmonious adaptations. Paradoxically, therefore, the therapist is not only a representative of the establishment (i.e., he or she helps contain deviance) but also a contributor to the ongoing evolution of community standards.

A problem always stands out in a person's languaging as something odd or peculiar–it is a conversational glitch of one sort or another. Something doesn't fit with something else. You don't go to a physician unless something out of the ordinary is happening: You feel a lump that was not there before or seem more out of breath than usual. In the psychological realm, you may perceive yourself as flying off the handle under circumstances that didn't previously bother you. Perhaps you've suddenly lost interest in your job, or in life itself, without understanding why. Falling asleep has become difficult, or sexual performance has become unexpectedly unreliable. Your employer has asked you to fly to other cities for conferences and you are neither willing to turn down the assignment nor able to admit to a profound fear of flying. You keep eating and gaining weight, although you desperately want to be thin. In all these cases, something seems out of place.

In each instance, the clash can be traced to an insufficiency in frame of reference. For instance, a client recently complained that she was desperately unhappy because she was being forced to pursue a goal dictated by others: She was applying to medical school, even though she really wanted to be an elementary school teacher. She said she was doing it simply to please her aging parents. From the frame of reference she was using, the goal of being a doctor belonged to her parents, not to her. However, from an expanded frame of reference, it became apparent that the goal she was actually pursuing–which *did* belong to her–was to enable a dream of her parents to come true. Medical school was an unpleasant and costly side effect of making that dream happen. When viewed that way, she at least regained a sense of ownership over her career behavior–it fit with who she wanted to be. In addition, it placed her in a better position to reevaluate benefits and costs. Would her parents really be happy if they understood that their daughter had no real enthusiasm for medicine and was potentially sacrificing a large piece of her life just to keep a family illusion in place?

FRAMES THAT LIMIT

M. C. Escher's whimsical drawings are able to create impossible and entertaining images because the artist takes liberties with the conventions of representing three-dimensional space on a two-dimensional surface. He purposely creates "problems" for the perceiver, in his case in order to surprise and fascinate. However, like all problems, intentional or otherwise, he creates these by leaving something out of the picture—usually something that isn't noticed as missing. A problem is always an *incomplete* or inadequate drawing of an event. And, just as Escher uses two-dimensional space to portray three dimensions, the person with a problem uses static, two-dimensional terms to represent a reality that is anything but static. (The daughter mentioned above temporarily "forgot" that it was *her* goal to keep the family dream intact.) A problem persists until the limitations of the frame are recognized. Just as the viewer fails to take into account the missing third dimension in Escher's portrayals, the person with a problem doesn't see what is missing, because the frame he or she is using is accepted as a given. The missing elements can be identified and included only when the constraining characteristics of the current frame are appreciated from an enlarged perspective.

A number of years ago, if we can believe the newspaper reports, some soldiers were secretly given doses of LSD as part of research experiments conducted by the CIA ("No one told them," 1975; Shuy, 1986). Since they did not know that they were being used as guinea pigs, they had no ready explanations for the bodily and perceptual effects they began to experience. They were operating within a limited frame. Had they been told that they were participants in an experiment using LSD, they would presumably have had less difficulty dealing with their reactions to the drug. The frame in which they were operating, and in which they tried to understand themselves, did not include the concept "you have been drugged." A set of problems was generated—in this case artificially—by requiring them to language phenomena in a framework woefully insufficient for the task. We are arguing that *all* problems arise in exactly that way, except that they usually do not involve an explicit, planned conspiracy. (Most paranoid individuals only *presume* the FBI or CIA is conspiring against them.) A person cannot resolve a mystery until or unless the language framework in which resolution is being attempted has been acknowledged.

Consider several individuals, all of whom are having difficulty falling asleep. One is about to undergo surgery the following morning. A second has just lost a spouse. The third is unclear about why she is having trouble sleeping. Only the third has a "problem" that is apt to require the intervention of a therapist or counselor. For the first two individuals, there is no mystery. Their situation, while inconvenient, fits easily into the explanatory frame being used. The third person is both unable to sleep and unable to explain her difficulty in sleeping. If she were to suddenly recall that she had just switched to a new brand of coffee—one with a higher concentration of caffeine—then she too would cease to be a likely candidate for psychotherapy. In the new and expanded framework, which now includes attention to changes in stimulants, the inability to sleep, although still annoying, ceases to be "problematic."

In short, problems involve somebody *making something* of something. Take something out of context, and it becomes meaningless. Put it in a new context, and it becomes something else. Problems might be thought of as "rubs" experienced by people attempting to reconcile different aspects of their lives within prescribed frameworks of meaning. In addition, they keep bumping up against the limitations of the frames they have adopted. As Wittgenstein (1922/1971) warned, the limits of our language become the limits of our world.

Imagine, for example, a child crayoning a picture. The child suddenly discovers that the green crayon is missing, and therefore the grass in the picture cannot be colored in. The child's "game" has been disrupted. A major upset ensues. With the teacher's help, however, the child comes to appreciate that (a) not all grass is green; (b) not all good pictures are fully colored; (c) pictures can be fantastic as well as realistic; (d) additional crayons can be bought or borrowed; (e) blue and yellow make green; and (f) in life, you don't always get what you want. All those learnings involve a breaking of the original frame within which the child's upset occurred. The obstacle of the missing crayon blocked the next move in the child's game; the teacher's interventions helped break the grip of the frame within which that limited game was being played. Without the first, there would be no real need for the second. Without the second, there could not be a satisfactory resolution of the first.

TWO-WAY INFLUENCE

In interpersonal couplings, such as the one between client and therapist, it is never possible to separate out influences or to fully predict what will happen next. Furthermore, the process is inevitably bi-directional. Teachers are changed by their students, and therapists are changed by their clients.

The senior author recalls working, early in his career, with a young sociopathic client. This man would tell one set of lies while still in the process of wiggling out of the previous set. His promises of reform were as frequent as they were insincere. He had an uncanny ability to keep going and to get people (including his therapist) to give him "just one more chance." In the process, he endured setbacks the rest of us might have found monumentally discouraging. Yet, nothing seemed to faze him. He always got caught, and always went back for more. When he had exhausted the good will of one group of acquaintances, he simply cultivated a new group of potential "resources." After each interlude with a girlfriend—sometimes ending in violence, arrest, pregnancy, and a flurry of restraining orders—he found someone else to romance and fleece. He traveled around the country, taking odd jobs, getting fired, getting hired, making nefarious deals, and moving on.

It is doubtful that anything therapeutic happened in the course of our sessions together. However, being with this individual turned out to be an eye-opener for the author. It drove home how utterly dependent we are on everyone's agreeing to play by a certain set of rules and how easily and completely those rules can be abrogated. Prison meant nothing to this fellow—he enjoyed it and used his stays there to make new contacts. Even getting beaten up was not really a deterrent for him. For example, he found the sadistic initiation rites of a motorcycle club to his liking. The initiation didn't bind him to the club, as it was intended to do—he left soon thereafter. However, he would have jumped at the chance to participate in another initiation just for the thrill of doing something daring. At one of our sessions, the author realized the futility of talking—the words being used by client and therapist may have sounded the same, but their meanings to each of the participants couldn't have been more different. Nothing said could be taken at face value; no one—not even the police—had the power to make any agreements with this individual "stick." By viewing life through the eyes of this individual, the therapist could see just how fragile and malleable our arrangements with one another are—an abject and invaluable lesson in living that has stuck with him ever since.

SUMMARY

Life consists of couplings, some of which, when judged from the perspective of an alternative domain, represent orthogonal interactions. When therapy is effective, it constitutes an orthogonal interaction that then affects the person's operation elsewhere. The therapist is like a court jester—inside the "club" enough to know what is needed and outside enough to bring a fresh perspective to the proceedings.

Clients' problems stem from the fact that desirable consequences come packaged with undesirable elements. Cultural discontinuities stretch the person between competing modes of operation, leading to his or her having to live in "emotional contradiction." As with all issues, the resolution involves moving to a larger, more encompassing frame. It is the therapist's job to help make that frame available. However, when client and therapist spend too much time together or start off being too similar to one another, therapy is apt to be less effective. Their points of view are insufficiently distinct to generate the needed perspective.

In the next chapter we tackle emotion—although we define the term differently from how others define it. We will, in that context, be able to explain Maturana's principle about the arationality of human functioning. Life, and therapy, are about people's wants and desires, which have more to do with their structural "bodyhood" than their systems of logic.

CHAPTER 10

Emotions, Preferences, and Attachments

Human functioning has traditionally been divided into separate subsystems – cognition (thinking), affect (feeling), and behavior (acting). This set of distinctions, derived from classical thinking, has proved to be an obstacle to theorizing in psychology. It "confuses everything and clarifies nothing" (Kelly, 1969, p. 91). Cognition (including all the categories of self-observation) is not a separate mental process; it is a specialized form of action. Actions involve the entire body. Affects – which we will later define as bodily dispositions – underlie all action states.

When "faculty psychology" was popular, the operation of the person was divided into many separate categories, such as memory, perception, intelligence, volition, and language (Bunge & Ardila, 1987). However, the more that psychologists divided functioning into parts – some of them quite metaphorical – the more complex became the task of determining how those parts might be reassembled into an integrated whole. This approach became increasingly cumbersome and has now largely been abandoned. However, the vestiges that remain, including the tripartite model of cognition, affect, and behavior, still impede our efforts to understand how people function.

The current literature on thoughts, feelings, and actions is dominated by two broad concerns – the issue of primacy and the issue of interdependence. Included in those categories are questions such as the following: Does affect precede or follow thought? Do behaviors generate feelings and thoughts or vice versa? What proportion of an affect is really a cognitive evaluation? Can one have affectless thought? (Izard, Kagan, & Zajonc, 1984; Kleinginna & Kleinginna, 1985; Lazarus, 1984; Zajonc, 1984). In our view, all these questions derive from premises that are disadvantageous and outmoded.

American psychology has cyclically emphasized each of the three categories of functioning. From 1900 until about 1960, behaviorism dominated the scene, and observable behavior was considered by many to be the only legitimate target of scientific investigation. In the '60s, the field underwent the so-called "cognitive revolution," which brought thoughts back into the picture. Today, there are signs that emotion is staging a comeback (Greenberg & Safran, 1989).

Once the tripartite division has been reified, the debates we mentioned above are as unresolvable as they are inevitable. They are the contemporary residuals of the age-old problem of mind-body dualism. When you reify the distinction between the mental and the physical, locating some phenomena in the head and others in the body, you conjure up conceptual problems that then cannot be readily solved or disposed of (Ryle, 1949). For example, if one process is corporeal—of the body—and another incorporeal—of the mind—through what common vehicle can the two be expected to communicate or influence one another?[1] However, the recognition that language is communal action and that cognitive domains are no less and no more "mental" than any others frees one from the conceptual straitjacket imposed by dualistic theorizing.

In any discussion of an alternative approach to the "emotions," two interrelated factors must be taken into account: first, that people, as living systems, have bodies that are situated in time and space; second, that all conceptual schemes—even those that seem most rational—are based on starting premises that are actually arational. Our conceptual premises are related to how our bodies are constructed and how they function. Our bodies determine both what we *want* to do and how we go about doing it. We each have a "bodyhood" that is implicated in every action, including all those activities we typically label cerebral, theoretical, or abstract. In other words, the ultimate reference point for everything we think and do is our own activity. We are animals first and civilized humans second.[2] Our systems of logic and rhetoric are founded, first and foremost, on how we operate as physical beings.

---

[1]We are reminded of Tevye's comment in *Fiddler on the Roof*, "A bird may love a fish, but where would they build a home together?" (Stein, Bock, & Harnick, 1964, p. 100).

[2]In other words, "First comes the grub, then come the morals" (Weill & Brecht, 1928).

DISTINCTIONS ARE PREFERENCES

As we indicated in a previous chapter, the basic operation of human beings is the drawing of distinctions. However, distinguishing is an activity, and as such it creates values (Brown, 1972; Durkin, 1981). Therefore, acts of valuing—preferences—determine even the basic logical units or categories with which we think and reason. For example, a wine connoisseur makes many fine distinctions that give one vintage greater or lesser value than another. To the uninitiated, such distinctions are meaningless—they either don't exist or don't make any sense. The casual wine drinker may view anything beyond "red," "white," and "rosé" as much ado about nothing. Again, distinctions, as well as the values they create, are linked directly to human activities. Even abstract notions, such as "democracy" or "freedom," are anchored in concrete human practices (in this case, activities such as voting, going to public libraries, and laughing at political cartoons in the newspaper).

The way people talk enables them to sound more ***reasonable*** than they actually are. When decisions are made, people go to great lengths to convince themselves that they are making those decisions rationally and logically rather than simply on the basis of visceral preference. In an earlier example, we pointed out that humans may go through the exercise of making elaborate lists of pros and cons, but they "sneak" their preferences into the process by monitoring what gets added to the list, what gets subtracted, and how the items are subsequently described, arranged, and weighted. If it still isn't coming out "right," they stall, seek additional inputs, try an alternative decision-making method, or decide to trust their "intuition" just this once. Life's important decisions—getting married, having children, going to school, changing careers—are made on the basis of inclination, justified by amassing supportive "facts" and mounting reasonable-sounding arguments. This is true also in the presumably hallowed halls of science, where, in the final analysis, an experimenter's "hunch" often rules the day.

Everything we do is accompanied by a bodily predisposition. These dispositions are sets or attitudes that make classes of behavior more probable or less probable. For example, when a person sits down to a large meal or curls up in bed with a good book, he or she is less likely to launch into a vigorous exercise program or initiate a session of complicated problem-solving. Although fighting and fleeing are the classic examples of opposite directional sets—each "disables" the other—all behaviors involve elements of directionality. The person is always "pointing" toward or away from something.

When you are pointed one way, it takes extra effort to get you reoriented in a different direction. You can't easily kiss and make up while you are in the middle of an argument, and if you set out to buy a brand-new car the salesperson may have trouble interesting you in a used model, even if it is a steal. A person having trouble falling asleep may be stuck between two opposing dispositional modes. He or she wants to get some rest but is still invested in resolving an important life issue. Each of these tasks requires a different form of support from the musculature, the visceral system, and so on. Therefore, the person experiences the frustration of vacillating between two incompatible goals. The person is "stretched" between two incompatible bodily attitudes—repose and problem-solving.

In such situations, it is often useful to "ride the horse in the direction it's going," as people were often reminded during Werner Erhard's *est training* (Efran, Lukens, & Lukens, 1986). You cannot automatically detach yourself from your problem-solving concerns, but you may be able to achieve completion for the moment by getting up and jotting your thoughts down on a piece of paper or by drafting a letter relevant to the situation. Here, as elsewhere, we favor a strategy of *inclusion* rather than exclusion; the frame needs to be expanded rather than contracted. Attempts to "forget" about the problem just lead to more tossing and turning. Giving your concerns their due by taking an action that moves toward a completion point works better.

AN ALTERNATIVE DEFINITION OF EMOTION

We define emotions as the bodily predispositions that underlie, support, and create readiness for actions (Frijda, 1986, 1988). In this usage of the term there is always an ongoing emotion; at any point in time, we are moving one way or another, even if that motion isn't one of high intensity. A person operating at a fever pitch may be called "emotional," but *emotion*, as we define it, isn't something that comes and goes or exists in connection with only a few select activities. Emotion is with us all the time, as our system continually changes state in connection with shifting internal and external circumstances. This fact alone should dash any hopes that the thorny questions of primacy (which comes first—thought, feeling, or behavior?) can be satisfactorily answered.

The erroneous notion that we are sometimes emotional but otherwise rational is one of the bulwarks sustaining the belief in a tripartite system. We hope it is becoming clear that such a conception is an oversimplification and a liability. Every "rational" act rides piggyback on an underlying emotional predisposition, even when that predisposition is not being noticed or made explicit in language.

People implicitly understand this. They know that even presumably rational judgments and decisions are influenced by the ebb and flow of emotion. That's why they talk about waiting to "catch the person in the right mood." One parent, acting as friendly advisor, may tell children "not now" when they ask whether to address a request to the other parent. People realize that their propositions will get a more favorable hearing if the other person is already positively inclined to move in a direction compatible with their request.

Thus, emotion doesn't precede or follow action—it is the bodily support that a class of actions requires. Language, of course, is just one of the classes of action that emotions support. Just as it is difficult to walk over and shake hands with a person with whom you are currently annoyed, it is also hard to apologize or exchange social niceties with him or her.

When you are lying in bed talking to yourself about buying a new car, you are *already* involved in the process of buying it. You are poised in the right direction and taking the preliminary steps along the route. The person who protests that he or she was "just thinking about it" is merely reminding us that he or she is not yet at a point along the path where a reversal would be socially or financially costly—the deal is still tentative. Later, after signing a formal purchase agreement at the showroom, backing out will not be as easy; a lawyer's services may be required to implement a later "change of mind."[3]

Saying "I do" at a wedding ceremony is an example of a substantial language action. It embodies a fundamental emotion—moving into union with another. It also makes people queasy because they realize that if they should experience any additional, sudden "changes of heart," they will not be able to gracefully back up or get out of the agreement they are consummating.

LOVE, HATRED, AND INDIFFERENCE

In the hierarchy of emotions, the emotion of love—what Maturana (unromantically) calls "the passion for living together in close proximity"—is most basic to the building of community and the construction of language. Language and the building of civilization require the kind of recurrent

---

[3]People talk about a "change of mind." Sometimes exactly the same experience is described as a "change of heart." Neither description is fully accurate, although the second is closer. In using such expressions, people are indicating that the bodyhood as a whole has shifted to a different posture—an "about face" has occurred.

interaction that happens only when people have the desire to associate closely with each other. Here again we see that our most rational achievements are built on an a priori biological given. For Maturana, the opposite of love isn't hate—it is indifference. Hatred signifies continued attachment and involvement, whereas indifference moves the person off in another direction altogether, dissolving the association.

Once we look beyond therapists' preoccupations with techniques and the appearance of professionalism, we see that therapy is a human conversation founded on love.[4] The recognition of this tends to embarrass those who like to think of themselves as objective scientists or mechanics of the mind. But one doesn't tinker with the mind the way an auto mechanic tinkers with a car engine. Bad thoughts aren't plucked out and replaced the way a technician replaces defective spark plugs (Coyne, 1982). Instead of tinkering with thoughts as if they were discrete, easily interchanged entities, the therapist "embraces" the thinker, creating a space in which that person can allow his or her own pattern of thinking and planning to unfold and be observed. The emphasis is not on directly changing those thoughts or plans but on permitting them to be viewed against the wider background the client-therapist nexus provides. Under those circumstances, thoughts and plans change by themselves.

Partly because of the discomfort therapists have about admitting to themselves or others that love is at the heart of the therapy enterprise, they often go to extremes to avoid, minimize, or deflect expressions of appreciation and affection from clients. Some, for example, have an ironclad rule—no gifts. When therapists give pejorative connotations to ordinary and positive impulses, it is difficult for clients to give voice to their feelings of gratitude and sense of connectedness. In our practices, we accept (but don't solicit) such expressions of thankfulness—books, poems, food, and other tokens of appreciation. In many cultures, refusing a gift is considered an insult to the person offering it. Some gifts are, of course, not gifts at all—they are bribes. True gifts do not commit the recipient to reciprocate in any way. If a gift is intended as a bribe, that fact becomes apparent when it fails to have its intended effect. A client once offered a gift (which we politely accepted) and immediately thereafter asked to schedule additional sessions (which we just as politely declined). That was all that needed "to be said" about the matter. In this setting, a bribe accepted as a gift may ultimately

[4]This is perhaps akin to the Rogerian concept of "nonpossessive warmth" (Truax & Carkhuff, 1967), the general affiliative dimension that shows up in client ratings of therapists (Elliott & James, 1989), or aspects of the so-called therapeutic alliance (Luborsky, Crits-Christoph, Mintz, & Auerbach, 1988).

become a gift, even if it wasn't what the person originally intended. On the other hand, a gift accepted as an obligation ceases to be a gift.

EMOTIONAL CONTRADICTION

Conflicts, such as finding yourself married to a person you no longer like, are never struggles between feelings and thoughts, thoughts and actions, or feelings and actions (Akillas & Efran, 1989). They are contradictions between goals that simultaneously require opposing bodily predispositions. If people want to push away others whom they also need to keep close at hand, they are forced to live, as we have indicated, in "emotional contradiction" (Mendez, Coddou, & Maturana, 1988). They are quite literally coming and going at the same time.

The same dynamics hold true even with regard to life's minor, temporary hassles. The phone rings while you are engrossed in a TV program or are finally getting down to work on a problem. You don't want to be rude to the person who is calling, but nevertheless you feel wrenched away from your initial involvement. You are being "split down the middle," "torn in two," and so on. With friends, too, we sometimes run hot and cold. One minute we seem a million miles away and the next minute we are available to be in close relationship. When there is a mismatch in these moods, friction develops. Yet such emotional shifts are inevitable and, by themselves, relatively insignificant. Unfortunately, when these are misinterpreted by others as personal affronts, they can jeopardize the status of a relationship. Because of their needs, people are driven to overpersonalize everything. We need to remind them frequently that these matters aren't necessarily personal.

However, in these rapid shifts, it isn't that our cognitive apparatus has gone off in one direction and our guts or feet have taken a different route. The *entire* system, as a whole, is being subjected to conflicting demands.

Because of the nature of the projects involved—for example, joining a friend for a movie versus continuing to do homework—you may *language* one goal as being more visceral and another more cerebral. This, however, is a metaphorical language distinction and has no literal validity. Conflicts are between enactments—not subsystems of the body.

THE LANGUAGE OF EMOTION

The attempt to affiliate and disaffiliate at the same time leads to trouble, and so does the desire to simultaneously submit and dominate. Emotions can therefore be classified as pairs of opposites, because they usually move us in alternative directions (de Rivera, 1977). However, if there is smooth movement toward a goal—if nothing interferes with our progression—we will not usually describe the situation as "emotional." The commonsense language of emotion tends to be applied only when we "sense" ourselves shifting gears. The gear-shifting occurs when there is an obstacle blocking our path.

If we were totally free to do as we pleased, words like "anger" would not be needed. When something got in our way, we would simply destroy it—zapping the obstruction with a ray gun. However, because such ease of action isn't possible except in science fiction, we stand before many obstacles with clenched teeth—in a state of emotional contradiction—wanting to attack but being compelled to exercise partial restraint. Anger is our term for the experience of blocked or inhibited fighting or annihilating. The underlying desire is to strike full force, but the circumstances and potential costs force a mitigation of forward action. When we are in this state of emotional contradiction, we usually describe ourselves as being "angry." The vocabulary of affect is therefore a vocabulary of passive or partially blocked actions (Peters, 1970).

If a person loses his or her keys, a search-and-retrieval campaign can be launched—there isn't necessarily an emotional contradiction. However, if a close friend or relative dies, the person is stymied. There is no appropriate way to "search and retrieve" what has been taken away. Therefore, the person experiences a futile, blocked, aimless form of retrieval—grief. Some people, while grieving, actually make partial, aborted retrieval motions into empty air, as if they might somehow be able to summon the person back. They have a "longing" for something to be found and returned to them. They also plead, implore, apologize, and go through a variety of other activities that might result in a restoration of the relationship—if the person were still living. Again, the "feel" of an emotion is actually the feel of blockage—of contradiction.

In this regard, descriptions of children in playground fights are instructive. Before a fight breaks out, a boy might describe himself as "fighting mad." However, once the fight gets going full blast—when action is no longer blocked—his anger disappears. One youngster who repeatedly banged his opponent's head against the pavement later reported that he did so "for no particular reason" and without any accompanying sensation—neither anger, joy, or regret. He was operating on automatic pilot and had to be stopped by a bystander. Just as we drive a car automatically, without later being clear which route we took, full-fledged action may be executed without the generation of an "observer" to evaluate or feel anything. People do not necessarily experience fear while actively running from danger or avoiding a pursuer. If, however, their path is cut off, they will describe the resulting blockage in terms of fright or terror—thwarted escape.

We have interviewed dental phobics who report that it isn't simply the "pain" that gets to them—it is the passive, helpless, blocked state in which they find themselves during dental procedures. They are awake, but their mouths are open, they can't speak or leave, and they are unable to predict exactly what is coming next or when it will end. Similarly, torture is always an arrangement calculated not just to create raw physical sensation but also to deprive the victim of opportunities to predict or control the progression of events.

Actors, both amateur and professional, will tell you that stage fright—a self-imposed torture—rarely strikes in the middle of a performance. It occurs in the wings, while they are waiting for a performance to begin. Again, the sensation derives from enforced passivity—and the emotional contradiction that it generates. The actors want both to get on with the show and to cancel the appearance altogether. At the time, they can do neither.

Positive feelings, too, including excitement and sexual arousal, involve blocked action (Tripp, 1987). For instance, spectators at a ball game, unable to participate directly, are reduced to engaging in partial, substitute activities, such as shouting directions at the team, hollering, and jumping up and down within their confined spaces. Paradoxically, they thus *experience* more excitement than the players do—at least during the game itself. The players, being in full action, have neither the time nor the need for emotional display. Of course, between plays or after the game ends, they too may attempt to keep action going in substitute channels. The winners will pour champagne on one another, carry the coach on their shoulders, hug each other, and cause a commotion. The losers, experiencing "the agony of defeat" will replay the game over and over in conversations with themselves, longing to reverse time and begin again.

Sexual practices in all cultures provide for forms of blockage that help stir up and sustain erotic intensity. These sexual "obstacles" take many forms, from limiting full access to the sexual partner (chaperones, elaborate courtship rituals, required clothing) to building behavioral blockages into the sex act itself (biting, hitting, hesitation, and so on). When there is easy and continuous partner accessibility, sexual desire wanes. Similarly, full nudity quickly becomes asexual, as nudist colonies have more than adequately demonstrated. Striptease artists intuitively understand that to create arousal, they must use partial concealment skillfully, offering a series of promissory notes that might soon be redeemed. In other words, in the sexual arena, playing "hard to get" works—up to a point. Hope and discouragement must be kept in balance to keep the fires of emotional contradiction burning.

STEAM-KETTLE THINKING

Many therapists still act as if they believed that people "contain" emotions, such as anger, more or less the way a steam-kettle contains heated water. They want the person "boiling" with rage to "vent" his or her emotions, lest pressure build up and cause an external or internal explosion. The steam-kettle metaphor is widespread but unfortunate. It does not articulate well with human physiology, nor does it provide a reliable guide to clinical practice. Emotions are not stored quantities, nor do they disappear when "discharged." Such metaphors persist because they contain a grain of truth—they capture an element of commonsense experience. A man who is angered by his employer's curt denial of a raise *does* feel better after bashing a pillow a few times, but not because he has gotten the anger out. Someone who has "had a good cry" after an upsetting experience *does* report relief, but not because sadness has been "drained" away.

In fact, one could create circumstances in which people could pound pillows from today to tomorrow and end up just as angry as when they started, or even angrier. On the contrary, there are times when a person's anger diminishes while he or she sits quietly, listening to others talk. The amount of relief experienced is not related to the amount of energy expended. The relief relates, instead, to whether the blockage has been eliminated. People believe strongly in cathartic or steam-kettle approaches because, more often than not, the expressive process leads to collateral shifts in social process—while the person emotes, positions are softened or changed, realignments occur, permissions are given, and bonds are formed. In other words, it is the action implications of catharsis that are critical—not the energy expenditure or whether or not something has been "gotten off one's chest."

In a catharsis-oriented group session, a member was asked to yell at the "internal wall" that presumably inhibited him from communicating with women. After some elaborate carrying-on, he received hugs of support from the women in the group—including one on whom he had a crush—and the men rallied to assure him that they, too, had parallel difficulties in approaching members of the opposite sex. The man experienced "cathartic relief" and shared more freely about himself with the other group members. In situations like this, many things are happening at once. Therefore, it is easy to lose sight of the critical social realignments that are taking place and to focus instead on the signs of emotional display that accompany them. If the person were alone or with a therapist of the same sex, the outcomes might have been far different.

Years ago, one of the authors had the unfortunate experience of co-leading a group where things didn't go according to plan. One of the members was moved to acknowledge publicly, for the first time, that he was gay. Moreover, he expressed his deep love for a male member of the group. Instead of giving him the kind of support and understanding that is typical in such groups, a different and unexpected dynamic took hold, and the man who made the disclosures was essentially isolated from his peers. Instead of "joining" with him and attempting to close the perceived distance between his experience and their own, other group members rushed away in all directions.

It was like being present at a ceremonial "shunning." Nothing the co-leaders did seemed able to reverse or ameliorate the polarities that rapidly developed. The members of this particular group seemed much more homophobic than anyone might have guessed. The man took a risk, anticipated group acceptance, and struck out. In the week following the meeting, he was understandably depressed. His friend in the group wanted nothing further to do with him, and he began contemplating suicide as the only way out. Only massive amounts of support from the co-therapists and others kept the situation from ending in tragedy. In this instance, a person "got something off his chest" but experienced additional distress instead of relief. Here, emotional contradiction was heightened rather than resolved.

DISCHARGE PATTERNS

Tears, laughter, tantrums, and trembling—discharge patterns—are often considered to be "emotions." Indeed, these outwardly impressive displays are often viewed as the epitome of emotional expression. Yet, the evidence is strong that these reactions are not emotions, per se, but represent system *recovery* from blocked action patterns (e.g., Efran & Spangler, 1979; Frijda, 1988; Jackins, 1965; Nichols & Efran, 1985). Accommodation to obstacles consists of an arousal or activation stage—gearing up for battle—and then a recovery phase, right after the obstacle has been removed or surmounted. The discharge patterns we mentioned above are part of the *recovery* stage rather than the arousal stage. Thus, people cry not directly because they are sad or distressed, but because they have been released from the clutches of a contradiction. A child lost in a supermarket is most prone to cry *after* the parent has been spotted or when help appears to be on the way—not when he or she is most thoroughly and hopelessly lost. Similarly, when there has been an automobile accident, adults on the scene are most apt to cry when the ambulance arrives and they can "go off duty" or when relatives arrive and they see a familiar face.

Friends or relatives waiting at an airline counter for news about a crash are—if you watch the evening news—grim-faced. When the news comes—whether it is good *or* bad—tears flow. The tears represent the release of the tension or high state of activation in which the people have been functioning. Something has, one way or another, been resolved.

Likewise, at weddings or other joyous events, tears occur when a tension-arousing sequence comes to completion. When the bride says "I do," a phase of her mother's life has come to a successful conclusion, and she can stop holding her breath. The tears that flow are labeled tears of joy in honor of the occasion, but tears are tears—the mechanism is always the same, regardless of the particular circumstances that created the prior elevation in tension. Laughter and the other forms of discharge operate similarly, with certain distinctions that need not concern us here. Discharge forms have more in common with one another than we generally recognize. Thus, a person who is crying may easily break into giddy laughter, and vice versa. In fact, if you are unaware of the provoking situation and are listening from the next room, you may be unable to distinguish whether the person you hear is laughing or crying.

After people have had a good cry, a belly laugh, or a no-holds-barred tantrum, they generally report that they feel better. The tendency therefore is to think that crying, laughing, or tantrums have healing powers. However, these are simply the outward signs that people have been released from an emotional contradiction. Escaping from the bonds of the contradiction is what feels good.

Those who are familiar with ***reevaluation counseling*** (Jackins, 1965) know that it is often useful to invite someone who is caught in emotional contradiction to mimic a body posture inconsistent with the content of the statement he or she is making: The person says, "Both my parents died this year," and the therapist replies, "Can you say that with a big smile?" Surprisingly, if the setting is right, a person is enabled to let go and cry at that point. It is as if, in attempting to enact these conflicting postural demands at the same time, the person's composure is undermined and he or she "flows" in the path of least resistance—toward equilibrium. Obviously, this technique can only be used effectively when the alliance between client and therapist is strong, so that the person does not interpret the suggestion as an indication of disrespect or indecent mockery.

Recently, a client reported confusion about whether or not he should leave his wife. He had felt distant from her for a number of years and had now, quite unexpectedly, fallen in love with a co-worker. She, too, was married but less than satisfied at home. However, her husband had multiple sclerosis, and the prospect of leaving him – in his state – filled her with guilt. In fact, both lovers felt enormously remorseful about their secret meetings and the web of lies and fabrications in which they had become embroiled. At one point, the therapist said to the man, "So, it looks like you want out of your marriage, doesn't it?" He burst into tears and cried uncontrollably for many minutes.[5]

When the reaction was over, he thanked the therapist for "clarifying everything." The therapist had merely stated something that seemed obvious but that hadn't yet been verbalized in declarative form. Even the client's wife, when she later heard about the interaction, said, "Your therapist just put into words what you already – in your heart – knew to be true." His wife, who had previously resisted seeing a therapist, decided, after hearing about this incident, to avail herself of his services. She felt an affinity for the therapist, even though his statement might have been interpreted as being opposed to her interests. People appreciate being told what's so, even when they don't like what it is. Some therapists like to "build rapport" first, before they say what they believe to be so. We tend to tell the truth right off the bat. We consider telling the truth to be the major element in establishing trust and rapport. (When we visit a physician, we appreciate knowing immediately what he or she thinks is wrong – we don't expect to be buttered up first.)

The therapist's comment put an open secret into words. Until that point, the client could neither avoid thinking about that alternative nor give himself permission to entertain it forthrightly. When people are in emotional contradiction, they play games with themselves, games that they cannot possibly win. (Remember, one cannot win an argument with oneself.) The therapist's comment ended an unproductive and emotionally costly cat-and-mouse game. All options were now on the table and could be openly discussed. A door that had been slightly ajar was opened wide, and the tears were a sign of the tension reduction that the change in framework produced.

When we attempt to navigate between emotionally conflicting demands, we all engage in multilayered discussions with ourselves in which we try to mask or circumvent what we already know. This is not an

---

[5]For therapists who are uncomfortable with discharge – which includes most of us – a minute or two of tears seems like an hour. It is no accident that tears can make us edgy. When children cry, we as responsible grownups are supposed to "do something to help make them feel better." When we are unable to figure out how to get them to stop crying, we often become frustrated and frantic – sometimes even abusive. When adults cry, we are also moved to assist them, even though it is less clear what needs to be done. Thus, we feel helpless, and wish the crying would stop.

unconscious mind at work—merely tricks of self-observational conversation. Recall what happens when you learn that a couple who seemed to have an "ideal marriage" are getting divorced. At first, you are surprised and shocked. Within moments, however, you remember that you suspected this all along. There were those times when they behaved awkwardly, gave implausible excuses for being late or absent, answered the phone abruptly, and so on. You knew all along that something was amiss, but until the formal announcement was made it was more convenient for you to "not discuss" with yourself what you already knew.

Consider, too, people who receive an envelope from a college to which they have applied for admission. They debate whether to open the envelope now or after lunch. Should they first hold it up to the light and attempt to make out some of the writing? Should they have someone else open and read it? Should they feel the thickness of the envelope, on the theory that an acceptance letter might have more pages than a rejection? This is an instance of emotional contradiction in action (and in miniature). People both want to know and want to postpone knowing. Of course, if they could be sure that the news was good (or bad), they would be able to decide how to proceed.

DEPRESSION, DEPENDENCY, HOPELESSNESS

Human beings live within a continuous flux of emotions and moods. Words flow through our bodies, and bodily states are expressed partly through our verbal expressions. Thus, when a person is depressed, he or she can easily entertain one class of thoughts, but may have trouble embracing other lines of thinking. As the emotional stance shifts, so does the availability and perceived relevance of other patterns of action and thought. As we suggested in earlier chapters, the cognitivist hypothesis that depression is caused by flaws in thinking cannot be accurate (Coyne, 1989). From the point of view we have been describing, depressed thoughts are *part* of depression—not the cause of it. Depression, as a bodily disposition, involves treating options pessimistically. Experientially, the connections between immediate options and meaningful goals have been eroded or weakened. Once that has occurred, the depressed person "uses" available circumstances to support his or her stance—that nothing is working or workable. It isn't so much that particular circumstances cause the person to become depressed. On other occasions, those same circumstances would be taken in stride. The person "does depression" with any circumstances that happen to be lying around; if those prove insufficient, the person draws upon more distant events to help make the case.

Clinically, it has often been noticed that people who have been depressed do better when they shift into anger and aggression. Bergner (1988), in fact, recommends a treatment along these lines. Two directions cannot peacefully coexist, and anger trumps depression and renders it obsolete. Anger is generally the preferable state because it is compatible with many more action possibilities. The angry person actively complains (leading to possible resolutions); he or she more readily seeks, rather than avoids, interaction. One strategy for converting "hopelessness" into something more active is to challenge the person to explain why—if something is truly hopeless—he or she would bother bringing it up? (After all, people don't spend much time talking about flying without the help of machinery, since the project appears futile.) Thus, the person taking the trouble to proclaim the hopelessness of the situation must harbor—in that secret conversation with self—some expectation that matters might improve, if only the proper button could be pushed. An acknowledgment of that fact paves the way for getting to work on finding an appropriate button.

A different but analogous shift occurs with people who complain they are overly *dependent*—always feeling obliged to do what others want. Of course, they do no such thing. They do precisely what they want, but blame misfortunes on others. In our practice, we often request (without explanation) that such individuals follow some simple direction, such as standing up or moving from one seat to another. They invariably hesitate, protesting that the request doesn't make sense. They want to know all the whys and wherefores before taking action. These presumably "meek" individuals can be surprisingly bold and pugnacious in insisting on their rights. This gives us an ideal opportunity to illustrate that their level of blind compliance is a far cry from what they had been "advertising." We made only one request—and it was harmless and easy to fulfill—yet we got nothing but hesitation, protest, and argument. What happened to the excessive dependency they had promised?

ATTACHMENTS

Tasks that are incomplete continue to command attention (Klinger, 1977). The Eastern term "attached" captures the image of a person who is caught in emotional contradiction—wanting something that he or she is unable to devise a way of obtaining. You don't choose your attachments. The best you can do is be aware of what they are. That way you are apt to make provisions to include them in your activities, so that completions can be achieved. Consider, for example, someone whose spouse has died and who is having difficulty getting on with life. Well-meaning friends suggest that the person should stop dwelling on the past, find a new partner, keep busy, and so on. These admonitions ignore essential aspects of the attachment phenomenon. Of course, even if such advice were fully valid and would improve the person's life immeasurably, it couldn't be followed. How can someone "keep busy" when every fiber of the person's being moves him to sit and ruminate about the person who is gone?

Besides, the survivor ought *not* forget or bury what has come before. That would serve only to invalidate the meaningfulness of his or her life story. It would make the job of reconstructing a productive life harder—not easier. Instead, what is needed are links that help cement the past to a viable future. The death of a loved one is not to be forgotten, abandoned, or trivialized—it is to be incorporated in future plans and projects (Marris, 1974). In some cultures, the person is given substantial aid in this task through sacred rituals and ceremonies. In our own more individualistically oriented and secularized society, establishing the necessary links can be more difficult. What is needed are suitable formats for memorializing the past relationship as an aspect of ongoing endeavors. Although the person who died cannot, as a physical entity, continue into the future, essences of the relationship can be sustained.

When Senator Hubert Humphrey died, his wife was offered an opportunity to complete the remainder of his term in the Senate. Here was an ideal vehicle for her to commemorate and help perpetuate what she and her husband stood for, and to play an active role in completing projects on which they had both been working. Similarly, Coretta Scott King has had opportunities to sustain her memories of her husband through her work for the cause to which they both devoted their lives. In circumstances like these, less is lost, and the process of mourning becomes smoother.

Not all widows and widowers have ready-made opportunities for continuing meaningful involvements. However, possibilities can always be created. A couple whose daughter dies of leukemia can incorporate into their activities fund-raising efforts on behalf of cancer research. Mothers Against Drunk Driving provides a socially useful outlet for many angry, grieving parents. These and other more private solutions tend to be more constructive than urging the person to "be busy" or "to try and forget." A parent who only spends his or her days looking through old photographs or who makes a frozen shrine of a deceased child's bedroom misses an opportunity to convert a loss into an effective and satisfying plan for future living.

Freeing people of outmoded attachments consists largely of expanding the frame of reference in which they live, so that dead goals can be rehabilitated into live ones. Nicholas Cummings (1979) gives a good example of this in describing his work with addicted individuals. He discusses the importance of reawakening a person's abandoned dream—of helping him or her connect something important from the past to something that might yet come to fruition: "The therapist discerns some unresolved wish, some long-gone dream that is still residing deep in that human being, and then the therapist pulls it out and ignites the client with a desire to somehow look at that dream again" (p. 1123). In other words, with the therapist's help, the person must distinguish a frame of reference that generates worthwhile goals and activities. Although it may no longer be feasible for the person to become an Olympic swimmer—a dream he or she had as a teenager—satisfaction may still be found in coaching a swim team, writing about sports, collecting money for the Special Olympics, or starting a neighborhood sports competition.

The project doesn't have to strike others as essential or substantial; it can be a hobby as well as an occupation. It does have to be significant to the person who undertakes it, enabling him or her to weave a story of the "self" that seems sustainable. If you listen at Alcoholics Anonymous meetings to recovering alcoholics who have done well, they have all found ways to successfully "use" the elements of their lives, including periods of drunkenness, to develop a viable narrative. Despite whatever misfortunes they may have experienced along the way, they have managed to engineer a workable identity that they can "sell" to themselves and others. Notice that in solving emotional difficulties the focus is always on action alternatives, not on the release of quantities of feeling from imaginary internal containers.

UNEXPECTED OCCURRENCES

When the continuity of a person's life has been disrupted by a severe and unexpected event—a death, an accident, a job layoff, a mugging, a rape, a divorce—continuity needs to be restored. If therapy is to help in this process, the entirety of the person's experience of the event must be the jumping-off place. There is a tendency to disallow aspects of the person's experience because it doesn't happen to fit current social expectations. As times change, different aspects of experience tend to be discounted or dismissed as "illegitimate." Vietnam veterans have long complained that no one has wanted to hear their story. In the past, women who had been raped had similar difficulties. The process is so automatic that even the individuals themselves may not realize how thoroughly their report of the experience is being filtered through and shaped by the prejudices and needs of community members.

For example, a person who has been in an automobile crash may be permitted to freely express fear about the event, and even anger at the other driver, but may be subtly dissuaded from talking about his or her glee upon hearing about the severity of the other driver's injuries. It only takes a slight change in expression or interest on the part of the listener to "shape" a person's story in one direction or another. In the next retelling, only the pain of the accident will be emphasized, and the desire for revenge will have been softened or omitted altogether. People want to listen only to what they expect to hear—what fits with current philosophical premises. After all, we are "attached" to our assumptions just as surely as we are to other aspects of our action patterns. Yet, it is exactly when a story doesn't fit our preconceptions that the person's experience most desperately needs to be validated by being put into words and shared with members of the community.

As we have said, it used to be more difficult for women who had been raped to tell their whole story. It was automatically assumed that they had done something to provoke or entice the rapist—therefore, at some level, rape was routinely considered to be their own fault. In some sections of the country, this attitude may still prevail. Even among "enlightened" mental health workers, that underlying bias probably still affects how such narratives are edited. However, whereas in the past women who were raped couldn't communicate their innocence, they now are unable to communicate the psychic guilt they may be experiencing. Lawyers are now adamant that women *not* talk about any aspects of the experience that might be the least bit incongruent with the "victim" role.

For example, one woman recalled returning a man's glance and smiling at him, not realizing what was going to happen next. In another instance, a woman had a fleeting fantasy about having a daring romantic fling with the stranger she saw ahead of her. Obviously, her lawyer forbade her from reporting this aspect of her experience. Because we have so long been battling the bias of rape's being the woman's fault, there is now the danger of suppressing any portions of her story that appear to lend credence to that interpretation.

Experiences are complex and multifaceted—we go through many moods and readjustments as an incident unfolds and as it is replayed. There is never, for very long—in the theater of our minds—one clear-cut villain and one clear-cut victim. Everyone and everything is implicated and is suspect. People wonder whether they should have been walking alone on a particular street, why they didn't purchase a whistle, whether it was right to keep an apartment in that neighborhood. They ruminate about whether they should have resisted more (or less), whether they might have screamed louder, what others are thinking about them, and so on. All such thoughts—because they have occurred—need to be legitimized. The elements that seem ugly are as crucial as those that are expected and socially sanctioned. It is the unshared and unvalidated pockets of secrecy and hypocrisy that keep people up at night. The experiential truth—different from either the legal or historical truth—is what needs to be told (Bruner, 1986; Mahrer, 1978/1989; Spence, 1982).

We avoid referring to a woman who was raped as a "victim," since that is just one role out of many, and not necessarily the one that she has chosen to occupy. Moreover, she was attacked by a person—not a "rapist." Abstractions and labels always get in the way when we are attempting to share experience—they eclipse and condense experience. Every "rape" is different from every other, and one moment in the event is different from every other moment. In working with women who have been raped we try to aid in the sharing of the experience by asking questions such as "Who did he remind you of?" "Who else?" We also ask, "What would you like to say to him?" "What were you thinking?" "What thought did you have but wished you hadn't?" and so on.

Individuals in reevaluation counseling have learned to ask "What were you thinking?" instead of "What were you feeling?" Ironically, the first question works better than the second in helping the person identify his or her emotional stance. Once the stance is clear, feelings take care of themselves. Evaluations by the listener, even sympathetic ones, get in the way of experiential reports. They signal what the listener expects to hear, and they therefore distort the process. What is called for from the listener is relaxed attention—not sympathy or judgment.

In multiple retellings, the person's story keeps changing, with richer details being added all the time. Aspects that were initially withheld become integrated into the narrative. On the other hand, if the listener is impatient or opinionated, the retellings become shorter and more circumscribed. Perhaps many details of experience can be profitably edited out of judicial proceedings—but in the therapy context, they need to be given the space they deserve. For example, a woman who has been raped has to be given an opportunity to confront her concerns that she might have planned better or been cleverer in handling her attacker. Such thoughts flash through us in milliseconds, but those that cannot be shared may linger as unfinished business for months, years, or even lifetimes.

As people have an opportunity to tell a story in all its detail, their relationship to it shifts. They decenter—moving into the role of storyteller (Rosen, 1985). In other words, there is a recognition that the storyteller and the story being told are not identical. Instead of *being* the story, they begin to *have* a story. The storyteller becomes the frame—the space—

within which all such stories happen. Later the storyteller can decide what to do next with any particular aspect of the story. Will it make the "best stories of the decade" list or will it be tucked away on a back shelf as being too gruesome to be displayed? What might the story be good for? It can be added to a growing reservoir of wisdom. It can be regarded as an initiation rite, marking the end of innocence. It can vindicate a particular position. It can serve as a purple heart, a badge of courage, or a scarlet letter. As storyteller, the person begins to gain a sense of mastery over that which is being told.

In one instance, a woman who had been raped spoke about her need to get away from people—from the city, from the streets where the crime happened, and so on. She even imagined escaping to a mountain cave, where she wouldn't be bothered by anyone—particularly men. As she developed this fantasy, she began to have an idea that was first alarming and then amusing. She realized that there was another person who might, at that particular moment, also be trying to get away from the city—away from the police. She envisioned the man who attacked her as having taken up residence in a nearby cave. He'd probably want to come over some morning to borrow some sugar or linger over a neighborly cup of coffee. In having this image, her sense of fear was replaced by a strange bemusement. The "rapist" had, in a very real sense, become "her own rapist," about whom she could invent things, change interpretations at will, and—in short—do whatever she wanted with him.

PREFERENCES—THE GOOD, THE BAD, AND THE UGLY

People are preferential creatures, but what we want is not always convenient, practical, consistent, socially sanctioned, or logical. Our desires dominate our existence—and unacknowledged desires dominate most of all. Yet, in every sphere, desires keep changing. At one time you could probably have eaten your way through a drugstore's supply of candy; these days a single Snickers bar is about all you can manage. Perhaps, as a child, you gleefully crushed frogs with rocks, just to see what was inside them, or you pulled the legs off daddy-longlegs to watch them twitch and jump around. Now even the thought of doing such things sends shivers up your spine. In the domain of preferences, we frequently delude ourselves and deceive others with an aplomb that would be the envy of any con artist. In responding to questions about what we want, we almost automatically mix together what we think we should want, what we once wanted, what we might someday want, what we have led others to believe we want, and so on.

A therapy that does not address people's preferences is doomed, no matter how valid it may otherwise appear to be. Tapping into the unacknowledged wants embedded in clients' stories is critical to successful therapeutic work. For example, when a pregnant woman says (for the third time), "I really need to quit smoking," she means just the opposite. She wants to keep right on smoking and correctly intuits that her trips to the therapist's office to discuss the matter will get her husband off her back for a while. After all, by seeing a therapist she can *claim* to herself and to him that she is doing something about the problem.

The woman we are describing doesn't need additional education about the adverse effects of smoking, particularly while pregnant. She isn't stupid. Nor does she lack information on methods for quitting. Her problem-solving skills are entirely intact. Some therapists are too quick to infer that their clients are deficient organisms, incapable of functioning at a high level of efficiency.[6] Because we view things from our own perspective, we assume they want what we want, but don't know how to get it—that they are playing our game, but playing it poorly. More often than not, they are playing their own game, and doing it rather well.

The smoker in this example is irresponsible—not because she is imposing risks on an unborn child, or because she is placing herself at increased risk for heart disease, cancer, and other afflictions—but because she is lying to the therapist and to herself as well. Her smoking is a "disclaimed action" (Schafer, 1983), and it renders her false to herself. She is neither willing to give up cigarettes nor willing to face the consequences of asserting her commitment to continue smoking. As Alfred Adler (1930) might have said, using a potent language that is now out of fashion, she is a "moral coward." She lacks the courage of her convictions. In fact, she lacks conviction. She wants everything to be made easy for her. Her words and other actions do not mesh.[7]

People who do not mean what they say—who are being hypocritical in conversations with themselves—cannot derive much satisfaction from their performances. Something always seems out of kilter. By the time people

---

[6]We recall the example of a mental health worker who attempted to teach "social skills" to a group of delinquent youths. Well into the program, he discovered what might have been suspected at the outset—that the delinquents had as much skill in some of these areas as he did. They used them well when arranging drug deals or keeping their parents off balance, but had little interest in phoning up prospective employers or reporting for work on time. They were not unskilled—they were playing a different game.

[7]We have begun to discover (e.g., Schachter, 1982) that many people give up smoking readily using a variety of techniques. The notion that it is nearly impossible to extinguish smoking behavior is an exaggeration that derives from taking at face value what a subset of individuals report. Those who attend smoking groups or talk to their therapists about their smoking are a biased sample. Many of them would rather talk and grouse than quit.

have reached adulthood, they have made so many compromises—there have been so many "sellouts" en route—that it becomes difficult to recollect the destination of the journey (Powers, 1973). For example, some of our graduate students report that they tend to lose sight of what initially attracted them to the field. Since they find themselves doing work that doesn't fit their interests, they are prone to experience themselves as powerless victims, doing the bidding of others.

It is the therapist's job to help clients be clear about the relationship between what they describe wanting to do and what they actually do. The therapist helps the person distinguish, for example, between wanting to quit and *wishing* he or she wanted to quit. In the case of the pregnant smoker, it was the latter. Once that is clear, it may soon shift to the former.

As therapists, it is crucial that we avoid inadvertently becoming accessories—before or after the fact—to a presentation of self that is inauthentic. Agreeing to accept a client's stated goals—unless they are being actively achieved—is signing a pact with the devil. It is precisely those goals that sound good but do not correspond to actual preferences that keep the client stuck. The actual preferences cannot be legitimized within the narrow framework in which the person is operating, and he or she is forced to live in emotional contradiction. All too often, the therapist accepts a false statement of goals at the outset of therapy—they sound reasonable—and the therapy thus gallops off in the wrong direction, heading merrily nowhere. Worse yet, the therapist's agreement sustains the very pattern that has been consternating the client. Thus, instead of helping with a solution, the therapist becomes part of the problem.

We once made a heroic but entirely misguided attempt to come to the aid of an undergraduate student who was flunking out of school. She was unquestionably bright, and she came from a politically important family. The school's advisors were sympathetic to her plight and granted her an additional semester to prove herself. Her instructors, too, all gave this likeable individual "incompletes," extra chances, and endless extensions. We assumed, as had everyone else, that this woman really *wanted* to stay in school. She said she did. However, no matter what was tried, she would drop the ball at the last minute. Her successes were accidental. In this case, we were initially blinded by our own definitions of life success, which, like those of her family, placed academic accomplishment high up in the list of noble causes. We confused her game with our own. Her older brother had been very successful in both school and the business world, and everyone had automatically assumed that she would follow a similar path. In any event, it slowly began to dawn on us that success in school was someone else's agenda—not hers. Furthermore, we had inadvertently joined the forces of those who made it difficult for other options to be heard and taken seriously.

After we got off the "we must help you finish school" bandwagon, we were able to help her identify what she really wanted to do. She decided to take an indefinite leave of absence from school, moved to another city, took an apartment with a roommate, and has been working for a number of years as a buyer for a clothing outlet. There is now some talk about her returning to complete a degree, but without the sense of high drama that accompanied her earlier educational foray.

GOAL FUSION

Although therapists inevitably have their own goals for clients, problems are created when there is a confusion—perhaps it would be better to say a fusion—between what a client wants and what the therapist expects or wants the client to want. Under these circumstances, the therapist begins to get the feeling that he or she is single-handedly dragging a reluctant individual to the shores of salvation. When the client does not seem to be picking up his or her share of the load, it is time to question whose goals are whose. Since clients often give lip service to reasonable-sounding goals—they even may initially think they are serious about them—it is easy to get confused. However, the rule of thumb is that live goals are those toward which people are discernibly moving, not those that are simply topics for prolonged and repetitive discussion.

Recently, a therapist in a clinic decided to train a male client to be more comfortable about being touched by other males. He was convinced that this would be advantageous to the client, so he proceeded to "desensitize" him by touching him in casual ways when he arrived and when they said goodbye. He would give him an occasional encouraging pat on the shoulder or a slap on the back. The client, of course, had no idea his reactions were being "shaped" by the therapist. Putting aside the question of whether these procedures were effective—we doubt that they were—we wonder on whose authority they were being employed? The therapist was "treating" a problem for which no actual contract existed. Occasionally a therapist may ask a client's permission to "do something behind his back" for purposes of demonstration or strategy. However, in our view, there must be some contractual legitimization for services being rendered if they are to be construed as psychotherapeutic.

It is in domains in which clients' values depart most sharply from commonly held beliefs that great courage is required for clients to notice and take responsibility for personal preferences. They don't have to advertise their desires on billboards, but they do need to take them into account and appreciate that they exist. To the extent that people distance themselves from their own "wants," they lose the opportunity for satisfaction and intimacy. Intimacy, of course, goes beyond sheer physical proximity. It consists of letting others know who you are—that is, what you want. If what they think you want has been fabricated, then others never get to know who you are, and their approval or acceptance cannot be self-satisfying. We all know how easy it is to be lonely in a crowd. On the other hand, true intimacy—letting your wants be known in the presence of others—is the antidote to loneliness. As Matthew Arnold said, "Resolve to be thyself: and know, that he who finds himself, loses his misery."

To assist the client in the domains in which relatively unpopular wants reside, the therapist must resist the strong temptations to (a) buy the client's disavowals of responsibility (which take every conceivable form), (b) misread the client's goals as being more logical or socially acceptable than they actually are, or (c) substitute personal goals for those of the client. Ironically, a therapist who is truly "on the job" with regard to these difficult issues may sometimes seem to be tolerating or perhaps even encouraging the continuation of pathological or foolhardy actions on the part of the client, rather than rushing to "change behavior." On the other hand, "changing behavior" often misses the point entirely, and produces only temporary, superficial, irrelevant, or unsatisfying outcomes. In fact, what some people consider changed behavior is, from the point of view of the establishment of meaning, merely the same old routines in new and improved guises.

SUMMARY

People are preference machines. Preferences arise out of people's operations as physical entities. All spheres of activity—including the abstract, the linguistic, and the intellectual—are founded on arational preferences. People do not choose their preferences, but learning what they are is a step toward making adequate provision for their being fulfilled. A therapy that doesn't acknowledge the centrality of preferences cannot succeed.

Emotions are bodily dispositions that undergird action. Love—the passion for living together in close proximity—is the fundamental emotion on which civilizations are founded and languages are developed. The opposite of love is not hate, but indifference—the willingness to drift apart.

Living is a process of valuing—making some things more important than others. Values are *real-ized* by being enacted in the community. A person operating hypocritically, with large pockets of "disclaimed action," cannot experience intimacy or self-satisfaction. As people's frameworks for living are expanded, they can find new ways to attain goals that had previously been disclaimed. Therapy creates a space in which people can listen to their own stories and can come to appreciate the unacknowledged wants and assumptions these stories contain.

CHAPTER 11

Therapy as Inquiry

Not all influential therapists began their careers as health care professionals. Carl Rogers studied for the ministry at Union Theological Seminary, Sigmund Freud began by conducting basic neurological research, Harvey Jackins was a labor organizer, Carl Jung had strong commitments to classical and religious studies, George Kelly was a speech teacher, Carl Whitaker was a gynecologist, David Epston was an anthropologist, and Jay Haley was in communications. The diversity of backgrounds perhaps accounts for the fact that, in addition to its official characterization as a mental health treatment, psychotherapy has sometimes been construed as personal education, moral or spiritual redemption, and social reform or correction (Orlinsky, 1989).

Of course, these models are not mutually exclusive—they blend into one another. Physicians educate, clergymen participate in social reform, truant officers moralize, and so on. Therapy as conversation unites all these concerns. A client comes in with particular complaints, but just beneath the surface are the fundamental existential questions: Who am I? Who are you? How should we interact? What does life mean? At one level, therapy is about getting free of the pain of living in emotional contradiction. However, resolving the contradiction requires inquiring into these larger questions.

The term psychotherapy was coined by combining "psyche" (mind) and "therapeia" (treatment) into a single word (*Oxford English Dictionary*, 1982). It was hoped that treatments for the mind would evolve to parallel those being used to heal the body. Unfortunately, when the term was invented, no such methods existed—the concept represented wishful thinking. Today, more than a hundred years later, such analogous treatments have yet to be devised. It is time to abandon the analogy altogether. Note that the term *patient*—when applied to individuals seeking psychotherapy—is doubly misleading. It not only implies that something "medical" is about to happen but, as George Kelly used to argue, also conjures up the inappropriate image of a passive human being waiting *patiently* to be cured by someone else's ministrations. Therapy, as conversation, isn't like that.

In our own work as therapists we accept the fact that therapy is not—and never will be—precisely like fixing broken or defective machinery. Therapy is primarily concerned with matters of morality and values, responsibility and ethics—patterns of living together. As such, it is a small aspect of a more inclusive ongoing social negotiation process. The participants—clients and therapists—do not operate in a vacuum. They represent not only themselves but also the larger "clubs"—families, subcultures, professional guilds, and philosophical schools of thought—in which the meaning of their actions is embedded (Rabkin, 1970).

THERAPY AS EDUCATION

In such matters, therapy is much like other forms of group or individual education. Education is an inculcation of values and beliefs, sponsored by people who wish to sustain and advance particular traditions. A curriculum is never objective or static—even if it appears to consist of nothing more "political" than algebra (Sampson, 1981). Furthermore, the dialectical process of teaching and learning leads to the continual revision and evolution of the sponsoring tradition. For us, therapy is a specialized form of education—an inquiry into how better living arrangements can be devised (Efran, Lukens, & Lukens, 1988b).

For whom can therapy—construed as inquiry—be useful? The answer is: practically everyone, but not for everything that ails them. Therapy will *not* necessarily free a schizophrenic of hallucinations, nor will it wipe out the biological distinctions that make an individual susceptible to bouts of manic-depression. Talking about life patterns is not going to *directly* alter the biochemistry of the diabetic or the autonomic system characteristics of the person with ulcers. On the other hand, each of these individuals might well profit from exploring his or her raison d'être and place in the community. Becoming clearer in these domains will, of course, impact secondarily on other facets of living, including blood sugar levels, autonomic system functioning, and the willingness to comply with drug regimens or other treatment procedures. Thus, the relevant question is not "Who can profit from psychotherapy?" but, instead, "What, realistically, can we expect psychotherapy to do for a person?"

Calling what we do "education" brings it down to earth and helps eliminate that misplaced aura of technocracy—scientism—that has too often cloaked the therapist's role, mystifying clients and their therapists alike. In therapy, clients and therapists pose questions to themselves and each other about the meaning of life and about their relationship to others in society. Clients come in for tutoring when their own inquiry process bogs down, when they weren't finding the answers they needed within the limited framework they were using. As therapist-educators, we teach, lead, explore, and influence. We help in the formulation of better questions that lead toward more productive and interesting answers. Good questions are those that generate additional options for living.

Conceiving of life as a fixed arrangement that must inexorably follow set rules from the past is antithetical to the therapeutic venture as we understand it. As Kelly puts it, the philosophical stance that underlies the therapist's craft is the notion that "whatever exists can be reconstrued" (1969, p. 227). Each reconstruction leads to different outcomes. "Some . . . may open fresh channels for a rich and productive life. Others may offer one no alternative save suicide" (p. 228).

A LABORATORY SETTING

As part of the services provided, the therapist helps the client establish a kind of research laboratory (including field sites) in which the implications of his or her life assumptions can be tested. In reputable laboratories, arrangements are made for keeping risks at acceptable levels. In a chemical lab, for example, such provisions take the form of goggles, aprons, gas hoods, insulated tongs, heat-resistant glassware, pressurized containers, and sprinkler systems. The equipment used and the procedures followed never eliminate risk altogether, but they reduce it substantially.

In therapy, too, precautions are taken. New alternatives are most apt to be explored if there are assurances that any resulting explosions can be satisfactorily contained. To achieve this aim, therapy sessions are partly insulated from larger life contexts and are conducted in accordance with a contract designed to help insure integrity of purpose. Opportunities are provided to test hypotheses in sheltered waters before they have to be implemented in potentially treacherous open seas. The therapist—an experienced guide – is on hand to help plan, monitor, and evaluate the progress of the experiments performed. The therapist helps spot loopholes and weaknesses in experimental design.

Although initial experimentation can take place in protected environments, people must ultimately test the usefulness of their discoveries and inventions out in the real world. They cannot know whether they can climb Mt. Everest if they just stay at home and read *National Geographic* articles about it. For example, teenagers who really want to know how their parents will react if they stay out beyond curfew must at some point stay out and see what happens. After all, parents will not necessarily back up their verbal threats. Furthermore, even parents do not know in advance how they will react to an actual transgression. Like the rest of us, they can only suppose how they will act, based on past experience. But a person cannot achieve satisfaction living a life of suppositions and hypotheticals. The questions worth asking are those tied directly to consequences.

Not all clients arrive with well-formulated or interesting questions in hand. In fact, much of the work of therapy is in reestablishing – in clients' experience – a connection between ostensibly isolated and free-floating "symptoms" and their life constructions, so that the inquiry process can proceed to a meaningful conclusion. Symptoms are not malignancies that attack from the outside but "urgent questions, behaviorally expressed, which have somehow lost the threads that lead either to answers or to better questions" (Kelly, 1969, p. 19). A therapist helps clients follow those threads, shedding light on linkages that have gone unnoticed. In a sense, a person can only be "cured" of a question when a satisfactory answer emerges or when the question itself merges into larger, more inclusive foci of concern. At that point, the original question no longer haunts the person.

A client we saw couldn't understand why he procrastinated about getting his work done. He had tried everything to get himself in gear – behavioral contracts, bets with others, inspirational audiotapes, self-help books, and so on – all to no avail. Yet, in other spheres of activity, such as working on his car or caring for his lawn, he was a bundle of energy and ambition. Why couldn't he transfer his enthusiasm from these areas into the work arena, he wondered. Procrastination was, for him, a mysterious curse – he didn't know where it came from. He didn't initially see that his system was trying to tell him something – namely, that he hated his work as an accountant but loved tinkering with automobiles and working in his garden. Although he complained about his inefficiency on the job, he did manage to meet firm deadlines; what didn't get done was the work that was more optional. Thus, he was successfully treading water but not advancing – a perfect arrangement for a person who wishes he were elsewhere. His circumstances, discussed in therapy, led to questions such as, "What would they have to pay you to make it truly worthwhile to continue doing what you dislike?" "What would life look like if you left accounting and took a job managing a garden supply shop, repairing cars at a service station, or running a paperback bookstore?"

Psychologist Dan Kiley, author of *The Peter Pan Syndrome*, recently went undercover and visited 115 professional "helpers" to see how they practiced. He made remarkable discoveries. For example, a male therapist attempted to seduce him, a female therapist exposed herself to him, several professionals prescribed medications hastily and needlessly, and still others seemed more concerned with the state of his finances than the state of his mental health. However, one therapist—whose counsel he found especially valuable—helped put him in touch with his need to explore some of life's larger questions. This led to major changes: He moved to another state, where he could be closer to nature, and he decided to spend more time writing and less time seeing private clients (Sifford, 1990). The "symptoms" he presumably reported to each of the therapists, for which some prescribed major tranquilizers or advised complex personality overhauls, related to unresolved value issues. As with the procrastinator, when such questions have been successfully identified and answered, "symptoms" of emotional disturbance are often transformed into ordinary choices.

SIMPLICITY

Important questions are not necessarily complicated, although they are often housed in a framework that prevents satisfactory answers from emerging. Some therapists are experts at making even commonplace issues sound convoluted. They seem to prefer elaborate formulations and interventions to simple ones. (Raise a simple question with them and you get a pageant.) On the contrary, we want to keep things as basic as possible—following the "law of parsimony" (Efran, Lukens, & Lukens, 1988a). We don't believe that good living requires a Ph.D. or that high-priced experts need to be consulted at every turn in the road.

In an overly rationalized and intellectualized society such as our own, there is a tendency to *explain* life using fancier concepts than those we use to *live* it. It is important that our analyses not become so heady that they lose their connection with experience. Therapists can become so engrossed in listening with the "third ear" that they neglect to make use of the first two. Everyday emotional contradictions are not necessarily best understood in terms of deviously operating unconscious mechanisms or internal mind entities continually vying for control. In this regard, we recall the admonition of a former instructor—a social worker by training—who wisely reminded us that psychologists and psychiatrists can get so preoccupied with their studies of the superego and the id that they forget how to say "hello."

PERMISSION TO POUND

Obviously, therapeutic dialogue differs in significant ways from what typically goes on in social conversations. Otherwise, why write special books about it? A primary function of therapy is to break up patterns of activity (including thinking) that aren't readily challenged in other contexts. Objectivity is continually being converted to "objectivity" in quotation marks. In the service of doing this, conversational gambits that would be considered impolite or rudely asymmetrical in other social settings are licensed by the therapy contract.

The therapeutic contract—like the implicit contract between a coach and an athlete—prevents the therapist from being seen as intrusive, adversarial, or sadistic. It enables the client to tolerate and make proper use of the battering of assumptions that needs to take place. Of course, a client continually pounded can still feel as if he or she is being beaten up. On the other hand, too much sympathy keeps unproductive assumptions intact. Artful therapists therefore create and maintain a climate of love in which a modicum of friendly pounding is acceptable and, later, appreciated.

A couple came to see us because the wife had had an affair. Although it was over, it had left behind a wake of resentment and distrust. At one point, the husband threatened to do bodily harm to his wife's lover, and the wife, for her part, justified the affair on the basis of her husband's insensitivity to her needs. Both spouses arrived with strong but implicit assumptions about life and marriage. However, they were also willing to put their assumptions aside long enough to reexamine them. The attitudes they held in common included that (a) affairs don't happen unless something is wrong in a marriage; (b) the rate of sex in a healthy marriage is relatively constant over time; (c) the only reasonable reaction of a husband toward the "other man" is one of anger and hatred; (d) if the affair hadn't happened, the marital relationship would be healthier or at least easier to repair; and (e) complete forgiveness, with the reestablishment of full trust, would be virtually impossible to achieve.

As therapists with "objectivity" in quotation marks, we did not accept any of these assumptions as either factual or immutable. As we've said, such discrepancies between the starting points of therapist and client are what makes therapy a potentially productive (and exciting) venture. However, clients must sense that the therapist's commitment is not simply to undermine or invalidate their starting positions—but to help them enlarge the framework within which these positions can be examined and evaluated. (The goal isn't to pound the client into oblivion, but to hammer out a larger conceptual context.)

In this instance, we invited the husband and wife—separately—to explore alternatives to each of the stated assumptions (as well as some minor beliefs nested within the larger conceptions). Therapy, as we practice it, is a series of such invitations. In this case, we listened to bits of the husband's and the wife's narratives. Based on what we heard, we were able to visualize the kinds of allegations that must have been flying back and forth in their household. In the preceding months, the couple's relationship had indeed been punctuated by what Maturana describes as conversations of "recrimination, accusation, and characterization"—an unholy triumvirate that arises when "objectivity" cannot be kept firmly in quotation marks (Mendez, Coddou, & Maturana, 1988). These are manifestations of the process whereby people find ever more ingenious ways to make themselves and each other "wrong" in life.

However, this couple obviously had strong bonds with one another, and both the wife and the husband wanted to "conserve" the positive aspects of their relationship. These factors allowed us to go quickly to the heart of the matter. We suggested that they contemplate throwing away the rule book upon which their marriage had thus far been based and "make up" some new rules that might work better for them. After all, there was nothing sacrosanct about the particular set of assumptions with which they started—except that they were traditional. In the several joint and individual sessions that followed, the focus was almost entirely on what each of them really wanted out of life—both as individuals and in the context of the relationship. Primary importances were separated from secondary distractions. When people—such as this husband and wife—are clearer about what is really important to them, they are less apt to become preoccupied with finding fault, casting blame, or occupying the victim role to justify what they didn't get.

TRADING GAME PLANS

This couple was able to take hold of the idea that they could let go of one game plan (a set of distinctions that wasn't working well) in favor of another. They saw that they had the authority to play by new rules. In the new, experimental context they created for themselves, the wife forgave her husband for being, perhaps by nature, a somewhat insensitive "dolt." She accepted the possibility that he would *forever* have to be reminded to send flowers or to pick his clothes up off the floor. She decided he was worth living with anyway. He, in turn, was willing to forgive her for having been involved in an affair. He realized that she still loved him and very much wanted their marriage to go forward. They both realized that their situation was not that unusual. Statistics make it clear that neighbors up and down the block have also had extramarital relations, often without anyone else knowing about it. In many cases, marriages are destroyed by infidelities; in other cases, the marital union is unaffected or may even be strengthened.

Personally, we do not condone violating marriage vows, and we do not take instances of infidelity lightly. Subterfuge is a hazardous policy, and living with broken agreements invalidates both oneself and others. However, it is a mistake to underestimate people's ability to surmount apparently detrimental circumstances and generate something new and unexpected out of adversity. Furthermore, people say all sorts of things that, when push comes to shove, they don't mean. (Sometimes they didn't know they didn't mean it.) Life changes, and opinions change. For example, many spouses steadfastly assert that if their mate were to commit even a single infidelity it would spell the end of their relationship. However, when such an event actually occurs, they may be quite willing to forgive and begin again.

It would be better if people were a little more tentative when they make such pronouncements about themselves. That way, they would less often have to eat humble pie when their self-predictions don't pan out. It is particularly sad and ironic when, for example, a man goes on and on about how he wouldn't put up with a wife who was unfaithful, when everyone else in the room knows that his wife has been sleeping around behind his back for years. We know so little about ourselves that our stance should be one of continual curiosity and discovery rather than of doctrinaire pronouncement. In discussions about oneself and the future, the expression "we shall see" ought to be used more often.

Notice that in the case we reported, the therapist wasn't interested in modifying a specific behavioral pattern or dispelling an errant thought pattern. The couple was not being advised to set up behavioral contracts with each other, to keep charts, or to work at improving their communication skills.[1] There was little emphasis on tracing their assumptive structure back to family-of-origin patterns. (A person is responsible for his or her

[1]Therapists theorize about the value of "open" communication, but communication between spouses can also be "too open" for anyone's good. People need permission to have personal spaces for fantasies, daydreams, and secrets. Moreover, spouses who say they "aren't communicating" often know all too well what their partners are thinking. When they say they "can't communicate," they mean they don't know how to change what the other person thinks or does.

assumptions, regardless of where they came from or who else does or doesn't support them.) The therapeutic conversation took the form of a series of *invitations* to each individual to spend a bit of time in a *different* frame of reference—to base life on alternative distinctions. These premises are broader in scope, thereby permitting problems that loomed large from the old perspective to be downsized into petty annoyances in the new purview. Notice, also, that these options would not easily emerge out of the conversations a person might have had with his or her usual associates. One of the values of therapy as conversation is that some of the ordinary "club" rules can be temporarily suspended. Therapy is an opportunity to be pried loose from the constraints imposed by local ordinances.

In our experience, handling bigger questions results in smaller questions disappearing automatically. When you have begun to figure out who you are in life, issues about who will take the garbage out or who will drive the kids to soccer practice pale into relative insignificance. Therefore, as therapists, we reach for the largest frame we can manage. As clients tell their stories, we continually ask ourselves: What is the overall presupposition that must be in place for this sort of tale to be produced and taken seriously? We then try to reveal the dimensions of that frame from the vantage point of a still larger context.

A woman we saw was concerned about how to get her husband to show up at work on time. He was constantly late and she feared that this would cost him his job, or at least a promotion. To deal with this at the level of concrete behaviors would—in our opinion—miss the boat. Buying a louder alarm clock, contracting to have him retire earlier or be roused at the right time by someone in the family—such immediate solutions fail to come to grips with the essentials of the problem. As Kelly asserted, behavior is man's way of asking questions of the universe. Thus, the goal is to clarify the question, not to banish the behaviors that make it visible.

In this case, for example, a relevant question might be: What support did this husband agree to provide for his family when he got married? Is he fulfilling those contractual agreements? For what or for whom does he work? What will his contribution to society be? What does he want his life to represent? Instead of attending to specific behaviors, the focus shifts to larger frameworks of meaning. In our view, oversleeping isn't necessarily a maladaptive behavior in need of elimination. It is a ramification of a particular set of values and commitments. It may, for example, be a muted protest against a contract the person didn't want to sign in the first place and has no intention of fully honoring. (In this case, the couple got married because the wife was pregnant—not because they were ready to have a family.) Once such matters are examined, arranging wake-up calls or buying alarm clocks turns out to be a secondary consideration. As one client said, when asked by a friend to explain why he found therapy valuable, "My therapist *forces* me to think clearly about who I am and what I want."

SMALLER QUESTIONS

The first couple we described made the therapist's job comparatively easy. They had good questions and were willing to explore alternatives courageously. Some clients have something quite different in mind when they arrive at the therapist's office. They are not interested in examining frames of reference—they want a pill for the pain, they want somebody to pay for what was done to them, they want to stall for time, they want an ally in a battle, or they want to stave off loneliness. Such clients are not "resisting" treatment—they are simply pursuing their own goals as they construe them. They have every right to see if the therapist can be used in those ways. However, if the therapist accepts these alternative contracts or fails to recognize that there may be a mismatch of goals, the "therapy" will be stalemated.

One reason so-called "borderline" clients have garnered an unsavory reputation in some circles is that they often succeed, at least initially, in hoodwinking therapists into presuming that a proper therapy contract has been negotiated when, in fact, it has not. The therapist may be busy "exploring," but the client is, instead, merely proving a point or invalidating a stance. Therapists can thoroughly accept—and enjoy—"borderline" individuals—provided they distinguish an actual commitment to inquiry from look-alike pursuits. One of the tests is that in genuine inquiry outcomes aren't preordained—it is neither about finding individuals guilty nor exonerating them from blame.

As therapists, we hope to entice those without much "research experience" to join us in an inquiry process. In the classroom, the teacher may arouse sufficient curiosity so that students are temporarily willing to give up their single-minded concern with earning high grades or finessing difficult assignments. Similarly, the therapist raises sufficiently intriguing questions to induce clients to do something other than playing out their repetitive scripting. As one client—who had previously seen other therapists—put it, "Now, *this* is something else again."

LETTING GO OF CONCEPTS

Inquiry demands that the questioner temporarily let go of a concept. By definition, all concepts—even good ones—are hostile to changing experience. A concept, as long as it is in use, demands allegiance to itself.

Experiences that do not fit must be reshaped, discounted, or ignored. For example, a boyfriend who doesn't call when he is supposed to is forced—if he values the relationship—to explain away his negligence. He must convince his girlfriend that her concepts about him were not in error. He must pretend to be what he is not. Yet, what would ultimately improve the relationship would be a willingness to draft new concepts to encompass their experience of each other, rather than having to continually force-fit their experience into preconceived and narrow conceptual frameworks. The tragedy is that in the relationship model they are applying—even if they should stay together and marry—he is apt to be making excuses for not calling year in and year out, while she will be repeatedly obliged to pretend that she believes him "this particular time." They become prisoners of a conceptual framework that prevents them from relaxing into who they are. However, to escape that framework, they must risk facing the unknown. Clients are in that same predicament. The therapist helps them see that the risks might be worth taking.

INDIVIDUALS VERSUS SYSTEMS

Invitations to inquiry are posed by therapists to individuals—not groups. In many cases, such as with the couple we described above, joint meetings may be useful. However, every person who is present at such a meeting has the right to decide individually which invitations to accept or reject. Only individuals have ears and mouths—couples, family systems, and social organizations do not speak and do not hear. Social organizations do not take action—people do. Social groups are composites of the actions of their constituent members. One asserts one's membership in an organization by acting the way its members act (Maturana, 1980).

When members of an organization act differently, the organization changes. As Maturana states, authority is always created by concession—it isn't imposed from the outside. Even a direct act of oppression requires two interlocking components—someone willing to do the oppressing and someone willing (for whatever reasons) to play the role of victim.

We bring up the issue of the relationship between groups and group members because sometimes therapists—especially those espousing family and system approaches—adopt a reified view of system functioning. They talk as if certain "powers" resided in a system, apart from the combined preferences and behaviors of the people who are the component parts. Although the whole may indeed be greater than the sum of the parts, it has no greater "power" than those parts.

A corps de ballet creates effects that may be more dazzling than those that could be created by individual dancers operating alone. However, the choreography only goes forward because each dancer is willing to play out his or her assigned role. If any dancer falls, forgets, or rebels, a changed choreography results. In that sense, every dancer has the "power" to revise the dance. Similarly, a fox may be said to play an important role in balancing an ecological system. However, the ecological perspective is an observer's purview—the fox is unaware that it has an ecological function to fulfill. It eats rabbits because it has a taste for them—not to help keep nature in balance or to keep the ecologist happy. A die thrown upon a table is *not* forced to abide by the laws of chance. On the contrary, the die, by how it lands, helps establish what we—as observers—will declare the laws of chance to be.

WHY BOTHER?

A teacher can lecture to an entire classroom, and a family therapist may elect to meet with many members of the same family at once. However, each individual in the classroom is learning something different, and each client at a family meeting is pursuing an individual agenda. The analysis is complicated because everyone is together—each interaction can therefore trigger multiple responses—but the basic principle is unchanged. Each person is on his or her own therapeutic journey.

As we have already suggested in earlier chapters, neither classroom dialogue nor therapeutic interaction consists of a simple transmittal of information from one person to another. Information is not like a grocery-store commodity that can be stored, brought up from a stockroom when needed, and delivered intact to a waiting customer. People hear what they are ready to hear—in the way they are ready to hear it. Each person in the room hears something different, and each proceeds at a unique pace. A behavior therapist gives an unassertive client an assignment intended to encourage independent action; this particular client, in carrying out the assignment, engages in one more dutiful act of compliance with an authority figure. Thus, in this instance, the lesson taught was definitely not the lesson learned.

Since therapy is a participatory process, a therapist cannot repeat a session or even an intervention. In a sense, every session involves a different—changed—client. Similarities drawn between sessions, moments, or clients are language simplifications. So, too, are attempts to identify which link in the chain of events was critical in producing a given change (itself an arbitrary punctuation). Every act identified as indispensable was preceded by some other act, which can also be said to have been essential. All this complexity has caused some therapists to throw up their hands and say, "Why bother?"

Why formulate plans? Why think about the details of a case? Why consider using one strategy of intervention rather than another? Why not just sit back and do nothing in particular? This laissez-faire policy has been considered by some to be the embodiment of an enlightened approach to therapy, in which "information," "influence," and "power" are eschewed (see, e.g., the debate between Hoffman, 1985, 1988b, and Golann, 1988a, 1988b). Some therapists working in this mode refuse to voice their opinions; they may even deny that they have any. They don't take stands, give definite assignments, or make specific predictions. By being passive and "neutral," they believe they are respecting the autonomy of a living system or a family system. They have convinced themselves that "objectivity" in quotation marks requires a dispassionate approach. Since nothing can be proven objectively correct, why assert the value of one position over another?

This reminds us of the apocryphal college sophomore who, after hearing in an introductory philosophy course that free will doesn't exist, decides to sit and do nothing for the rest of his life. Of course, his friend—an "A" student—hastens to point out to him that "doing nothing" would require exercising as much "free will" as any other option. Moreover, when the two get invited to join the crowd for a beer at a nearby pub, the "sit and do nothing" plan quickly fades into oblivion—free will or no free will. Similarly, theoretical assertions that systems are (and always have been) autonomous entities doesn't imply that one should treat them any more gingerly than one did before recognizing that fact.

The autonomy of the organism is actual and potent—it doesn't require that therapists be still or remain neutral. Therapists can even continue to have plans and make predictions—they just cannot anticipate that everything will work out as expected.

THE ILLUSION OF NEUTRALITY

To the structure determinist, true neutrality is an illusion. It is neither desirable nor possible. As nondirective therapists learned years ago, you cannot be in the presence of another individual and avoid potentially biasing the proceedings in one direction or another. When you withhold your opinions, people begin to read more subtle cues—they watch for a shift in position, a change in facial expression, a sigh, or a break in breathing pattern. In the terminology of communication theory, you cannot *not* communicate (Watzlawick, Beavin, & Jackson, 1967). There is nothing in life but opinion—points of view—including the opinion that neutrality is desirable. Putting "objectivity" in quotation marks destroys the last shred of justification for the neutral defense. Everything said or done by the therapist represents personal preference, not objective necessity. Even if a therapist were to claim that he or she was simply doing what the canons of the profession demanded, he or she would still be accountable for upholding such traditions rather than working for their demise.

Neither the therapy enterprise as a whole nor any action within it can be justified as ultimately correct. Therapists practice because it is what they want to do and because others are willing to let them. A client of ours once asked, "What is therapy supposed to be?" The crisp answer to that question is, "Whatever the client and therapist decide to make of it." In this particular instance, the client was asked to glance around the room and describe what he saw. He described himself, the therapist, and the various accoutrements of the room—rug, desk, chairs, books, and so on. No "therapy" was to be found anywhere in the room. Thus, credits or complaints about what had transpired—or might soon transpire—would have to be attributed to either the client, the therapist, or the interior decorating. This was our way of illustrating to him that therapy is just a label for whatever he and his therapist decided to do together.

In a chapter cleverly titled "You can't go far in neutral" Paul Wachtel (1987) argues that the false attachment to neutrality has been a fundamental liability of the analytic approach. Putting theoretical differences aside altogether, it may be that the main practical distinction between the newer therapies and traditional analysis is the willingness of therapists from the newer schools to jump in with both feet, urging clients to take definite actions.

Of course, not all analysts fit the stereotypical "blank screen" image. One psychoanalyst with a reputation as a superb clinical instructor and an effective clinician frequently surprised his students by always being on the move, keeping people slightly off balance with ingenious probes. On one occasion, he began modeling an animal out of clay and handing a lump of the clay to a reputedly uncommunicative psychotic client, with the instruction, "Make a leg." That gave them a shared project and quickly opened a channel of communication between them. On another occasion, working with a client who had difficulty expressing his ambivalence toward his father, he took a shiny half dollar out of his pocket, rubbed it between his fingers, and then asked the client if he would like to have it. This psychoanalyst never telegraphed where he was going next, but his methods continually forced both students and clients to think about who they were and what they were doing.

Clients *want* to be confronted, chided, shown startling demonstrations, and introduced to bold new conceptualizations and formulations. This is also what we, as therapists, want to do with them. Because clients (like all living systems) are conservative, they need others to break their usual patterns and help stir the conceptual and experiential pot. Clients may not know in advance exactly what they will need—nor do we. Neither of us could sit down and write out a precise recipe for how the dialogue should go. If we could, the process would probably be unnecessary, and it certainly wouldn't be very exciting. However, when clients and therapists actively pursue questions, try out plans, and devise new methods, they gradually discover what works for them. Traditions of studied neutrality or reverent worship at the altar of system autonomy need to be replaced by a commitment to the spirit of vigorous debate.

Family therapists have often championed a kind of "neutrality" because they so frequently find themselves amidst swirling family controversies. In those situations, it seems the better part of valor to stand clear of the fray and avoid taking sides. However, those are precisely the situations in which it might have been better to avoid seeing the family together in the first place. This is heresy in some circles. Some family therapists define themselves in terms of the penchant for seeing everyone at the same time. However, what was originally a theoretical breakthrough—and is sometimes a good idea—has deteriorated into just another professional shibboleth. In our view, there is no point convening a group if their being together merely perpetuates defensiveness and fighting. Sometimes you have to get people far enough away from their cohorts in order to generate room for them to think independently. Again, the notion that the family "is a system" gets in the way. The United States is a system, but helping a few citizens doesn't necessitate seeing them all.

From our perspective, some family therapists work at cross purposes. Many of the methods they have invented over the years might best be construed as "loosening" techniques (Kelly, 1955) that help therapists as well as clients gain new perspectives. (These methods include allowing long time periods between visits, inviting suggestions from observers behind a one-way mirror, handing family members written messages, changing team compositions, and periodically bringing in new co-therapists.) All such approaches serve to shake up expectations, increasing the possibility of orthogonal interaction. On the other hand, if therapists insist on always treating the family as a unit, they limit the possibility of individuals' escaping their "club" roles long enough to play with other alternatives.

In working with families, it is often necessary for the therapist to support one family member's conception over another, even if this means taking sides. This is no different from what labor mediators do in negotiating contracts. Although they are not employed by either side, they frequently tell participants from both sides (behind the scenes) which of their strategies are apt to make sense and which demands they should consider modifying. They may also make proposals of their own. When this is done in the interest of moving the parties toward settlement, the mediator who makes specific suggestions does not necessarily lose credibility or sacrifice the good will of the participants. Clients are often willing to be called wrong. They are even able to tolerate a certain amount of unavoidable loss of face if they are convinced it is in the service of a worthwhile cause. Therapists need not be shy about venturing opinions and suggesting options. They must also be willing to make mistakes and to be wrong. An Adlerian once shared with us the following story: Word got back to Adler, through a colleague, that a former client was angry with him in connection with something he had suggested to her. He told his colleague to remind the client, "Dr. Adler always reserves the right to be wrong."

INTERCHANGEABLE THERAPISTS

The illusion that there are objective treatments that can be described in psychotherapy "shop manuals" has dissuaded some clients from shopping for a therapist who might truly suit their purposes. They think of therapies and therapists as basically interchangeable, except for relatively minor differences in experience, competence, or "bedside manner." Thus they go about picking a therapist the way they might choose a physician, lawyer, or real estate agent. They fail to appreciate that the essence of therapy is the match between client and therapist, not the therapist's technical competence in applying set procedures. Choosing a therapist is more like choosing a coach, an art teacher, or a research co-investigator. It should be more widely recognized that not all client-therapist pairings will adopt similar goals or choose similar routes to achieve them.

A person who says, "I've tried therapy and it didn't help me," is subscribing to a version of the uniformity myth (Kiesler, 1966)—that therapy with one person is just like therapy with another. Rejecting therapy because you tried it once is like denouncing education because you once took a boring course. Also, it is inadvisable to base the choice of a teacher or conversational partner strictly on the diplomas the person possesses or on recommendations of local medical or mental health groups. (A friend's recommendation might prove more helpful, but the adequacy of the "fit" still needs to be tested directly.) A certain amount of trial and error is therefore practically inevitable. In that sense, selecting a therapist is more like dating than people generally like to admit.

SOLIDIFYING THE CONTRACT

After an initial session with our own clients, we frequently ask them to go home and think over what took place. If, within the next few days, they experience perceptible improvement—the fog starts to lift, life becomes more interesting, or they feel that they "clicked" with us—then they should consider making another appointment. If, however, life seems just as dreary or distressing as before, then perhaps they would be better off seeking help elsewhere. We want clients to assess this issue for themselves when they are out of our presence, so that they aren't overly swayed by the demands of the immediate social situation. Furthermore, we take some pains to establish our willingness to have the person look elsewhere—the issue of fit takes precedence over the possibility of bruised egos, lost finances, or logistic complications. If the fit is right, everything else can usually be worked out. If it isn't, everything else may prove irrelevant.

In our view, progress (and improvement) ought to be sensed from the outset. A student returning from the initial session of a class ought to say to himself or herself, "I can already tell that it's going to be an exciting semester." Likewise, our clients ought to leave that first session having at least glimpsed new possibilities. If the session went well, a different spin will have been put on an old set of problems. In the interests of getting a basic fix on the therapeutic question, we are willing to postpone gathering all the details about symptom duration, family history, and Blue Cross numbers. These matters can wait a bit; beginning the formulation of a viable therapeutic question cannot.

For this reason, we object to those lengthy and routine clinic intake procedures that keep individuals endlessly treading water. By the time therapy gets underway, the energy that generated the contact may have long since dissipated. Many individuals who call or who come in to seek services are so turned off by the intake procedures that they never get any further. Intake procedures must be carefully structured so that they communicate something other than bureaucratic indifference.

TRIVIAL AND NONTRIVIAL MACHINES

Part of the confusion about whether to be active or passive, neutral or opinionated, planful or spontaneous, derives from a fundamental misunderstanding about the distinction between trivial and nontrivial systems. A trivial machine—like a computer—repeats the same sequence with absolute predictability. In its operation, it follows the "garbage in—garbage out" principle. It does exactly what it is told—no more, no less. However, nontrivial systems—such as human beings—are never fully predictable. What comes out may bear very little resemblance to what went in. Sometimes garbage goes in and gems come out, and sometimes it is the other way around. For a nontrivial system, the future is never just the past with some more time added. There is always the possibility of transcendence. In the hands of human beings, language always creates new and different possibilities, the implications of which can never be fully anticipated in advance.

However, nontrivial machines can always be *considered* to be trivial machines for purposes of prediction and production. This is a simplification, to be sure, but it is a useful and permissible strategy. Thus, even though everyone recognizes that no two students are alike, an instructor chooses one textbook for the entire class. Not every student will read the book in the same way, and some will sell their copies back to the bookstore the moment finals are over. However, the instructor, to be practical, has to play the percentages. In picking this text, he or she assumes that a larger number of students will resonate to it than to the other texts that were being considered.

We are sufficiently similar to one another (in structure and experience) so that crude guesses can be made about how people will respond to a given situation. These are just hunches, and in particular cases they will prove to be way off base. However, one has to begin somewhere. Structure determinism reminds us to remain experimentalists. We must be "two-headed"—we plan and predict but are not surprised when predictions go awry and plans need to be updated. Good scientists design experiments and apply for grants, but they also know that their most important discoveries are apt to occur when they least expect it. They need to be ready to shift gears and take advantage of serendipitous events. Therapy, like team research, is a form of brainstorming—it involves full, vital participation in an evolving conversation that is only partly predictable.

TWO CRITICAL MISCONCEPTIONS

Clients and therapists are responsible for perpetuating two misconceptions that adversely affect their own health and welfare. The first forms the foundation for many clients' complaints. It is the notion that each client is special and has special entitlements. Clients often act as if life had made them certain promises that now aren't being honored. They feel shortchanged. As David Reynolds, a leading American proponent of Japanese Naikan therapy, has said, "I have never seen a neurotic person who was full of gratitude" (Reed, 1986). The stance of being special and entitled works against the achievement of personal responsibility and self-satisfaction. Responsible people understand that they have created their own expectations and obligations—the world doesn't owe them anything.

The second misconception, promulgated mainly by mental health professionals themselves, is that therapy is a "treatment." By fostering this illusion, professionals create conundrums in which they and their clients become ensnared. Psychotherapy—and we wish the name could be changed to something less misleading—is a unique conversational process. As a treatment, it falls flat on its face. As a context in which to devise and test better ways to live, it can work very well indeed.

THE MEANING OF PSYCHOTHERAPY

In therapy, two or more individuals meet and form a novel coupling that enables them to carve out new distinctions. In the process, as we have noted, they breathe life into alternatives that had no previous existence. At its best, psychotherapy begins with a particular "glitch" in a client's life and moves toward redefining and expanding the possibilities of living. That's what can make it an exciting and enriching endeavor for clients and therapists alike.

References

REFERENCES

Ackerly, G. D., Burnell, J., Holder, D. C., & Kurdek, L. A. (1988). Burnout among licensed psychologists. *Professional Psychology: Research and Practice, 19*, 624–631.

Adler, A. (1930). *The education of children*. London: George Allen & Unwin.

Akillas, E., & Efran, J. S. (1989). Internal conflict, language and metaphor: Implications for psychotherapy. *Journal of Contemporary Psychotherapy, 19*, 149–159.

Alloy, L. B., & Abramson, L. Y. (1979). Judgement of contingency in depressed and nondepressed students: Sadder but wiser? *Journal of Experimental Psychology: General, 108*, 441–485.

American Psychiatric Association (T. B. Karasu, Chairperson). (1989). *Treatments of psychiatric disorders: A task force report of the American Psychiatric Association* (Vols. 1–3). Washington, DC: American Psychiatric Association.

American Psychological Association. (1982). *Report of the task force on the evaluation of education, training, and service in psychology*. Washington, DC: Author.

Arond, M., & Pauker, S. (1987). *The first year of marriage: What to expect, what to accept, and what you can change*. New York: Warner Books.

Atkinson, R. (1989). *The long gray line*. New York: Houghton Mifflin.

Bach, R. (1977). *Illusions: The adventures of a reluctant messiah*. New York: Delacorte Press (Creatures Enterprises, Inc.).

Bales, J. (1988). The advocates: NAMI grows in size, impact. *APA Monitor, 19*(3), 8.

Bandura, A. (1978). The self system in reciprocal determinism. *American Psychologist, 33*, 344–358.

Barker, L. M., Best, M. R., & Domjan, M. (Eds.). (1977). *Learning mechanisms in food selection*. Waco, TX: Baylor University Press.

Barnett, P. A., & Gotlib, I. H. (1988). Psychosocial functioning and depression: Distinguishing among antecedents, concomitants, and consequences. *Psychological Bulletin, 104*, 97–126.

Bateson, G. (1972). *Steps to an ecology of mind*. New York: Ballantine Books.

Bateson, G. (1979). *Mind and nature: A necessary unity*. New York: E. P. Dutton.

Bayer, R. (1990). Psychiatry, psychoanalysis, and the status of homosexuality. [Review of *Male homosexuality: A contemporary psychoanalytic perspective*]. *Contemporary Psychology, 35*, 12–13.

Bergner, R. M. (1988). Status dynamic psychotherapy with depressed individuals. *Psychotherapy, 25*, 266–272.

Berk, S. N., & Efran, J. S. (1983). Some recent developments in the treatment of neurosis. In C. E. Walker (Ed.), *Handbook of clinical psychology* (Vol. 2, pp. 531–562). Homewood, IL: Dow Jones-Irwin.

Berman, J. S., & Norton, N. C. (1985). Does professional training make a therapist more effective? *Psychological Bulletin, 98*, 401–407.

Bernard, C. (1927). *An introduction to the study of experimental medicine*. New York: Henry Schuman. (Original work published 1865)

Bogdan, J. (1986). Do families really need problems? *The Family Therapy Networker, 10*(4), 30–35, 67–69.

Breger, L., & McGaugh, J. L. (1965). Critique and reformulation of "learning-theory" approaches to psychotherapy and neurosis. *Psychological Bulletin, 63*, 338–358.

Breger, L., & McGaugh, J. L. (1966). Learning theory and behavior therapy: A reply to Rachman & Eysenck. *Psychological Bulletin, 65*, 170–173.

Brilliant, A. (1979). *I may not be totally perfect, but parts of me are excellent*. Santa Barbara, CA: Woodbridge Press.

Brown, G. S. (1972). *Laws of form*. New York: Julian Press.

Bruner, J. (1986). *Actual minds, possible worlds*. Cambridge, MA: Harvard University.

Buie, J. (1989). Psychologist prevails despite schizophrenia. *APA Monitor, 20*(10), 23.

Bunge, M., & Ardila, R. (1987). *Philosophy of psychology*. New York: Springer-Verlag.

Campbell, J. (1949). *The hero with a thousand faces*. Princeton, NJ: Princeton University Press.

Camus, A. (1946). *The stranger*. New York: Knopf.

Capra, F. (1976). *The Tao of physics*. Berkeley, CA: Shambhala Publishers.

Carpenter, M. (1990, January 19). Debating "boot camps" for inmates. *The Philadelphia Inquirer*, p. B4.

Carson, R. C. (1990). Needed: A new beginning. [Review of *Diagnosis and classification in psychiatry: A critical appraisal of DSM-III*]. *Contemporary Psychology, 35*, 11–12.

Costello, C. G. (1963). Behavior therapy: Criticisms and confusion. *Behaviour Research and Therapy, 1*, 159–161.

Cowen, E. L. (1982). Help is where you find it: Four informal helping groups. *American Psychologist, 37*, 385–395.

Coyne, J. C. (1982). A critique of cognitions as causal entities with particular reference to depression. *Cognitive Therapy and Research, 6*, 3–13.

Coyne, J. C. (1989). Thinking postcognitively about depression. In A. Freeman, K. M. Simon, L. E. Beutler, & H. Arkowitz (Eds.), *Comprehensive handbook of cognitive therapy* (pp. 227–244). New York: Plenum.

Cummings, N. A. (1979). Turning bread into stones: Our modern antimiracle. *American Psychologist, 34*, 1119–1129.

Dance, K. A., & Neufeld, R. W. J. (1988). Aptitude-treatment interaction research in the clinical setting. A review of attempts to dispel the "patient uniformity" myth. *Psychological Bulletin, 104*, 192–213.

Dannenberg, L. (1976, September). The amazing job club. *Family Circle*, pp. 41–44.

de Rivera, J. (1977). *A structural theory of the emotions*. New York: International Universities Press.

Dell, P. F. (1982a). Beyond homeostasis: Toward a concept of coherence. *Family Process, 21*, 21–41.

Dell, P. F. (1982b). Family theory and the epistemology of Humberto Maturana. *The Family Therapy Networker, 6*(4), pp. 26, 39, 40, 41.

Dell, P. F. (1985). Understanding Bateson and Maturana: Toward a biological foundation for the social sciences. *Journal of Marital and Family Therapy*, *11*, 1–20.

Dohr, K. B., Rush, A. J., & Bernstein, I. H. (1989). Cognitive biases and depression. *Journal of Abnormal Psychology*, *98*, 63–67.

Dollard, J., & Miller, N. E. (1950). *Personality and psychotherapy: An analysis in terms of learning, thinking, and culture*. New York: McGraw-Hill.

Durkin, J. E. (1981). *Living groups: Group psychotherapy and general system theory*. New York: Brunner/Mazel.

Durlak, J. A. (1979). Comparative effectiveness of paraprofessional and professional helpers. *Psychological Bulletin*, *86*, 80–92.

Efran, J. S., & Caputo, G. C. (1984). Paradox in psychotherapy: A cybernetic perspective. *Journal of Behavior Therapy and Experimental Psychology*, *15*, 235–240.

Efran, J. S., Chorney, R. L., Ascher, L. M., & Lukens, M. D. (1989). Coping styles, paradox, and the cold pressor task. *Journal of Behavioral Medicine*, *12*, 91–103.

Efran, J. S., Germer, C. K., & Lukens, M. D. (1986). Contextualism and psychotherapy. In R. L. Rosnow & M. Georgoudi (Eds.), *Contextualism and understanding in the behavioral sciences: Implications for research and theory* (pp. 169–186). New York: Praeger.

Efran, J. S., Heffner, K. P., & Lukens, R. J. (1987). Alcoholism as an opinion: Structure determinism applied to drinking. *Alcoholism Treatment Quarterly*, *4*(3), 67–85.

Efran, J. S., & Lukens, M. D. (1985). The world according to Humberto Maturana. *The Family Therapy Networker*, *9*(3), 23–25, 27–28, 72–75.

Efran, J. S., Lukens, M. D., & Lukens, R. J. (1986). It's all done with mirrors: Some reflections on the Forum. *The Family Therapy Networker*, *10*(2), 41–43, 47–49.

Efran, J. S., & Lukens, R. J. (1986). The quest for causes: What the constructivists are saying about us these days. *The Family Therapy Networker*, *10*(6), 65–68.

Efran, J. S., Lukens, M. D., & Lukens, R. J. (1988a). Cultivating simple-mindedness: An antidote for complexity. *The Family Therapy Networker*, *12*(2), 17–18.

Efran, J. S., Lukens, R. J., & Lukens, M. D. (1988b). Constructivism: What's in it for you. *The Family Therapy Networker*, *12*(5), 27–35.

Efran, J. S., Lukens, R. J., & Lukens, M. D. (1989). Comments on "The volcano and the computer." *The Family Therapy Networker*, *13*(5), 78–79.

Efran, J. S., & Marcia, J. E. (1972). Systematic desensitization and social learning. In J. B. Rotter, J. E. Chance, & E. J. Phares (Eds.), *Applications of a social learning theory of personality* (pp. 524–532). New York: Holt, Rinehart & Winston.

Efran, J. S., & Spangler, T. (1979). Why grownups cry: A two-factor theory and evidence from "The miracle worker." *Motivation and Emotion*, *3*, 63–72.

Elliott, R., & James, E. (1989). Varieties of client experience in psychotherapy: An analysis of the literature. *Clinical Psychology Review*, *9*, 443–467.

Emery, S. (1977). *Actualizations: You don't have to rehearse to be yourself*. Garden City, NY: Doubleday & Co.

Erhard, W., & Gioscia, V. (1977). The *est* standard training. *Biosciences Communications*, *3*, 104–122.

Eysenck, H. (1988). Psychotherapy to behavior therapy: A paradigm shift. In D. B. Fishman, F. Rotgers, & C. M. Franks (Eds.), *Paradigms in behavior therapy: Present and promise* (pp. 45–76). New York: Springer.

Fiester, A., & Rudestan, K. (1975). A multivariate analysis of early droupout process. *Journal of Consulting and Clinical Psychology*, *43*, 528–536.

Fish, J. M. (1973). *Placebo therapy*. San Francisco: Jossey-Bass.

Foa, E. B., & Emmelkamp, P. M. G. (Eds.). (1983). *Failures in behavior therapy*. New York: Wiley & Sons.

Foa, E. B., Steketee, G., Grayson, J. B., & Doppelt, H. G. (1983). Treatment of obsessive compulsives: When do we fail? In E. B. Foa & P. M. G. Emmelkamp (Eds.), *Failures in behavior therapy* (pp. 10–34). New York: Wiley & Sons.

Frank, J. D. (1973). *Persuasion and healing: A comparative study of psychotherapy* (rev. ed.). Baltimore: Johns Hopkins University Press.

Frank, J. D. (1987). Psychotherapy, rhetoric, and hermeneutics: Implications for practice and research. *Psychotherapy, 24*, 293–302.

Franks, C. M. (1987). Behavior therapy: An overview. In G. T. Wilson, C. M. Franks, P. C. Kendall, & J. P. Foreyt, (Eds.), *Review of Behavior Therapy: Theory and Practice. Vol. 11* (pp. 1–39). New York: Guilford Press.

Fraser, J. T. (1987). *Time: The familiar stranger*. Amherst: University of Massachusetts Press.

Freud, S. (1959). Beyond the pleasure principle. In J. Strachey (Ed. and Trans.), *The standard edition of the complete psychological works of Sigmund Freud* (Vol. 18, pp. 3–64). New York: W. W. Norton. (Original work published 1920)

Frijda, N. H. (1986). *The emotions*. New York: Cambridge University Press.

Frijda, N. H. (1988). The laws of emotion. *American Psychologist, 43*, 349–358.

Garfield, S. L., & Kurtz, R. M. (1974). A survey of clinical psychologists: Characteristics, activities and orientation. *Clinical Psychologist, 28*(1), 7–10.

Garfield, S. L., & Kurtz, R. M. (1976). Clinical psychologists in the 1970's. *American Psychologist, 31*, 1–9.

Geisel, T. S. ("Dr. Seuss"). (1940). *Horton hatches the egg*. New York: Random House.

Gergen, K. J. (1982). *Toward transformation in social knowledge*. New York: Springer-Verlag.

Gleick, J. (1987). *Chaos: Making a new science*. New York: Viking Penguin.

Gochman, S. I., Allgood, B. A., & Greer, C. R. (1982). A look at today's behavior therapists. *Professional Psychology, 13*, 605–611.

Goffman, E. (1959). *The presentation of self in everyday life*. Garden City, NY: Doubleday.

Goffman, E. (1961). *Asylums: Essays on the social situation of mental patients and other inmates*. Garden City, NY: Doubleday Anchor.

Goffman, E. (1971). *Relations in public: Microstudies of the public order*. New York: Basic Books.

Golann, S. (1988a). On second-order family therapy. *Family Process, 27*, 51–65.

Golann, S. (1988b). Who replied first? A reply to Hoffman. *Family Process, 27*, 68–71.

Gold, M. S. (1989). *The good news about panic, anxiety & phobias*. New York: Villard Books.

Goldfried, M. R. (1980). Toward the delineation of therapeutic change principles. *American Psychologist, 35*, 991–999.

Goldiamond, I. (1972). Toward a constructional approach to social problems: Ethical and constitutional issues raised by applied behavioral analysis. *Behaviorism, 2*, 1–84.

Goleman, D. (1986, September 23). Psychiatry: First guide to therapy is fiercely opposed. *The New York Times*, pp. C1, C12.

Goleman, D. (1989, October 17). Critics challenge reliance on drugs in psychiatry. *The New York Times*, pp. C1, C6.

Goolishian, H., & Anderson, H. (1987). Language systems and therapy: An evolving idea. *Psychotherapy, 24*, 529–538.

Gould, S. J. (1989). *Wonderful life: The Burgess Shale and the nature of history*. New York: Norton.

Goulding, M. M., & Goulding, R. L. (1979). *Changing lives through redecision therapy*. New York: Brunner/Mazel.

Green, R., & Herget, M. (1989). Outcomes of systemic/strategic team consultation: II. Three-year followup and a theory of "emergent design." *Family Process, 28*, 419–437.

Greenberg, L. S., & Safran, J. D. (1989). Emotion in psychotherapy. *American Psychologist, 44*, 19–29.

Greer, G. (1984). *Sex and destiny*. New York: Harper & Row.

Haley, J. (1973). *Uncommon therapy: The psychiatric techniques of Milton H. Erikson, M.D.* New York: Norton.

Haley, J. (1980). *Leaving home: The therapy of disturbed young people*. New York: McGraw-Hill.

Hargens, J. (1989). *Systemic therapy—A European perspective*. Broadstairs, Kent, U.K.: Borgmann Publishing.

Hattie, J. A., Sharpley, C. F., & Rogers, H. J. (1984). Comparative effectiveness of professional and paraprofessional helpers. *Psychological Bulletin, 95*, 534–541.

Hoffman, L. (1985). Beyond power and control: Toward a "second order" family systems therapy. *Family Systems Medicine, 3*, 381–396.

Hoffman, L. (1988a). A constructivist position for family therapy. *The Irish Journal of Psychology, 9*, 110–129.

Hoffman, L. (1988b). Reply to Stuart Golann. *Family Process, 27*, 65–68.

Hofstadter, D. R. (1979). *Gödel, Escher, Bach: An eternal golden braid*. New York: Basic Books.

Horvath, P. (1988). Placebos and common factors in two decades of psychotherapy research. *Psychological Bulletin, 104*, 214–225.

Howard, K. I., Kopta, S. M., Krause, M. S., & Orlinsky, D. E. (1986). The dose-effect relationship in psychotherapy. *American Psychologist, 41*, 159–164.

Issacs, W., Thomas, J., & Goldiamond, I. (1960). Application of operant conditioning to reinstate verbal behavior in psychotics. *Journal of Speech and Hearing Disorders, 25*, 8–12.

Izard, C. E., Kagan, J., & Zajonc, R. B. (1984). *Emotions, cognition and behavior*. New York: Cambridge University Press.

Jackins, H. (1965). *The human side of human beings*. Seattle: Rational Island Publishers.

James, W. (1890). *The principles of psychology* (Vols. 1–2). New York: Dover.

Janov, A. (1970). *The primal scream*. New York: Dell.

Jaynes, J. (1976). *The origin of consciousness in the breakdown of the bicameral mind*. Boston: Houghton Mifflin.

Jenkins, J. J. (1974). Remember that old theory of memory? Well, forget it. *American Psychologist, 29*, 785–795.

Johnson, D. L. (1988a). A father: The search for help leads to NAMI. *APA Monitor, 19*(3), 9.

Johnson, D. L. (1988b). Schizophrenia and the family: A how-to manual for treatment. [Review of *Schizophrenia and the family: A practitioner's guide to psychoeducation and management*]. *Contemporary Psychology, 33*, 245–246.

Johnson, W. (1946). *People in quandaries: The semantics of personal adjustment*. New York: Harper & Row.

Kazdin, A. E. (1979). Fictions, factions and functions of behavior therapy. *Behavior Therapy, 10*, 629–654.

Keeney, B. P. (1983). *Aesthetics of change*. New York: Guilford Press.

Kellum, B. A. (1974). Infanticide in England in the later Middle Ages. *History of Childhood Quarterly: The Journal of Psychohistory, 1*, 367–388.

Kelly, G. A. (1955). *The psychology of personal constructs* (Vols. 1 & 2). New York: Norton.

Kelly, G. A. (1969). *Clinical psychology and personality: The selected papers of George Kelly* (B. Maher, Ed.). New York: John Wiley & Sons.

Kendall, P. C. (1989). The generalization and maintenance of behavior change: Comments, considerations, and the "no-cure" criticism. *Behavior Therapy, 20*, 357–364.

Kendall, P. C., & Bacon, S. F. (1988). Cognitive behavior therapy. In D. B. Fishman, F. Rotgers, & C. M. Franks (Eds.), *Paradigms in behavior therapy: Present and promise* (pp. 141–167). New York: Springer.

Kiesler, D. J. (1966). Some myths of psychotherapy research and the search for a paradigm. *Psychological Bulletin, 65*, 110–136.

Klein, M. H., Dittman, A. T., Parloff, M. B., & Gill, M. M. (1969). Behavior therapy: Observations and reflections. *Journal of Consulting & Clinical Psychology, 33*, 259–266.

Kleinginna, P. R., & Kleinginna, A. M. (1985). Cognition and affect: A reply to Lazarus and Zajonc. *American Psychologist, 40*, 470–471.

Klinger, E. (1977). *Meaning & void: Inner experience and the incentives in people's lives.* Minneapolis: University of Minnesota.

Kovacs, A. L. (1987). Perspective on the training of professional psychologists: Storm clouds ahead. *The Psychotherapy Bulletin, 22,* 13–16.

Kuhn, T. (1970). *The structure of scientific revolutions* (2nd ed.). Chicago: University of Chicago Press.

Langs, R. (1989). *The technique of psychoanalytic psychotherapy.* (Vols. 1 & 2). New York: Jason Aronson.

Lawrence Erlbaum (Publisher). (1989, April). *Introducing the affective revolution* [Advertisement]. Hillsdale, NJ: Lawrence Erlbaum.

Lazarus, A. A. (1971a). *Behavior therapy and beyond.* New York: McGraw-Hill.

Lazarus, A. A. (1971b). Where do behavior therapists take their troubles? *Psychological Reports, 28,* 349–350.

Lazarus, R. S. (1984). On the primacy of cognition. *American Psychologist, 39,* 124–129.

Ledwidge, B. (1978). Cognitive-behavior modification: A step in the wrong direction? *Psychological Bulletin, 85,* 353–375.

Ledwidge, B. (1979a). Cognitive behavior modification or new ways to change minds: Reply to Mahoney & Kazdin. *Psychological Bulletin, 86,* 1050–1053.

Ledwidge, B. (1979b). Cognitive behavior modification. A rejoinder to Locke and to Meichenbaum. *Cognitive Therapy & Research, 3,* 133–139.

Lerner, M. J., & Simmons, C. H. (1966). Observers' reaction to the "innocent victim": Compassion or rejection? *Journal of Personality and Social Psychology, 4,* 203–210.

Levinson, H. N., & Carter, S. (1986). *Phobia free.* New York: M. Evans & Company.

Levis, D. J. (1988). Observations and experience from clinical practice: A critical ingredient for advancing behavioral theory and therapy. *The Behavior Therapist, 11,* 95–99.

Lewinsohn, P. M., Zeiss, A. M., & Duncan, E. M. (1989). Probability of relapse after recovery from an episode of depression. *Journal of Abnormal Psychology, 98,* 107–116.

Lieberman, D. A. (1979). Behaviorism and the mind: A limited call for a return to introspection. *American Psychologist, 34,* 319–333.

Locke, E. A. (1979). Behavior modification is not cognitive—and other myths: A reply to Ledwidge. *Cognitive Therapy & Research, 3,* 119–126.

Loftus, E. F. (1980). *Memory: Surprising new insights into how we remember and why we forget.* Reading, MA: Addison-Wesley.

Loftus, E. F., & Loftus, G. R. (1980). On the permanence of stored information in the human brain. *American Psychologist, 35,* 409–420.

London, P. (1986). *The modes and morals of psychotherapy* (2nd ed.). Washington, DC: Hemisphere Publishing Corp.

Luborsky, L., Crits-Christoph, P., Mintz, J., & Auerbach, A. (1988). *Who will benefit from psychotherapy? Predicting therapeutic outcomes.* New York: Basic Books.

Luborsky, L., & Singer, B. (1975). Comparative studies of psychotherapies: Is it true that "everyone has won and all must have prizes"? *Archives of General Psychiatry, 32,* 995–1008.

Lukens, M. D. (1989). Commitment, rational cognition, or skill enhancement? Comparison of three approaches to the treatment of test-anxiety. *Dissertation Abstracts International, 49,* 2382B. (University Microfilms No. 88-12, 180)

Made for the shade. (1990, January 9). *Time,* p. 53.

Mahoney, M. J., & Kazdin, A. E. (1979). Cognitive behavior modification: Misconceptions and premature evaluation. *Psychological Bulletin, 86,* 1044–1049.

Mahrer, A. R. (1989). *Experiencing: A humanistic theory of psychology and psychiatry.* Ottawa: Uiversity of Ottawa Press. (Original work published 1978)

Malcolm, J. (1984). *In the Freud archives.* New York: Knopf.

Marks, I. M. (1982). Toward an empirical clinical science: Behavioral psychotherapy in the 1980's. *Behavior Therapy, 13,* 63–81.

Marris, P. (1974). *Loss and change*. New York: Pantheon Books (Random House).
Masson, J. M. (1984). *The assault on truth: Freud's suppression of the seduction theory*. New York: Farrar, Straus & Giroux.
Masson, J. M. (1988). *Against therapy*. New York: Atheneum.
Maturana, H. R. (1970). *The biology of cognition*. Biological Computer Laboratory Research Report 9.0, University of Illinois, Urbana.
Maturana, H. R. (1980). *Man and society*. Unpublished manuscript.
Maturana, H. R. (1984, November). *The observer and reality*. Paper presented at the Annual Meeting of the American Society for Cybernetics, Philadelphia, PA.
Maturana, H. R. (1988a). *The biological foundations of self consciousness and the physical domain of existence*. Unpublished manuscript.
Maturana, H. R. (1988b). Reality: The search for objectivity or the quest for a compelling argument. *Irish Journal of Psychology, 9*, 25–82.
Maturana, H. R., & Varela, F. J. (Eds.) (1980). *Autopoiesis and cognition: The realization of the living*. Boston: Reidel.
Maturana, H. R., & Varela, F. J. (1987). *The tree of knowledge: The biological roots of human understanding*. Boston: Shambhala.
McCulloch, W. S. (1965). *Embodiments of mind*. Cambridge, MA: MIT Press.
Mehren, E. (1989, December 25). Harvard professor provides evolutionary perspective. *The Philadelphia Inquirer*, p. C5.
Meichenbaum, D. (1979). Cognitive behavior modification: The need for a fairer assessment. *Cognitive Therapy & Research, 3*, 127–132.
Mendez, C. L., Coddou, F., & Maturana, H. R. (1988). The bringing forth of pathology: An essay to be read aloud by two. *Irish Journal of Psychology, 9*, 144–172.
Merton, T. (1965). *The way of Chuang Tzu*. New York: New Directions.
Messer, S. B., & Winokur, M. (1980). Limits to the integration of psychoanalytic and behavior therapy. *American Psychologist, 35*, 818–827.
Metzner, R. (1963). Re-evaluation of Wolpe and Dollard & Miller. *Behaviour Research and Therapy, 1*, 213–215.
Miller, R. C., & Berman, J. S. (1983). The efficacy of cognitive behavior therapies: A quantitative review of the research evidence. *Psychological Bulletin, 94*, 39–53.
Mills, J. C., & Crowley, R. J. (1986). *Therapeutic metaphors for children and the child within*. New York: Brunner/Mazel.
Minuchin, S. (1974). *Families and family therapy*. Cambridge, MA: Harvard University Press.
Minuchin, S., & Fishman, H. C. (1981). *Family therapy techniques*. Cambridge, MA: Harvard University Press.
Minuchin, S., Rosman, B. L, & Baker, L. (1978). *Psychosomatic families: Anorexia nervosa in context*. Cambridge, MA: Harvard University Press.
Neill, J. R. & Kniskern, D. P. (Eds.). (1982). *From psyche to system: The evolving therapy of Carl Whitaker*. New York: Guilford.
Nichols, M. P. (1986). *Turning forty in the eighties: Personal crisis, time for change*. New York: W. W. Norton.
Nichols, M. P. (1987). *The self in the system: Expanding the limits of family therapy*. New York: Brunner/Mazel.
Nichols, M. P., & Efran, J. S. (1985). Catharsis in psychotherapy: A new perspective. *Psychotherapy: Theory, Research, Practice, Training, 22*, 46–58.
No one told them. (1975, July 21). *Time*, p. 15.
Norcross, J. C., & Prochaska, J. O. (1982a). A national survey of clinical psychologists: Affiliations and orientations. *The Clinical Psychologist, 35*(3), 1, 4.
Norcross, J. C., & Prochaska, J. O. (1982b). A national survey of clinical psychologists: Characteristics and activities. *The Clinical Psychologist, 35*(2), 1, 5–8.
Norcross, J. C., & Prochaska, J. O. (1984). Where do behavior (and other) therapists take their troubles?: II. *The Behavior Therapist*, 7, 26–27.

Norcross, J. C., & Wogan, M. (1983). American psychotherapists of diverse persuasions: Characteristics, theories, practices, and clients. *Professional Psychology: Research and Practice, 14,* 529–539.

Olson, D. H. L. (1986). Circumplex model VII: Validation studies and FACES III. *Family Process, 25,* 337–351.

Olson, D. H. L, Bell, R., & Portner, J. (1978). *Family adaptability and cohesion evaluation scales (FACES).* Unpublished manuscript, University of Minnesota.

Omer, H., & Alon, N. (1989). Principles of psychotherapeutic strategy. *Psychotherapy, 26,* 282–289.

Omer, H., & London, P. (1988). Metamorphosis in psychotherapy: End of the systems era. *Psychotherapy, 25,* 171–180.

Orlinsky, D. E. (1989). Researchers' images of psychotherapy: Their origins and influence on research. *Clinical Psychology Review, 9,* 413–441.

Ossorio, P. G. (1978). *What actually happens: The representation of real-world phenomena.* Columbia, SC: University of South Carolina Press.

Overbye, D. (1981, June). Messenger at the gates of time. *Science '81,* pp. 61–67.

Overton, W. F. (1984). World views and their influence on psychological theory and research: Kuhn–Lakatos–Laudan. In H. W. Reese (Ed.), *Advances in child development and behavior. Vol. 18* (pp. 191–126). New York: Academic Press.

Oxford English Dictionary. (1982). London: Oxford University.

Panati, C. (1987). *Extraordinary origins of everyday things.* New York: Harper & Row.

Panati, C. (1989). *Panati's extraordinary endings of practically everything and everybody.* New York: Harper & Row.

Parloff, M. B. (1987). Reanalysis: Terminable and interminable. [Review of *Forty-two lives in treatment: A study of psychoanalysis and psychotherapy. The report of the psychotherapy research project of the Menninger Foundation, 1954–1982*]. *Contemporary Psychology, 32,* 856–858.

Patterson, C. H. (1989). Foundations for a systematic eclectic psychotherapy. *Psychotherapy, 26,* 427–435.

Pekarik, G. (1983). Follow-up adjustment of outpatient dropouts. *American Journal of Orthopsychiatry, 53,* 501–511.

Peters, R. S. (1970). The education of the emotions. In M. Arnold (Ed.), *Feelings and emotions: The Loyola symposium* (pp. 187–203). New York: Academic Press.

Powers, W. (1973). *Behavior: The control of perception.* Chicago: Aldine.

Prioleau, L., Murdock, M., & Brody, N. (1983). An analysis of psychotherapy versus placebo studies. *The Behavioral and Brain Sciences, 6,* 275–310.

Prochaska, J. O., & Norcross, J. C. (1983). Contemporary psychotherapists: A national survey of characteristics, practices, orientations, and attitudes. *Psychotherapy: Theory, Research and Practice, 20,* 161–173.

Proffitt, D. R. (1977). Demonstrations to investigate the meaning of everyday experience. *Dissertation Abstracts International, 37,* 3653B. (University Microfilms No. 76-29, 667)

Rabkin, R. (1970). *Inner and outer space: Introduction to a theory of social psychiatry.* New York: W. W. Norton.

Randall, T., & Mindlin, M. (1989). *Which reminds me.* New York: Delacorte Press.

Reed, J. (1986, December 4). You are what you do: Interview with David K. Reynolds. *Woodstock Times,* pp. 45–47.

Reiss, S. (1987). Applying cognitive and social psychology [Review of *Behavior therapy: Beyond the conditioning framework*]. *Contemporary Psychology, 32,* 864–865.

Rescorla, R. A. (1988). Pavlovian conditioning: It's not what you think it is. *American Psychologist, 43,* 151–160.

Ribble, M. A. (1943). *The rights of infants: Early psychological needs and their satisfaction.* New York: Columbia University Press.

Rorer, L. G. (1989a). Rational-emotive theory: I. An integrated psychological and philosophical basis. *Cognitive Therapy and Research, 13,* 475–492.

Rorer, L. G. (1989b). Rational-emotive theory: II. Explication and evaluation. *Cognitive Therapy and Research, 13*, 531–548.
Rosen, H. (1985). *Piagetian dimensions of clinical relevance*. New York: Columbia University Press.
Rosenfarb, I., & Hayes, S. C. (1984). Social standard setting: The Achilles heel of informational accounts of therapeutic change. *Behavior Therapy, 15*, 515–528.
Rotter, J. B. (1954). *Social learning and clinical psychology*. Englewood Cliffs, NJ: Prentice-Hall.
Rotter, J. B. (1972). Some implications of a social learning theory for the practice of psychotherapy. In J. B. Rotter, J. E. Chance, & E. J. Phares (Eds.), *Applications of a social learning theory of personality* (pp. 554–573). New York: Holt, Rinehart & Winston.
Rushdie, S. (1989). *The satanic verses*. New York: Viking Penguin.
Rychlak, J. F. (1981). *Introduction to personality and psychotherapy* (2nd ed.). New York: Houghton Mifflin.
Ryder, R. G. (1987). *The realistic therapist: Modesty and relativism in therapy and research*. Newbury Park, CA: Sage.
Ryle, G. (1949). *The concept of mind*. New York: Barnes and Noble.
Sampson, E. E. (1978). Scientific paradigms and social values: Wanted—a scientific revolution. *Journal of Personality and Social Psychology, 36*, 1332–1343.
Sampson, E. E. (1981). Cognitive psychology as ideology. *American Psychologist, 36*, 730–743.
Sampson, E. E. (1989). The challenge of social change for psychology: Globalization and psychology's theory of the person. *American Psychologist, 44*, 914–921.
Sarason, S. B. (1981). *Psychology misdirected*. New York: Free Press.
Schachter, S. (1982). Recidivism and self-cure of smoking and obesity. *American Psychologist, 37*, 436–444.
Schafer, R. (1983). *The analytic attitude*. New York: Basic Books.
Scharff, D., & Scharff, J. S. (1987). *Object relations family therapy*. Northvale, NJ: Jason Aronson.
Schofield, W. (1964). *Psychotherapy: The purchase of friendship*. Englewood Cliffs, NJ: Prentice-Hall.
Schwartz, R. (1987). Our multiple selves. *The Family Therapy Networker, 11*(2), 24–31, 80–83.
Schwartz, R. (1988). Know thy selves. *The Family Therapy Networker, 12*(6), 20–29.
Shapiro, D. (1965). *Neurotic styles*. New York: Basic Books.
Shapiro, D. A., & Shapiro, D. (1982). Meta-analysis of comparative therapy outcome studies: A replication and refinement. *Psychological Bulletin, 92*, 581–604.
Sharma, S. L. (1986). *The therapeutic dialogue: A theoretical and practical guide to psychotherapy*. Albuquerque: University of New Mexico Press.
Shuy, R. W. (1986). Ethical issues in analyzing FBI surreptitious tapes. *International Journal of the Sociology of Language, 62*, 119–128.
Sifford, D. (1990, January 21). An undercover look at the nation's therapists. *The Philadelphia Inquirer*, pp. H1–H2.
Simon, R. (1985). Structure is destiny: An interview with Humberto Maturana. *The Family Therapy Networker, 9*(3), 32–37, 41–43.
Skinner, B. F. (1974). *About behaviorism*. New York: Alfred A. Knopf.
Skolnick, A. S. (1987). *The intimate environment: Exploring marriage and the family* (4th ed.). Boston: Little, Brown.
Slater, P. E. (1970). *The pursuit of loneliness: American culture at the breaking point*. Boston: Beacon Press.
Smith, M. L. (1982). What research says about the effectiveness of psychotherapy. *Hospital & Community Psychiatry, 33*, 457–461.
Smith, M. L., & Glass, G. V. (1977). Meta-analysis of psychotherapy outcome studies. *American Psychologist, 32*, 752–760.

Smith, M. L., Glass, G. V., & Miller, T. I. (1980). *The benefits of psychotherapy*. Baltimore: Johns Hopkins University Press.

Smothermon, R. (1979). *Winning through enlightenment*. San Francisco: Context Publications.

Spence, D. P. (1982). *Narrative truth and historical truth: Meaning and interpretation in psychoanalysis*. New York: W. W. Norton.

Spence, D. P. (1987). *The Freudian metaphor: Toward paradigm change in psychoanalysis*. New York: W. W. Norton.

Spitz, R. A. (1950). Anxiety in infancy: A study of its manifestations in the first year of life. *International Journal of Psychoanalysis, 31*, 138–143.

Spitz, R. A. (1965). *The first year of life: A psychoanalytic study of normal and deviant development of object relations*. New York: International Universities Press.

Stein, J., Bock, J., & Harnick, S. (1964). *Fiddler on the roof*. New York: Crown.

Steiner, G. (1978). *Martin Heidegger*. Chicago: University of Chicago Press.

Strupp, H. H., & Hadley, S. W. (1979). Specific vs. nonspecific factors in psychotherapy: A controlled study of outcome. *Archives of General Psychiatry, 36*, 1125–1136.

Sullivan, H. S. (1962). *Schizophrenia as a human process*. New York: W. W. Norton.

Szasz, T. (1973). *The second sin*. New York: Anchor Press/Doubleday.

Szasz, T. (1980). *Sex by prescription*. New York: Doubleday.

Tarasoff v. Regents of the University of California, 131 Cal Rptr. 14, 551 P.2d 334 (1976).

Tellegen, A. , Lykken, D. T., Bouchard, T. J., Wilcox, K. J., Segal, N. L., & Rich, S. (1988). Personality similarity in twins reared apart and together. *Journal of Personality & Social Psychology, 54*, 1031–1039.

Thompson, W. I. (Ed.). (1987). *Gaia, A way of knowing: Political implications of the new biology*. Great Barrington, MA: Lindisfarne Press.

Tierney, J. (1983, December). The myth of the firstborn. *Science '83*, p. 16.

Tischler, G. L. (Ed.). (1987). *Diagnosis and classification in psychiatry: A critical appraisal of DSM-III*. New York: Cambridge University Press.

Tomm, K. (1989). Foreword. In Jurgen Hargens (Ed.), *Systemic therapy: A European perspective. Systemic studies, Vol. 1* (pp. 7–11). Broadstairs, Kent, U. K.: Borgmann Publishing.

Torrey, E. F. (1972). What Western psychotherapists can learn from witch doctors. *American Journal of Orthopsychiatry, 42*, 69–76.

Treatment book is born in controversy. (1989, August). *APA Monitor*, pp. 19–20.

Tripp, C. A. (1987). *The homosexual matrix* (2nd ed.). New York: New American Library.

Truax, C. B., & Carkhuff, R. R. (1967). *Toward effective counseling and psychotherapy: Training and practice*. Chicago: Aldine.

Varela, F. J. (1979). *Principles of biological autonomy*. New York: Elsevier-North Holland.

Varela, F. J. (1989). Reflections on the circulation of concepts between a biology of cognition and systemic family therapy. *Family Process, 28*, 15–24.

von Foerster, H. (1981). *Observing systems*. Seaside, CA: Intersystems.

Wachtel, E. F., & Wachtel, P. L. (1986). *Family dynamics in individual psychotherapy*. New York: Guilford Press.

Wachtel, P. L. (1977). *Psychoanalysis and behavior therapy: Toward an integration*. New York: Basic Books.

Wachtel, P. L. (1987). *Action and insight*. New York: Guilford Press.

Wallach, A. (1989, March). Beautiful dreamings: Aboriginal art as a kind of cosmic road map to the primeval. *Ms. Magazine*, pp. 60–64.

Wallerstein, R. S. (1986). *Forty-two lives in treatment: A study of psychoanalysis and psychotherapy. The report of the psychotherapy research project of The Menninger Foundation, 1954–1982*. New York: Guilford Press.

Wallerstein, R. S. (1989). The psychotherapy research project of the Menninger Foundation: An overview. *Journal of Consulting and Clinical Psychology, 57*, 195–205.

Watson, P. (1981). *Twins: An uncanny relationship?* New York: Viking Press.

Watts, A. (1966). *The book: On the taboo against knowing who you are*. New York: Vintage Books.

Watzlawick, P., Beavin, J., & Jackson, D. D. (1967). *The pragmatics of human communication*. New York: W. W. Norton.

Watzlawick, P., Weakland, J. H., & Fisch, R. (1974). *Change: Principles of problem formation and problem resolution*. New York: W. W. Norton.

Weill, K., & Brecht, B. (1928). *Die Dreigroschenoper* [The Threepenny Opera]. Vienna: Universal Edition.

Weintraub, J. (1990, January 2). Umberto Eco: A scholar's rise in the world of bestsellers. *The Philadelphia Inquirer*, pp. E1, E8.

Wiener, M. (1989). Psychopathology reconsidered: Depressions interpreted as psychosocial transactions. *Clinical Psychology Review, 9*, 295–321.

Wiener, N. (1961). *Cybernetics: Or the control and communication in the animal and the machine* (2nd ed.). Cambridge, MA: MIT Press.

Wittgenstein, L. (1971). *Tractatus logico-philosophicus* (2nd ed.). London: Routledge & Kegan Paul. (Original work published 1922)

Wolpe, J. (1978). Cognition and causation in human behavior and its therapy. *American Psychologist, 33*, 437–446.

Wright, R. H., & Spielberger, C. D. (1989). Psychiatry declares war on psychology. *The Clinical Psychologist, 42*, 61–66. [Bound with *Clinical Psychology Review, 9*(4)].

Yalom, I. D. (1989). *Love's executioner: And other tales of psychotherapy*. New York: Basic Books.

Zajonc, R. B. (1984). On the primacy of affect. *American Psychologist, 39*, 117–123.

Zilbergeld, B. (1983). *The shrinking of America: Myths of psychological change*. New York: Little, Brown.

Zukav, G. (1979). *The dancing Wu Li masters*. New York: Bantam.

Name Index

Subject Index

Printed in the United States
96621LV00003B/34/A

9 780393 333732

Made in the USA
Lexington, KY
28 September 2010